JOURNAL FOR THE STUDY OF THE OLD TESTAMENT SUPPLEMENT SERIES
226

Editors
David J.A. Clines
Philip R. Davies

Executive Editor
John Jarick

Editorial Board
Robert P. Carroll, Richard J. Coggins, Alan Cooper, J. Cheryl Exum,
John Goldingay, Robert P. Gordon, Norman K. Gottwald,
Andrew D.H. Mayes, Carol Meyers, Patrick D. Miller

Sheffield Academic Press

Joshua and the Rhetoric of Violence

A New Historicist Analysis

Lori L. Rowlett

Journal for the Study of the Old Testament
Supplement Series 226

Copyright © 1996 Sheffield Academic Press

Published by Sheffield Academic Press Ltd
Mansion House
19 Kingfield Road
Sheffield S11 9AS
England

Printed on acid-free paper in Great Britain
by Bookcraft Ltd
Midsomer Norton, Bath

British Library Cataloguing in Publication Data

A catalogue record for this book is available
from the British Library

ISBN 1-85075-627-9

CONTENTS

PREFACE

The present work began as a doctoral dissertation for the University of Cambridge. I acknowledge the contribution of many other scholars, both in the literature and in personal conversations. Any imperfections are entirely my own, however.

I am especially grateful to my supervisor, Hugh Williamson, whose helpful comments and suggestions kept me on track. I would also like to acknowledge my fellow research students at Cambridge, particularly Judith Hadley, Madawi al Rashid, Tim Wright, Elizabeth Burr and Ginger Caessons, as well as the scholars (faculty and students) from other institutions who passed through Cambridge while doing their own research projects, most notably K. Lawson Younger and Richard Hess. Friends, family, and colleagues in the United States have also been a source of encouragement and support. I would like to thank my parents and my brother Larry, my cousins Richard Rieves and John Thomas, my friends Dave Webb and Jacques Berlinerblau, lifelong friends from the old neighbourhood Debra Allen and Carolyn Castro Stoup, and more recent friends Irene Baros-Johnson and magical Amanda Barker.

I dedicate this book to the memory of Hilary Whitehorn Pottinger, with whom I lived in Cambridge until her untimely death. I consider myself privileged to have known her and loved her.

ABBREVIATIONS

AB	Anchor Bible
AJSL	*American Journal of Semitic Languages and Literature*
ANET	*Ancient Near Eastern Texts Relating to the Old Testament*
AnOr	Analecta Orientalia
ARM	Archives royales de Mari
AS	*Anatolian Studies*
ATANT	Abhandlungen zur Theologie des Alten und Neuen Testaments
BASOR	*Bulletin of the American Schools of Oriental Research*
BDB	F. Brown, S.R. Driver and C.A. Briggs, *Hebrew and English Lexicon of the Old Testament*
BHS	*Biblia Hebraica Stuttgartensia* (3rd edn)
Bib	*Biblica*
BJRL	*Bulletin of the John Rylands Library*
BoTU	*Die Boghazköi-Texte in Umschrift*
BWANT	Beiträge zur Wissenschaft vom Alten und Neuen Testament
BZAW	Beihefte zur Zeitschrift für die Alttestamentliche Wissenschaft
CBQ	*Catholic Biblical Quarterly*
CTA	A. Herdner (ed.), *Corpus des tablettes en cunéiformes alphabétiques découvertes à Ras Shamra-Ugarit de 1929 à 1939*
DH	Deuteronomistic History
Dtr	Deuteronomistic Historian
FRLANT	Forschungen zur Religion und Literatur des Alten und Neuen Testament
GKC	*Gesenius' Hebrew Grammar*, ed. E. Kautzsch, trans. A.E. Cowley
HAT	Handbuch zum Alten Testament
ICC	International Critical Commentary
IEJ	*Israel Exploration Journal*
Int	*Interpretation*
ITL	International Theological Library
JBL	*Journal of Biblical Literature*
JCS	*Journal of Cuneiform Studies*
JNES	*Journal of Near Eastern Studies*
JSOT	*Journal for the Study of the Old Testament*
JSOTSup	*Journal for the Study of the Old Testament*, Supplement Series

JSS	*Journal of Semitic Studies*
KB	L. Koehler and W. Baumgartner (eds.), *Lexicon in Veteris Testamenti libros*
KBo	*Keilschrifturkunden aus Boqhazköi*
KEH	Kurzgefasstes Exegetisches Handbuch zum Alttestament
KHC	Kurzer Hand-Commentar zum Alten Testament
KTU	*Die Keilalphabetischen Texte aus Ugarit*
LD	Lectio divina
LXX	Septuagint
MIO	*Mitteilungen des Instituts für Orientforschung*
MVAG	Mitteilungen der Vorderasiatischen/Vorderasiatisch-Ägyptischen Gesellschaft
NCB	New Century Bible
NthG	Neue theologische Grundrisse
Or	*Orientalia*
OTL	Old Testament Library
OTS	*Oudtestamentlische Studiën*
OuTWP	De Ou Testamentiese Werkgemeenskap in Suid-Afrika
PEQ	*Palestine Exploration Quarterly*
Q	Qumran
RS	Ras Shamra
TDOT	G.J. Botterweck and H. Ringgren (eds.), *Theological Dictionary of the Old Testament*
ThWAT	G.J. Botterweck and H. Ringgren (eds.), *Theologisches Wörterbuch zum Alten Testament*
TLZ	*Theologische Literaturzeitung*
TRu	*Theologische Rundschau*
VT	*Vetus Testamentum*
VTSup	*Vetus Testamentum*, Supplements
WBC	Word Biblical Commentary
WMANT	Wissenschaftliche Monographien zum Alten und Neuen Testament
ZA	*Zeitschrift für Assyriologie und vorderasiatische Archäologie*
ZAW	*Zeitschrift für die Alttestamentliche Wissenshcaft*

Chapter 1

INTRODUCTION

Times of turmoil tend to foster narratives of identity. To provide a sense of order, people emphasize self-definition—that is, explanations of who they are, their origins and their perception of their destiny—during periods when chaos poses its most potent threat.

I shall attempt to demonstrate that the Book of Joshua is such a narrative. Although Joshua relates a story of the assertion of power through violent conquest, it does not function primarily as national battle epic nor as an anti-foreigner polemic, although these are elements of the story. Rather, those who produced the text used the rhetoric of warfare and nationalism as an encouragement and a threat, aimed at their own population, to submit voluntarily to the central authority of a government struggling to organize itself and create its own ideological framework of inclusion. Because a work of art may assert precisely what is missing in the historical context which produced it, the concern in Joshua with a strong sense of national unity may provide a clue pointing precisely to what was not there when the text was produced.

Although it purports to relate 'historical' events which (allegedly) took place sometime between 1400 and 1200 BCE, most scholars agree that the Book of Joshua forms part of the Deuteronomistic History (henceforth called the DH), composed many centuries later. The date and purpose of the DH are disputed, with some scholars favouring an exilic date, while others argue for either Hezekiah's or Josiah's Reform. Nearly all scholars concur that the original History is interrupted by later additions to the text, which can be traced to either exilic or post-exilic times. These redactional theories receive detailed attention in my chapter on the contribution of other scholars to the discussion of the DH.

In my work, I shall argue that the DH was probably written during the seventh century BCE, when Assyrian power had begun to wane, and the Neo-Babylonians had not yet arisen as a great empire. I attempt to demonstrate how the text functions as part of a programme to consolidate political power. The Book of Joshua is a document of anxiety: anxiety about control, insurrection, and chaos. The text may be read as an attempt to assert a socio-political order in the chaos created by Assyrian collapse. Words and images which echo Assyrian war rhetoric would have had powerful emotional associations to a readership familiar with Assyrian military capabilities and Assyrian modes of intimidation. One of my chapters, therefore, sets forth the various ancient Near Eastern parallels to the language of warfare in Joshua in order to accomplish two related goals: first, to demonstrate the extent of Assyrian literary influence in both language and style; and secondly, to illustrate the use of a rhetoric of divine intervention in warfare as an ideological assertion of power in other literatures of the immediate region.

My work on the Book of Joshua uses Michel Foucault's observations on power relations, as applied to texts by the Berkeley 'New Historicists', particularly Stephen Greenblatt. As Greenblatt has pointed out, a work of art will not only reflect the negotiations and exchanges of power taking place in the society which produced it but will also be a part of the process.[1] Therefore, the text itself has an ideological function as an assertion of power which in turn affects the political environment of that context. The threat inherent in the Joshua text functions as an instrument of coercion, or at least encouragement, to submission. The rhetoric of violence is used to establish the lines of inclusion, authority and hierarchy desired by the central government, whose control was far from secure.

The Book of Joshua reflects a combination of coercion and an attempt to harness the energies of the population by invoking their loyalties through a sense of identity. Narratives of identity require a set of axiomatic principles, inscribed in the text, to distinguish between 'us' and 'them' (the Other). One of my chapters is therefore devoted to an analysis of the literary dynamics of the incidents in which a rhetoric of violence is used to establish or negotiate the boundaries of the community.

Although the 'Canaanites' are the ostensible victims (the 'Others') in Joshua, the goal of the document is not to incite literal violence against ethnic outsiders. The text of Joshua is concerned with voluntary submission to a set of rules and norms; it is directed at Josiah's own people,

1. S. Greenblatt, *Shakespearean Negotiations: The Circulation of Social Energy in Renaissance England* (Berkeley: University of California Press, 1988), p. 6.

not at real (ethnic) outsiders, but at insiders who pose a threat to the hierarchy being asserted. The message is that the punishment of Otherness is death and that insiders can easily become outsiders (Others) by failure to submit.

At the same time, the Book of Joshua reflects a positive attempt to win the voluntary loyalty of the people by making them feel a part of a collective entity. By appealing to their sense of belonging, the text is building their identity as a unified people endowed with a purpose. The Book of Joshua contains numerous examples of willing compliance and even enthusiastic identification with the leader in whom the power is concentrated.

The Assyrian palace reliefs from the time period immediately preceding Josiah's reign provide an instructive parallel in a different artistic medium. In their book on the palace reliefs, Leo Bersani and Ulysse Dutoit note the visual means by which the king is made a symbol of national identity.[2] The king is larger than the surrounding figures, who stand or kneel in rows. The king stands out of alignment with the others, which calls attention to his presence. In the words of Bersani and Dutoit, the king represents 'his own columns of subjects; he *is* their national identity'. The palace reliefs often picture a national deity participating in battle at the head of the Assyrian king, destroying the enemies of Assyria. The king, in turn, stands at the head of his troops.

In the text of Joshua, the figure of Joshua occupies the same position as the Assyrian king in the palace art. The hierarchical lines of authority are strongly overcoded throughout the Book of Joshua, placing the subjects in a patriarchal order with a military flavour. The rank and file are always arranged by tribe, clan and family, under the authority of 'commanders' or 'elders', with Joshua (under Yahweh) at the top. Joshua is the embodiment of national identity, with the national god Yahweh at his head in battle.

Some scholars consider Joshua to be a thinly disguised King Josiah (e.g. Cross, Nelson, Coote and Coote; see my third Chapter for further discussion). R.D. Nelson[3] remarks on the royal aspects of the Dtr's presentation of Joshua,[4] as well as the specific parallels between the two

2. L. Bersani and U. Dutoit, *The Forms of Violence: Narrative in Assyrian Art and Modern Culture* (New York: Schocken Books, 1985), pp. 3-7.
3. R.D. Nelson, 'Josiah in the Book of Joshua', *JBL* 100.4 (1981), pp. 531-40.
4. Some of Nelson's observations concerning Joshua 1 show his interest in the

leaders. When Joshua takes power immediately upon the death of Moses, the model is not the charismatic pattern of judges or prophets, but is, instead, the royal model of dynastic succession. The people pledge uncompromising obedience to Joshua as the successor of Moses, as in the Assyrian vassal treaties demanding obedience to a suzerain's successor.[5]

In the covenant renewal ceremony of Josh. 8.30-35, Joshua takes what would be the king's role in the time of the monarchy.[6] The only two cases in which Dtr recounts a true covenant mediation are Josh. 8.30-35 and 2 Kgs 23.1-3, which involve Joshua and Josiah, respectively.[7] Nelson also points out that the emphasis on Joshua as the covenant maker, along with the additional details provided in the text, make explicit parallels to Josiah. For example, Nelson draws attention to the reading from a book of divine law (v. 34), which he says would have been something 'rather new in 622 BCE'[8] as a projection back into the classical past. The Passover celebration performed by Josiah in his eighteenth year also corresponds to the ancient model provided by Josh. 5.13-15. The Dtr had apparently suppressed an important reforming Passover celebrated by Hezekiah (2 Chron. 30) in order to present Josiah's work as totally revolutionary and to draw attention once again to the parallel between Joshua and Josiah.[9]

Joshua's role as a war leader also resonates with Josiah. Although the extent of Josiah's expansion is difficult to determine with accuracy, the ideal frontiers of Deut. 11.24, laid programmatically before Joshua (Josh. 1.1-6), reflect Josianic ambitions.[10] Nelson says, 'But even if the ideology of the return of lost lands went far beyond pedestrian reality, the ideology did remain in force'.[11] The Joshua of the Dtr, Nelson concludes, is a Josianic figure 'who acts out the events of Dtr's own day on the stage of the classical past'.[12] From a New Historicist perpective, one

---

'installation genre' theory, but I defer discussion of it until my Chapter 6. However, his overall point does not hinge upon this theory.

    5.   Nelson, 'Josiah', pp. 531-32.

    6.   G. Widengren made the same observation in 'King and Covenant', *JSS* 2 (1957), pp. 1-32, which Nelson also credits.

    7.   Nelson notes that in 2 Kgs 11.17, it is the priest Jehoida who renews the covenant, apparently as a stand-in for the underage Joash (p. 535).

    8.   Nelson, 'Josiah', pp. 534-35.

    9.   Nelson, 'Josiah', p. 536.

    10.   Nelson, 'Josiah', pp. 537-38.

    11.   Nelson, 'Josiah', p. 538.

    12.   Nelson, 'Josiah', p. 540.

could add that non-events, problems, failures and controversial definitions of events were also being acted out.

Taking Nelson's observations regarding Joshua and Josiah as one of my central premises, I attempt to demonstrate how the Josianic authorities, asserting their power through religious, political, military and cultural control mechanisms, were using the text to establish boundaries of acceptability in the society they were creating. Josiah's monarchy was based on the concept of a cohesive identity under a highly centralized government. In the words of Mary and Robert Coote:

> Josiah's resolution and prowess had overwhelmed a host of opponents in the name of one God, one cult, one law, one ruling house, and one subject people.[13]

My work represents a discussion of the way that certain passages in the Book of Joshua reflect this ideology of centralization and their role in bringing about the desired political result. The passages which I have chosen as the focus of the present work are military exhortations, in particular, the war oracle which opens the conquest (Josh. 1.1-9) and subsequent passages which echo its language (Josh. 1.16-18; 10.24-26). Other incidents in the Book of Joshua and elsewhere in the DH are discussed in detail only when they have some special relevance to the above passages. I analyze the power relations in the rhetoric of violence, using Michel Foucault's theory that power is not so much something which is possessed, but instead is something which is *exercised* in the negotiation of the forces of social control.[14]

---

13. R.B. Coote and M.P. Coote, *Power, Politics and the Making of the Bible: An Introduction* (Minneapolis: Fortress Press, 1990), p. 62.

14. M. Foucault, *Surveiller et Punir* (Paris: éditions Gallimard, 1975); available in English (trans. A. Sheridan) as *Discipline and Punish: The Birth of the Prison* (New York: Vintage Press, 1979).

Chapter 2

METHODOLOGY

The discipline of biblical studies is in a state of ferment much like that which characterized literature departments two generations ago. At stake are not just the methodological practices, but also the aims of research which are regarded as legitimate objects of inquiry. In the politics of interpretation, a chasm has opened between historical (source and redaction) critics on one side, and literary critics on the opposite. Meanwhile, the debate over formalist and contextualist modes of interpretation has resurfaced in literature departments due to the influence of contemporary continental theories of textual interpretation. Michel Foucault's work in cultural criticism has been applied most successfully to the field of literature by Shakespearian and Renaissance scholars calling for renewed attention to historical context and power structures. This type of analysis is called the 'New Historicism'.

The New Historicism as a methodology has the advantage of giving historical context the attention it deserves, without making the history of a text's composition the primary point of research (as though determination of sources were an end in itself). On the other hand, the new historicists avoid the pitfalls of a literary formalism (in which the text is seen as a world unto itself), which denies the complex interaction between cultural context and the art produced within it.

As I mentioned in my introduction, an important tenet of Greenblatt's theory is that a work of art will not only reflect the negotiations and exchanges of power taking place in the society which produced it, but will also be a part of the process. Greenblatt goes on to say that Shakespeare's plays continue to interact with the social context in which they are produced, right up through the present time.[1] If the same is true for any text or work of art, then Biblical scholars must take a look at the loci of power in the field and how the shifting politics of

1. Greenblatt, *Negotiations*, pp. 6-11.

interpretation continue to impinge upon theoretical practices. The field is centred in two institutions: the academy and the religious organizations. This statement may at first glance seem so obvious as to appear unnecessary. But a closer look at the dynamics of interpretation as cultural practice reveals the importance of an analysis of how institutions function as repositories of power.

Academic disciplines have their own set of rhetorics and rituals. Each discipline decides for itself, in complex ways, what will be regarded as worthwhile objects of inquiry, where the boundaries will be, and what will count as legitimate findings, in other words, as truth. Michel Foucault says that:

> Truth is a thing of this world: it is produced only by virtue of multiple forms of constraint... Each society has its general politics of truth...[2]

Truth in our society, he goes on to say, is produced and transmitted by certain apparatuses, such as the university, the army, the media, the laboratory, and the hospital. Within the university, individual academic disciplines have their own 'politics of truth': that is, the types of discourse which are accepted as true, the mechanisms which enable one to distinguish true and false statements, the means by which each is sanctioned, the techniques and procedures accorded value in the acquisition of truth, and the status of those who are charged with saying what counts as true.

John Hermann, a scholar of Anglo-Saxon poetry, mentions in the methodological chapter of his book *Allegories of War*[3] the defensiveness of his fellow-Anglo-Saxonists, citing the many times he has heard remarks dourly exchanged at scholarly meetings about the 'solidity of philology' and the insubstantiality of literary theory. Few Anglo-Saxonists, Hermann observes, seem troubled that their discipline shows few traces of the best critical thought of the present. The New Criticism in the fifties made some impact, leading some scholars to emphasize the subtlety and 'craftsmanship' of Anglo-Saxon poets:

> When complexity and craftsmanship became the key terms for evaluating literature... (he said)... neglected poems quickly became skillfully crafted little gems... but the continuing defense of Old English poems as worthy

2. M. Foucault, *Power/Knowledge: Selected Interviews and Other Writings, 1972-1977* (ed. Colin Gordon; New York: Pantheon, 1980), p. 73.

3. J.P. Hermann, *Allegories of War: Language and Violence in Old English Poetry* (Ann Arbor: University of Michigan Press, 1989), pp. 204-207.

of attention... because they are well-crafted has become drone-like. The
point has been made and its reiteration is of doubtful value...[4]

The field of Biblical studies is in a similar condition. Objection to
theory generally means objection to literary theory. Historical criticism
and philology are accepted as the standard procedures, not as alternative
theoretical practices.

'Hostility to theory', according to Terry Eagleton, 'usually means an
opposition to other people's theories and an oblivion to one's own'.
Eagleton backs his position with a quotation from John Maynard
Keynes, who said that, 'those economists who disliked theory, or
claimed to get along better without it, were simply in the grip of an
older theory'.[5]

Reacting against the two-hundred year hegemony of historical criticism—by which we usually mean source and redaction criticism—literary critics of the Bible began in the 1970s and '80s to demand an end to
the fragmentation of the text into sources to be dated. They argued that
the meaning, beauty and richness of the biblical literature were being
defiled, obscured or perhaps even lost. In order to recover them, the
text had to be read as a whole.

For example, in the first chapter of *The Art of Biblical Narrative*,
Robert Alter discusses the story of Tamar and Judah, which is generally
considered to be an interpolated story. He quotes a historical biblical
scholar who calls it a completely independent unit, having 'no connection with the drama of Joseph which it interrupts...'. Alter goes on to
point out its 'intimate connections through motif and theme' with the
Joseph story. He says that 'pointed connections are made with the main
narrative through a whole series of explicit parallels and contrasts'. He
uncovers some correspondences of language and thematic matter in
order to demonstrate the advantages of reading the text as an 'intri-
cately interconnected unity', rather than 'assuming it is a patchwork' of
disparate documents, as modern biblical scholars often do.[6] Therefore, in
Alter's view, the biblical text too becomes a skillfully crafted little gem.

---

4.   Hermann, *Allegories*, p. 207.
5.   T. Eagleton, *Criticism and Ideology* (London: New Left Books, 1976),
p. 43; also cited by C. Norris, *The Contest of Faculties* (London: Methuen Press,
1985), p. 6.
6.   R. Alter, *The Art of Biblical Narrative* (New York: Basic Books, 1981),
pp. 3-11.

While Alter developed his own way of reading biblical narrative, borrowing from the field of Homeric studies the concept of the type-scene, other critics began to read French and American literary theory. Employing the techniques of structuralism, a plethora of diagram-laden books and articles appeared on the scene. Roland Barthes' structural reading of Genesis 32 became a standard reference-point. Other scholars discovered the New Critical concept of 'close reading', and any mention of authorial intention became a 'fallacy'.

At first, only a handful of fairly radical scholars were agitating to expand the methodological boundaries of the field. Then some theologically conservative scholars began to discover that treating the text as a continuous, literary whole had political advantages for them. For one thing, they no longer have to justify their claims on historical-critical grounds. They no longer have to make a case for Mosaic authorship of the Pentateuch or the unity of Isaiah. They can simply argue for setting those issues aside in order to analyse the literary structure of the whole or to discuss how a narrative works aesthetically.

The historical critics of the last two hundred years, after all, were the original liberals of biblical scholarship. The entire point was to find a scientific approach to the text by examining the Bible the way an Assyriologist looks at an Assyrian text or an Egyptologist looks at ancient Egyptian literature. Since then, the historical critics have become an entrenched power structure, enjoying, for a time, a monopoly on methodological credibility. They set the agenda for research. Their issues became *the* issues. Literary scholars felt very much like outsiders, rebels with a cause. Historical critics were criticized by the first generation of literary biblical critics for treating the text itself as an archaeological tel, to be excavated by digging through the layers for historical evidence, with no sensitivity to literary nuance and only scant interest in meaning. Fragments of text, they charged, were treated like pottery sherds. Now we are at a methodological crossroads. We are not even certain what the options are, or what axiomatic assumptions lie at the base of each option.

A brief look at the genealogy of the New Criticism and its impact on English literature departments in the 1950s might provide a few clues. Several of the leading theorists associated with the New Criticism were 'Southern Agrarians'. In fact, three of the most influential, Allen Tate, John Crowe Ransom and Robert Penn Warren, had been contributors to

I'll Take my Stand,[7] the manifesto of the agrarian movement, centred at Vanderbilt University in Nashville, Tennessee. The agrarians argued that the South was fundamentally a different culture from the North. They were resentful of Northern, American imperialism, which Ransom called a 'foreign invasion of southern soil'.[8] They believed that the South was an organic, agricultural society, and they opposed the inroads of Northern, Yankee technology. They resisted the twin evils of urbanization and industrialization. Lest I give the impression that I am talking about the (present-day) Green Party, I hasten to add that the agrarian version of an organic society was the hierarchical social structure of the Old South. The plantation was at the centre of life, and everyone had a role to play in its functioning.

Not all New Critics were Southern. Some were Northern; some were British. Even those Southerners who were formerly associated with the agrarian movement changed their political views over the years. However, they did carry over into their New Critical theories some of the principles which had guided them as agrarians. They favoured certain kinds of poetic structures, for they sought in works of literature what they had once admired in historical institutions: 'a harmonious system, an organism in which there was a place for everything and everything in its place—and which, ideally, was part of an identifiable tradition, referring back to systems of a similar kind'.[9] As Ransom indicated in 'Art and the Human Economy', the effect of an aesthetic order on those who perceived it was to produce a momentary feeling of balance and wholeness.[10] The poem or other text was an organic whole, a world unto itself.

Greenblatt himself was educated during the heyday of the New Criticism. He wrote in the introduction to his book on the circulation of social energy:

> The textual analyses I was trained to do had as their goal the identification and celebration of a numinous literary authority, whether that authority was ultimately located in the mysterious genius of an artist or in the

7.   *I'll Take My Stand* (New York: Harper & Brothers, 1930).

8.   J.C. Ransom, 'Reconstructed but Unregenerate', in *I'll Take My Stand*, p. 23.

9.   R. Gray, *Writing the South* (Cambridge: Cambridge University Press, 1986), p. 163.

10.   J.C. Ransom, 'Art and the Human Economy', *Kenyon Review* 7 (1945), pp. 683-88.

mysterious perfection of a text whose intuitions and concepts can never be expressed in other terms. The great attraction of this authority is that it appears to bind and fix the energies we prize, to identify a stable and permanent source of literary power, to offer an escape from shared contingency... This project... repeatedly fails for one reason: there is no escape from contingency.[11]

As I hope I have demonstrated, the New Critics were not free from socio-political contingency either. The relationship between their political views and their aesthetic theories were simply unspoken, perhaps even unconscious.

Today the politics of interpretation in literature departments are aligned along ideological lines. In North America the debate in the media over 'political correctness' has even propelled academic squabbles into public view. The glaring publicity has brought the whole question of historical/socio-political contingency into sharp relief.

On one side of the dispute are those who grant aesthetics a privileged place above matters of theory and ideological reflection. They are the intellectual heirs of the New Critics. At the present time, aestheticians usually speak in favour of a timeless order of permanent truths, beyond the reach of political theory and practice. For example, aesthetic philosopher Roger Scruton says that, 'Those thoughts which animate our perception when we see the realistic painting with understanding are true thoughts'.[12] He would find a kindred spirit in Ransom, who discovered not only truth but 'salvation' in works of art.[13]

Robert Alter, who teaches in a literature department at Berkeley, has written a polemical book called *The Pleasures of Reading in an Age of Ideology*.[14] The rhetoric of the title is striking in its exaltation of aesthetic reading pleasure and denigration of ideology, as though ideology were somehow a corrupting influence. Ironically, it was Alter's earlier book on biblical narrative which inspired some of the most radical of the present generation of biblical scholars. Nevertheless, the important point here is that we can see the logical outcome of his views on the primacy of aesthetic considerations over and above engagement with historical,

11. Greenblatt, *Negotiations*, p. 3.
12. R. Scruton, *The Aesthetic Understanding: Essays in the Philosophy of Art and Culture* (London: Methuen, 1983), p. 108.
13. Ransom, 'Art and the Human Economy', p. 686.
14. R. Alter, *The Pleasures of Reading in an Age of Ideology* (Berkeley: University of California Press, 1990).

sociological and political issues. Implicit in the title of Alter's recent book is an assumption about the autonomy of art. As Christopher Norris wrote of Scruton, aestheticians exhibit a 'resistance to theories which would seek to account for it (art) on non-aesthetic (Marxist or other) grounds. Given that the work of art 'bears its significance within itself', this (kind of) argument is self-confirming and aesthetics has justified its legislative role'; a legislative role, that is, which the aesthetician can use to declare politics out-of-bounds. As Norris observed, theory is considered 'suspect in so far as it raises questions which aesthetics must either rule out of court or treat as possessing a strictly limited, second-order interest'. Otherwise aesthetics would have to relinquish its right to impose those first-order principles like the autonomy of art, which in turn lend support to its own intellectual truth-claims.[15]

The purpose of the aestheticians' claim to detachment and disinterest from political concerns, according to Norris, is to avoid questions about the hidden ideological underpinnings of the aestheticians' own arguments, which are often couched in mystical language about culture, tradition and aesthetic understanding (not to mention truth and salvation). One of Norris's observations regarding the debate centres on the correspondence between the ultra-conservative view of a just society (which he ascribes to Scruton) and the attempt to subordinate critical theory in relation to aesthetics: 'What these ... have in common is the desire to set firm limits to the criticism of existing values and institutions'.[16]

As Gerald Graff points out, those on the other side of the chasm do not argue against aesthetic interpretation, but rather in favour of a multi-faceted understanding of what gives a work of art its aesthetic and cultural power. For example, Graff says, Greenblatt emphasizes the need to recognize the racism of *Othello*, the misogyny of *The Taming of the Shrew*, the anti-semitism of *The Merchant of Venice*, and the colonialism of *The Tempest*. He believes that it is all but impossible to understand these plays without grappling with the dark energies upon which Shakespeare's art so powerfully draws.[17]

However, observes Graff, Greenblatt does not reduce *The Merchant of Venice* merely to an example of anti-semitism but sees the play as a site of conflict between these dark energies and more humane impulses. This conflict is an inseparable part of the literary and aesthetic quality of

15. Norris, *Contest*, p. 127.
16. Norris, *Contest*, p. 128.
17. G. Graff, 'The Nonpolitics of PC', *Tikkun* 6.4 (1991), pp. 50-52.

the play. As Greenblatt said in the introduction to *Shakespearean Negotiations*: 'Even those literary texts that sought most ardently to speak for a monolithic power could be shown to be the sites of institutional and ideological contestation'.[18]

A conservative critic could, of course, challenge Greenblatt's assertion that one cannot understand the play without grappling with sociopolitical issues like racism and anti-semitism, by pointing out that generations of readers and audiences seem to have done exactly that. Graff too was aware of this possibility:

> ...if audiences and readers have often paid little attention to these issues this tells us more about the restrictions of attention that have operated on the reading of literature than about Shakespeare...[19]

Graff goes on to express amazement at the ability of the opponents of political readings and ideological literary theory to deny that they have any politics at all. His views concur with the observations of Christopher Norris (quoted earlier) on the hidden political underpinnings of the aestheticians, and the political usefulness of suppressing these ideological underpinnings in order to advance their claims.

At the moment, the politics of interpretation in biblical studies are almost the reverse of those prevailing in literary studies. With the exception of Robert Alter, who does not work in a biblical studies department, the people who originally clamoured for aesthetic literary readings of biblical narrative are precisely the ones who are most sensitive to the ideological aspects of the text. This is probably because the first generation of literary biblical critics were not theoretical purists but were innovators and experimenters who wanted primarily to open the gates to new methodological approaches in general. The result was an eclectic blend of New Criticism, structuralism (a movement which in France was allied with the political left), social scientific and psychoanalytical criticism.

As we move into the postmodern era, the political alignment in biblical studies will probably change. Conservative scholars will most likely tend to occupy the field of poetics, as has often been the case in literature departments. Historical criticism will eventually become fragmented into increasingly diverse schools of thought and practice. Meanwhile, aesthetics and historical context will be read as a seamless ideological construct by the New Historicists who recognize, with Greenblatt, that

18. Greenblatt, *Negotiations*, p. 3.
19. Graff, 'Nonpolitics', p. 52.

there is no escape from historical, socio-political contingency. Literary production, like claims of truth, is (to quote Foucault) 'linked in a circular relation to systems of power which produce it and sustain it, and to effects of power which it induces and which extends it'.[20]

The focus of the New Historicism is what Greenblatt calls the 'circulation of social energy'. The central premise is that works of art have encoded within them the traces of a powerful energy resulting from the context in which they arose:

> ... it is manifested in the capacity of certain verbal, aural, and visual traces to produce, shape, and organize collective physical and mental experiences. Hence it is associated with repeatable forms of pleasure and interest, with the capacity to arouse disquiet, pain, fear, the beating of the heart, pity, laughter, tension, relief, wonder.[21]

Greenblatt's stated aim is to understand how and why some cultural products aquire such compelling force. Although he is interested in the situation which gave rise to the work of art—in his case, the historical context of the Shakespearean theatre—he acknowledges that there is no 'originary moment', when a cultural product is first 'made up'. In practice, he says, '"made up" means inherited, transmitted, altered, modified, reproduced far more than it means invented'.[22] He does, nevertheless, focus on the 'early exchanges', when the energies were first 'collected and deployed and returned to the culture from which they came', even though there is no direct access to the exchanges, 'no pure moment when the energy was passed and the process began'.[23] One can still focus on the historical context in order to ask how the collective beliefs and experiences of that context acquired an energy manifested in literary production.

The play or other work of literature continues to be the conduit of this energy long after the author's death and the inevitable alteration of the social context by the processes of history. 'Plays are made up of multiple exchanges, and the exchanges are multiplied over time, since to the transactions through which the work first acquired social energy are added supplementary transactions through which the work renews its power in changed circumstances'. When we experience a work of art

20. Foucault, *Power/Knowledge*, p. 74.
21. Greenblatt, *Negotiations*, p. 6.
22. Greenblatt, *Negotiations*, p. 13.
23. Greenblatt, *Negotiations*, p. 20.

(or attempt an analysis of it), we do so 'under the terms of our own interests and pleasures and in the light of historical developments that cannot simply be stripped away'.[24] An argument could be made that the field of biblical studies needs to include among its axiomatic assumptions that our own historical context inevitably plays a part in the way we read.

Greenblatt's work is concerned primarily with one author (Shakespeare) in a sociological context about which we have a plenitude of information (relatively speaking). A picture of the ancient Near East is more difficult to piece together. We are limited to the texts and artifacts which happened to be preserved for one reason or another, whether it be accidents of climate (as in Egypt, for example) or the meticulous efforts of a group (such as the scribal class). Our picture of the civilizations is necessarily skewed, not only by the paucity of evidence, but by the fact that we can only guess how typical or atypical the evidence is for its period. Added to this already complex problem is the question of ancient censorship. One wonders how many texts and votive objects were deliberately destroyed or altered by various political and religious powers. For example, Pharaoh Akhenaton's reform and the subsequent reaction against it are well-documented. One can only speculate whether similar processes took place in other regions and other times throughout the ancient Near East, leaving evidence on less durable media.[25]

The biblical scholar also has to contend with a text which is most likely a composite, which has been through more than one redaction. Theorists and critics of modern literature speak of every text, including those with one single author, as made up of disparate citations and elements. For example, Julia Kristeva writes that 'every text takes shape as a mosaic of citations; every text is the absorption and transformation of other texts'.[26]

Kristeva states clearly that she is not referring merely to the separation of sources, but rather to a much more complicated process:

> The term intertextuality denotes this transposition of one (or several) sign system(s) into another; but since this term has often been understood in the banal sense of 'study of sources', we prefer the term transposition

24. Greenblatt, *Negotiations*, p. 20.

25. M. Barker, *The Older Testament: The Survival of Themes from the Ancient Royal Cult in Sectarian Judaism and Early Christianity* (London: SPCK, 1987).

26. J. Kristeva, *Séméiotiké: Recherches pour une Sémanalyse* (Paris: Seuil, 1969), p. 146.

because it specifies that the passage from one signifying system to another demands a new articulation of the thetic—of enunciative and denotative positionality. If one grants that every signifying practice is a field of trans-positions of various signifying systems (an intertextuality), then one understands that its 'place' of enunciation and its denoted 'object' are never single, complete and identical to themselves, but always plural, shattered...[27]

The fact (generally accepted in the field, but not universally so) that the biblical text actually is made up of different sources simply adds one more dimension to this polyvalence, making the process more complex. The task of the biblical scholar therefore has the facets common to all literary critics, with additional challenges. Not only is the original context especially difficult to determine, but the scholar must also take into account the reinterpretations of later (but still ancient) redactors and their contexts, listening carefully to the gaps and silences in the text which may indicate an omission.

If Kristeva is right about every text being a mosaic, then the interest-ing question (to me) is neither what the individual pieces consist of, although that may be one step in the process of analysis, nor is it limited to what the whole signifies (as though a totalizing vision could capture the whole), although that too may raise important issues. The most interesting question is, how does the process of signification work in this text and why? What are the sites and positions of the pieces, what traces of meaning do they bring with them, and what are the relations between each part and every other part?

Looking beyond the issue of sources, at the contradictions and 'places of dissension or shifting interests' (Greenblatt's terminology) within each particular source, one can ask, what do these mean? Also, for those in the field of biblical studies, with a tendency toward fragmentation, per-haps the more crucial question is how and why elements are fused in the text the way they are. Biblical scholars must examine not just the loca-tion and identity of disruptions, but must ask, what can be found by examining the seams where disparate things are brought together, both within any given source and between sources.

The New Historicism, therefore, can be distinguished both from the 'old historicism' (which in biblical scholarship means something a little bit different than the 'old historicism' as conducted in literature depart-ments) and from rhetorical criticism as currently practised by biblical

27. J. Kristeva, *La Révolution de la langue poétique* (Paris: Seuil, 1974), p. 45.

scholars. The 'old historicism' in literary studies, according to Greenblatt, tended to be 'monological':

> ...it is concerned with discovering a single political vision, usually iden-
> tical to that said to be held by the entire literate class or indeed the entire
> population... This vision, most often presumed to be internally coherent
> and consistent, though occasionally analyzed as the fusion of two or more
> elements, has the status of an historical fact. It is not thought to be the
> product of the historian's interpretation, nor even of the particular interests
> of a given social group in conflict with other groups.[28]

Biblical scholars were never guilty of this monologism. The version of historicism which developed in the nineteenth century took account of (and even concentrated on) the distinctions between sources composed by competing factions. Historical criticism tends to be a short-hand expression for source and redaction criticism, with the 'old' form criticism of Gunkel somewhere in the background as well. However, we still may be guilty of over-simplification, overestimating the coherence and consistency within any given source.

We, like our colleagues in literature departments, have been somewhat naive about the mixture of political ideology and rhetoric in the text. Greenblatt's work represents a challenge to:

> ...the assumptions that guarantee a secure distinction between 'literary
> foreground' and 'political background' or, more generally, between artis-
> tic production and other kinds of social production. Such distinctions do
> in fact exist, but they are not intrinsic to the texts; rather they are made up
> and constantly redrawn by artists, audiences, and readers. These collec-
> tive social constructions on the one hand define the range of aesthetic
> possibilities within a given representational mode and, on the other, link
> that mode to the complex network of institutions, practices, and beliefs
> that constitute the culture as a whole. In this light, the study of genre is an
> exploration of the poetics of culture.[29]

While Greenblatt is specifically setting himself in opposition to the 'New Critics' in his field, his words also apply to the distinction between literature and so-called 'ancient Israelite historiography' which has occupied so much attention in twentieth century biblical studies. In other words, clear, unambiguous distinctions between the two types of cultural

---

28. S. Greenblatt, *The Power of Forms in the English Renaissance* (Norman: University of Oklahoma Press, 1982), p. 5.

29. Greenblatt, *Forms*, p. 6.

production (literary writings and historiographical) may be a chimera.
Greenblatt again addresses a similar problem when he says that:

> Renaissance literary works are no longer regarded either as a fixed set of
> texts that are set apart from all other forms of expression and that contain
> their own determinate meanings or as a stable set of reflections of histori-
> cal facts that lie beyond them... recent criticism has been less concerned to
> establish the organic unity of literary works and more open to such works
> as fields of force, places of dissension and shifting interests, occasions
> for the jostling of orthodox and subversive impulses.[30]

To differentiate the New Historicism from the type of rhetorical criticism currently practised by biblical scholars is somewhat more challeng-
ing than differentiating new and old historicisms, because there are many
overlapping concerns. This is particularly true of the branch of rhetorical
criticism which grew out of the 'old' form criticism. Where the form
critics were concerned with the *Sitz-im-Leben* of a literary form or unit,
rhetorical critics staked out as their domain the *Sitz-im-Text*.[31] However,
the focus on the *Sitz-im-Text* places the critic back in New Critical territory. The New Critics privileged the context within the text at the
expense of the context in which it was embedded.

New Historicists are concerned with both dimensions at once and with
how they fit together. The aim is not just recreating the original *Sitz-im-
Leben* for the purpose of historical reconstruction but analysing the historical traces which a word, phrase or even an entire genre carries with
it from that setting (to the extent that it can be determined). One can
simultaneously look at the *Sitz-im-Text*, as well as other settings (in both
life and texts) which have affected the associations that it carries with it
into the new situation in which we find it located.

There is another fundamental difference between New Historicism and
rhetorical criticism as it is usually done by biblical scholars. Rhetorical
critics tend to focus on what Greenblatt calls the search for a stable core
of meaning within the text. He argues that even those texts which
attempt to speak for a monolithic power (such as propaganda) can be
shown to be the sites of institutional and ideological contestation.

---

30. Greenblatt, *Forms*, p. 6.
31. A.M. Vater, 'Story Patterns for a Sitz: A Form- or Literary-Critical
Concern?', *JSOT* 11 (1979), pp. 47-56.

Greenblatt's New Historical[32] approach proposes a way of reading which looks 'less at the presumed center of the literary domain' (by which he means, at this point, a particular text) 'than at its borders, to try to track what can only be glimpsed, as it were, at the margins of the text', in order to gain at least some fragmentary insight into the 'half-hidden cultural transactions through which great works of art are empowered'.[33] Consequently, my reading of Joshua is concentrated not on the edicts of royal propaganda, which many scholars have identified throughout the DH, but instead is focused on the processes of marginalization within the text and how the rhetoric of violence expressed in military language is used to set and negotiate boundaries of inclusion, exclusion and marginality.

---

32. Unlike scholars of the English Renaissance, the field in which most New Historicists are found, biblical scholars are working with an unknown historical context, or at least a historical context which cannot be definitively proven. Therefore more attention is given to discussions of historical context in the present work than would normally be expected in a New Historicist study.

33. Greenblatt, *Negotiations*, pp. 3-4.

Chapter 3

HISTORICAL CONTEXT

I. *Introduction*

In order for the historical context of the Book of Joshua to be determined, an examination of its relationship to other parts of the biblical
canon must be undertaken. Every step of the process involves the
thorny issues of authorship.[1] In this chapter I offer only a selective, but I
trust fairly representative, survey of previous research on the topic of
the historical context in which the Book of Joshua was composed.

II. *Older Christian and Rabbinical Traditions*

The older tradition in Jewish interpretation held that Joshua himself was
the author, except for the final verses which recount his death. Baba
Batra assumes that Joshua wrote the book. According to Baba Batra,
Eleazar, the son of Aaron added the account of Joshua's death, and then
Phinehas recorded the death of his father Eleazar.[2] A modern Jewish
scholar who comes close to the traditional view is Yehezkel Kaufmann,
who argues that the stories were collected from 'living tradition' and
written down at the beginning of the period of the Judges.[3]

The idea that Joshua was the author was retained in the most conservative branch of the Christian interpretive tradition also. The Christian
scholar Charles Ryrie, one of the rare contemporary scholars who maintains that Joshua actually wrote the book himself, argues that it must
have been written by an eyewitness. Ryrie's argument hinges on the
idea that the vivid descriptions in the text mean that it must have been

---

1.   'Authorship' does not necessarily refer to individual authorship, but may
instead be used to mean the faction or factions responsible for a text.
2.   Baba Batra 14b-15.
3.   Kaufmann, *The Biblical Account of the Conquest of Palestine* (Jerusalem:
Magnes Press, 1953), p. 97.

composed by someone with first-hand knowledge of the events.[4] However, there is no reason to suppose that the writer's descriptions were necessarily reliable. Good descriptions only indicate that the writer was a talented story-teller; they do not necessarily indicate that the text contains eyewitness accounts of events. At the present time, only a few scholars still hold the traditional view in its most extreme form.

III. *Modern Theories*

Jewish tradition placed the Book of Joshua at the beginning of the 'former prophets', in accordance with the division of the Hebrew scriptures into three parts: Torah (the first five books, supposedly authored by Moses), prophets, and writings. Some secular and Christian scholars retained the idea that the first five books (which they called the 'Pentateuch') belonged together, even though the tradition of Mosaic authorship came under question. In the late nineteenth and early twentieth centuries, some biblical scholars argued that Joshua belonged with what preceded it, thereby constituting a 'Hexateuch' rather than a Pentateuch.[5] Some attempted to trace the same sources through Joshua that they had found in the first five books. However, no scholarly consensus emerged regarding which passages could be attributed to J and which to E.

A. *Martin Noth and the Deuteronomistic History*[6]
Martin Noth is generally credited with the idea that the books from Deuteronomy to II Kings were written as a 'unified and self-contained whole', which he named the Deuteronomistic History. He gave four reasons in support of his theory:
   1. Chronological scheme;

4.   Ryrie, *The Ryrie Study Bible* (Chicago: Moody Press, 1978), p. 326.
5.   Driver, *An Introduction to the Literature of the Old Testament* (ITL; Edinburgh: T. & T. Clark, 9th edn, 1909); H. Holzinger, *Das Buch Josua* (KHC; Tübingen: J.C.B. Mohr, 1901); J. Wellhausen, *Die Composition des Hexateuchs und der historischen Bücher des Alten Testaments* (Berlin: de Gruyter, 1876–77); J.E. Carpenter and G. Harford-Battersby, *The Hexateuch* (London: Longmans, Green, 1900).
6.   M. Noth, *Überlieferungsgeschichtliche Studien* (Halle: Scriften der Konigsberger Gelehrten Gesellschaft, 1943); partially available in English as *The Deuteronomistic History* (Sheffield: Sheffield Academic Press, 1981). Page numbers cited refer to the English translation.

2. Style: the vocabulary, diction and sentence structure of the editorial material are uniform and easily recognizable;

3. Arrangement: at important points in the story, the writer has one of the leaders make a speech which looks forward and backward in an attempt to 'interpret the course of events', and to give the people practical instructions for their future behaviour;

4. Theological unity in interpretation of history, particularly the writer's concern with God's 'retributive activity' when the people fail to heed demands that God has made upon their conduct.

Noth theorized that the Dtr[7] was writing in the middle of the sixth century BCE,[8] using traditional material which he arranged according to 'a carefully conceived plan'. He compares the Dtr's mode of composition to that of Hellenistic and Roman writers who used older sources to compose a history of the distant past.[9] Later redactors added to the history what Noth calls a series of 'accretions'.

Noth thinks that the Dtr wrote to teach the people 'the true meaning of the history of Israel from the occupation to the destruction of the old order'. The history was not intended to provide entertainment nor was it intended to 'satisfy a curiosity about national history'.[10] The Dtr's primary concerns, in Noth's view, were the special bond between Yahweh and the people, and God's constant involvement in Israel's history. The meaning which the Dtr discovered was:

> that God was recognizably at work in this history, continuously meeting the accelerating moral decline with warnings and punishments, and, finally, when these proved fruitless, with total annihilation.[11]

Noth says that 'following tradition', the Dtr liked to describe the relationship between Yahweh and the people as a 'covenant'. What the Dtr meant (according to Noth) by covenant was the 'permanent regulation

---

7.   Although I usually refer to Dtr in the singular for efficiency's sake, I acknowledge that the plural would be equally appropriate, since we cannot know whether the DH is the work of a school, cf. M. Weinfeld, *Deuteronomy and the Deuteronomic School* (Oxford: Clarendon Press, 1972), some other aggregate of individuals, or a single historian. Even if a single individual composed the work, he probably would not have been working independently in the sense that modern authors do, but most likely would have represented a faction.

8.   Noth, *History*, p. 79.

9.   Noth, *History*, pp. 10-11.

10. Noth, *History*, p. 89.

11. Noth, *History*, p. 89.

as defined in the law of the relationship between God and people'. The real theme of the history according to Noth is:

> the conduct and fate of the people once they have settled in Palestine. Dtr constructed his history as he did in order to show that the early (pre-settlement) events committed the people to unbroken loyalty to God as manifested in observance of the law...[12]

Noth points out that in Deut. 9.9-11 the Dtr equates the concepts of covenant and law (cf. also Deut. 4.13), but Noth fails to attach any ideological significance to this rhetorical linkage. In Noth's interpretation of the Dtr, the demand for observance of the divine law has as its background the 'fact' that God was manifested and acted at the beginning of Israelite history and has repeatedly intervened to help. The special relationship between God and people is confirmed through the 'promulgation of the law'.[13]

Noth was not unaware of the Dtr's peculiar use of the word 'law'. He said that it 'foregrounded' the Dtr's concern with centralization of the cult in the one place of worship (Deut. 12.13-14). Noth commented that this stipulation gets a disproportionate amount of attention compared with everything else that is in the Deuteronomic law and even admits that 'such a treatment of the Deuteronomic law did not do justice to it as a whole'.[14] Noth goes on to acknowledge explicitly that while King Josiah is given credit for 'promulgating the law' and making the law binding through covenant (2 Kgs 23.1-3), the Dtr's concept of the law seems to have been extremely selective:

> Whenever the Dtr makes Moses, Joshua and others insist upon the 'law', that is the Deuteronomic law, and warn the people not to transgress it, and whenever he judges historical figures and events by the standard of the 'law', he obviously means the legal ordinances concerning the worship of 'other gods' and in the case of the monarchical period especially, the legal prescription that there should be only one place of worship; he apparently ignores the rest of the law.[15]

One thing is clear: most of the Book of Joshua is not concerned with the law, except in the most rudimentary sense. Although the word 'law' is frequently mentioned, the content of the legal code is virtually ignored

12. Noth, *History*, p. 91.
13. Noth, *History*, p. 90.
14. Noth, *History*, p. 81.
15. Noth, *History*, p. 81.

throughout, except for the stipulation that there be only one god and only one place of worship,[16] expressed in the strong prohibition against building other altars (Josh. 22.10-34) which might create alternative worship centres.

The 'law', therefore, was directly linked with the royal power which placed the clergy under centralized authority, bringing religious matters firmly under state control. Although Noth has a different explanation for the Dtr's particularly narrow usage of the word 'law', he recognized (to some extent) the significance of the monarchy's role in this redefinition of the 'law' to mean centralized royal control of religious functions:

> ... at the beginning of his account of the monarchy he (Dtr) completely departs from the intention of the law itself and transfers the responsibility for the maintenance of the relationship between God and people, as envisaged by the law, to the monarchy. This is in fact the central idea in his account of the monarchy.[17]

By making the monarchy responsible for observance of the 'law' and making the king a necessary mediator between god and the people, responsible for maintaining the nation's relationship with its deity, the Dtr's ideology essentially gave the king a monopoly on religious power, with the people and the clergy under his control.

The Dtr further solidified the centralization of power in the hands of the king by making the preservation of the divine-human relationship the 'central idea' (to use Noth's terminology) in his account of the monarchy, to the detriment of other possible aspects of kingship. If the monarchy was, by definition, a religious-mediatorial office, then the king had divine sanction (according to Deuteronomistic logic) to quash competing claims to power and to stamp out any attempts at popular insurrection.

Clearly, the Dtr's redefinitions both of the 'law' and of the role of the monarchy are much more ideologically significant than Noth recognizes for purposes of centralizing the forces of social control. For example, according to Noth, the institution of monarchy was presented by the Dtr as:

---

16. The leader is accordingly commanded to build an altar according to specific instructions (Josh. 8.30ff.; Deut. 27.4-8), but the primary focus is on the singularity of the place of worship.

17. Noth, *History*, p. 82.

> ...a late innovation inappropriate by its nature and hence categorically objectionable...it accomplished a positive good only under isolated, outstanding representatives.[18]

Noth seems blind to the fact that presenting Josiah as outstanding in comparison with other monarchs would have obvious ideological advantages for Josiah and his power structure. Although Noth favors a sixth century dating rather than a Josianic dating for the history,[19] he does say that events[20] during Josiah's reign are 'an especially important part of the historical presuppositions to the Dtr's work'. Noth credits the Dtr with elevating the events of Josiah's time to a general norm, making it the 'main function of the monarchy as such to uphold the religious prescriptions in the Deuteronomic law'. Noth naively assumes that the events of Josiah's reign have influenced the Dtr's conception of the Deuteronomic law, giving the Dtr the impression that Josiah's reign was the realization of the ideal that should have been in force throughout the monarchical period:

> The way in which Dtr describes Josiah's application of the law makes it even more clear that he saw the 'law' (the Deuteronomic law) in the light of its historical role under Josiah, i.e., in the task he ascribes to the king of carrying it out. The law itself gave no guidance on this point.[21]

Ignoring the ideological thrust of the passages pertaining to Josiah, Noth explains the Dtr's idealization of King Josiah by saying that the Dtr was still 'vitally close' to the traditions concerning the history of his people. Noth thinks the Dtr already had an ideal fixed in his mind for what a King should be: a mediator between deity and people, responsible for seeing that the 'law' was observed. This 'covenant' responsibility was originally that of the people collectively, according to Noth, but the Dtr mistakenly assumed that the monarchy belonged in a mediatorial role. Rather than looking for which class or institution would benefit from the Dtr's presentation of this role as the 'central idea in his account of the monarchy', Noth simply assumed a mistake on the Dtr's part, a mistake which arose because King Josiah set such a good example that people naturally began to assume that Josiah's time saw the realization

18. Noth, *History*, p. 83.

19. Noth, *History*, p. 80.

20. Noth means that 'events' such as the discovery of the law (2 Kgs 22.3–23.3) and King Josiah's Reforms (2 Kgs 23.4-15, 19-20a), determined Dtr's view of the history of Israel.

21. Noth, *History*, p. 82.

of an ideal that should have been operational throughout the monarchical period.[22]

Noth thinks that the Dtr allows the monarchy to have such a prominent place in the second half of the history simply because the Dtr felt 'obliged to take account of this historical phenomenon', because of the monarchy's role in bringing about the end of the nation, and because the monarchy played a vital role in those developments which determined the Dtr's view of history as a whole. Noth thinks that Josiah's measures did not have much real influence because of Josiah's sudden death and the impact of the contemporary events of world history, but that the influence of Josiah's reform was indirect through the work of the Dtr, which in turn influenced the view of history taken in later times. Noth overlooks the ideological aspect of redefining the king's role in the way that the Dtr does and the advantages it would have for consolidating control.

It is interesting that Noth should say that not all aspects of the law played a practical role under Josiah, and, therefore, not every aspect of the law received attention from the Dtr, without concluding that the whole DH could have been shaped by someone during the period of Josiah's reform. If Josiah is portrayed as ideal, there is probably a good reason. In this case, it is no accident that Josiah, who was trying to assert the power of the central government, was 'ideal' with respect to the portion of the law, religious exclusivity, which best served his purpose: power consolidation. Already, in the Book of Joshua, the concern with the building of other altars and the assertion that it should not be done (Josh. 22.10-34) can be seen. It is vitally important that the word law means only the aspect of the law which is concerned with the centralization of worship in Jerusalem, which limits the power of the rural clergy. This ideology certainly puts the rural clergy under legal monarchical control and cuts the independent power that they might have, especially in remote areas far from Jerusalem.

The Dtr presents the institution of monarchy as neither all good nor all bad; his message seems to be that the nation needs one strong figure at a time to embody national identity and to act as mediator between nation and deity. Centralization of power is the key to the Dtr's ideology, not the type of leadership institution. Although Noth tended to emphasize the Dtr's pessimism with regard to the institution of kingship, a close reading suggests that monarchy in the Dtr was only (in certain

22. Noth, *History*, p. 82

limited contexts) equated with decline and disappointment to Yahweh because of the potential for abuse of power, which the Dtr peculiarly defined as participating in or allowing religious diversity. On the other hand, Josiah's power was enhanced by convincing his subjects that he, like Joshua in the distant past,[23] was necessary as the mediator between the people of his kingdom and their god. The point was to demonstrate that any type of institution could be right if implemented correctly, and the standard for correctly wielding power was defined in terms of power centralization. What could be more advantageous to Josiah's consolidation of power?

Noth's most valuable contribution to the debate about source and redaction issues lies in his recognition that the Books from Deuteronomy through Kings constituted a continuous, chronological account, of which Joshua is a part. Other scholars have challenged his sixth century dating of the history and modified the redactional theories in ways which are detailed below, but most scholars still take seriously his concept of a Deuteronomistic History.

B. *Subsequent Theories concerning the Deuteronomistic History*
Most of the previous research on the DH has been concerned with sources and redaction. There has been some work done in the field of literary criticism, but most of the literary studies have a narrow focus on a segment of the DH other than the Book of Joshua. Exceptions are works by Hawk,[24] Polzin[25] and Jobling.[26] In an intermediate category is Norman K. Gottwald's socio-literary introduction to the Hebrew Bible,[27] which makes use of several approaches.

There are three major schools of thought concerning sources, dating and redaction of the DH, including Noth's hypothesis of an exilic date. While most scholars agree with Noth's hypothesis that the DH constitutes one continuous work, many now think that part of the history was

23. R.D. Nelson, 'Josiah in the Book of Joshua', *JBL* 100.4 (1981), pp. 531-40.
24. C.D. Hawk, *Every Promise Fulfilled: Contending Plots in Joshua* (Louisville: Westminster Press, 1991).
25. R. Polzin, *Moses and the Deuteronomist: A Literary Study of the Deuteronomic History* (New York: Seabury Press, 1980).
26. D. Jobling, *The Sense of Biblical Narrative II* (JSOTSup, 39; Sheffield: Sheffield Academic Press, 1983).
27. N.K. Gottwald, *The Hebrew Bible: a Socio-Literary Introduction* (Philadelphia: Fortress Press, 1985).

a pre-exilic edition. One group of scholars favours a Josianic date for the first redaction.[28] Another group believes the original history ended with the reign of Hezekiah.[29] Both factions agree that there were additions by a later redactor (or redactors), either exilic or postexilic.

1. *The Göttingen School*

Another group, called the Göttingen School because of the connection with theories originating with Rudolph Smend of that university, places the entire DH in the exile. The Göttingen School tends to emphasize the different hands which reworked, or augmented, the original history during the exilic period. Smend[30] attempted to trace the hand of a writer with legal (nomistic) interests, whom he designated DtrN, throughout the books of Joshua and Judges. The original historian he designated DtrG (for Geschichter). Smend's theory was that the nomistic writer not only made additions, but substantially reworked the material in accordance with his interest in the law.

28. F.M. Cross, *Canaanite Myth and Hebrew Epic* (Cambridge: Harvard University Press, 1973); R.D. Nelson, *The Double Redaction of the Deuteronomistic History* (JSOTSup, 18; Sheffield: Sheffield Academic Press, 1981); R.E. Friedman, *The Exile and Biblical Narrative: The Formulation of the Deuteronomistic and Priestly Works* (Chico, CA: Scholars Press, 1981); S. McKenzie, *The Trouble with Kings* (VTSup, 42; Leiden: Brill, 1992).

29. I. Provan, *Hezekiah and the Books of Kings: A Contribution to the Debate about the Composition of the Deuteronomistic History* (BZAW; Berlin: de Gruyter, 1988); H. Weippert, 'Die deuteronomistischen Beurteilungen der Könige von Israel und Juda und das Problem der Redaktion der Königsbücher', *Bib* 53 (1972), pp. 301-39; M. Weinfeld, *Deuteronomy*; B. Halpern, *The First Historians: the Hebrew Bible and History* (San Francisco: Harper & Row, 1988); A.D.H. Mayes agrees with Weippert with regard to the judgement formulae in Kings, but ultimately places more emphasis on Josiah, in *The Story of Israel between Settlement and Exile: A Redactional Study of the Deuteronomistic History* (London: SCM Press, 1983); A. Lemaire posits an even earlier version, dating to the reign of Jehoshaphat, in 'Vers L'histoire de la Rédaction des livres de Rois', *ZAW* 98 (1986), pp. 221-36; R.E. Clements traces the kernel of the history back to the reign of Zedekiah, in 'The Isaiah Narrative of 2 Kings 20.12-19 and the Date of the Deuteronomistic History', in A. Rofé and Y. Zakovitch (eds.), *Isaac Leo Seeligmann Volume: Essays on the Bible and the Ancient World* (3 vols.; Jerusalem: Magnes Press, 1983), pp. 209-20.

30. R. Smend, 'Das Gesetz und die Völker: Ein Beitrag zur deuteronomistischen Redaktionsgeschichte', in H.W. Wolff (ed.), *Probleme biblischer Theologie: Gerhard von Rad zum 70. Gebürtstag* (München: Kaiser, 1971), pp. 494-509.

Building on Smend's work, Dietrich[31] theorized that another writer, called DtrP because of his prophetic interests, had interjected material pertaining to prophetic concerns. DtrP wrote after the first historian, DtrG, according to Dietrich, but before the nomistic writer added his editorial contribution after the release of Jehoiakin. Another follower of Smend, Veijola,[32] added his voice to the discussion by analysing the different attitudes toward the Davidic dynasty in the text. He found three divergent attitudes. He judged DtrG to be consistently pro-monarchy; DtrP he found to be negatively disposed toward the monarchy, and in DtrN, the monarchy's fate was contingent on obedience to the law.

As Provan pointed out in his critique of the Göttingen School, the evidence does not adequately support a thoroughgoing distinction between DtrG and DtrP, since one writer could certainly be interested both in history and prophecy. Furthermore, as Provan also noted, the Göttingen scholars disagree among themselves as to which passages were contributed by which redactor. As arguments among them proliferate, the number of redactors posited also tends to increase.

2. *The Double Redaction Hypothesis*
A number of scholars have developed theories that the first edition of the DH was preexilic, with a second redaction during or after the exile. Concerning the first edition, John Gray argues for the period at the end of the monarchy.[33] He calls attention to several factors that indicate a date prior to 586 BCE, such as the repeated statement about an abiding promise to the Davidic monarchs, and, on the other hand, references to exilic or postexilic events which indicate later additions. Gray finds clear evidence of those two stages, though not of their respective dates, in

31. W. Dietrich, *Prophetie und Geschichte* (FRLANT; Göttingen: Vandenhoeck & Ruprecht, 1972).

32. T. Veijola, *Die ewige Dynastie: David und die Entstehung seiner Dynastie nach der deuteronomistischen Darstellung* (AASF/B193; Helsinki: Suomalainen Tiedeakatemia, 1975); and *Das Königtum in der Burteilung der deuteronomistischen Historiographie: Eine redaktionsgeschichtliche Untersuchung* (AASF/B198; Helsinki: Suomalainen Tiedeakatemia, 1977).

33. J. Gray, *Joshua, Judges, Ruth* (NCB; Grand Rapids: Eerdmans Publishing, 1986); *I and II Kings* (Philadelphia: Westminster Press, 1962). In the introduction to the Joshua commentary, he is vague in assigning a date and seems to be avoiding a definite commitment to a Josianic date for the original compilation of the DH, but, even so, he still agrees that a pre-exilic edition was composed late in the monarchical period. He is more specific in the Kings volume.

Joshua and Judges, especially in the two farewell addresses of Joshua, and in various passages which interrupt the pattern of the Dtr's compilation, using 'post-exilic language'.[34] In the introduction to his commentary (both editions) on Kings, he commits himself to a Josianic date for the first Dtr, whom he refers to as the 'compiler', while leaving open the possibility that some of the traditions might go back at least to the time of Hezekiah. After the collapse of the northern kingdom, he says, the record of events in Judah becomes much fuller. After the inauguration of Josiah's reform, from 622 BCE onward, 'the Deuteronomic compiler, if not describing events which he had personally witnessed, was certainly dealing with history which his 'school' had helped to make'.[35] Although Gray specifically mentions the date 622 for the inauguration of Josiah's reform, the dating is far from certain. In the Chronicler's version (2 Chron. 34.6-7), the reform predates the finding of the text (supposedly a version of what is now Deuteronomy) in the temple. As M. Cogan points out,[36] Josiah's first act upon taking over the reigns of government in the Chronicler's version of events is purging the entire kingdom of all idolatry:

> ...now that the reform precedes the discovery of the Torah book, the sudden recognition of guilt which the book prompts is pointless: the sins mentioned by the book had been abolished six years earlier.[37]

The Chronicler's version highlights Josiah's devotion to Yahweh from his youth. The Dtr's version (in 2 Kings 22 and 23) serves a different purpose rhetorically, one which places the emphasis on obedience to an (allegedly) authoritative text. The very same text (or some version of it) is then placed at the beginning of the DH, lending it the same air of authority. The implication is that those exposed to the text should be every bit as moved as the pious king and just as inspired to obedience. As mentioned above, however, the emphasis throughout the DH is not on the content of specific laws but is attuned to the issues of centralization and unity.

---

34. Gray, *Joshua*, pp. 5-6.
35. Gray, *Kings*, pp. 13-14, 34-36.
36. M. Cogan, 'The Chronicler's use of Chronology as Illuminated by Neo-Assyrian Royal Inscriptions', in J.H. Tigay (ed.), *Empirical Models for Biblical Criticism* (Philadelphia: University of Pennsylvania Press, 1985), pp. 197-209.
37. Cogan, 'Chronicler's Use of Chronology', p, 204.

Wright and Boling[38] argue for a Josianic dating, although the focus of their work is more on the early history and archaeology of the Syro-Palestine region. Much of their attention is devoted to a search for the sources used by the Dtr, such as temple archives and other documents. They seem to be hardly concerned with the ideological aspects of the composition and oblivious to the political thrust of the emphasis on centralization in Jerusalem. They hypothesize instead that the Dtr worked in Jerusalem and that, for him, Jerusalem was the center of the world.

In contrast, several scholars have argued that a date during the reign of King Hezekiah should be assigned to the original historical document. According to Helga Weippert,[39] the formulae of judgment applied to the kings of Israel and Judah appear to come from the three different redactions. The first, she argues, is Hezekian, with later additions made during Josiah's reign and again in the exile.

Provan argues that the DH ended with Hezekiah's reign, and was probably assembled early in the reign of Josiah.[40] The resulting document, he argues, is the only pre-exilic edition of the books. The document was first revised during the exile, and was subsequently augmented only by isolated additions.

Mayes, writing earlier, also thinks that Weippert's theory might have merit with regard to the judgment formulae in Kings. The early edition, according to Mayes, was prompted by the reform movement of Hezekiah. It was then updated and set in a 'wider context' during the time of Josiah, whose reform was given a positive evaluation on the basis of Hezekiah's earlier reform.[41] Mayes's theory, however, does not take into account the greater attention given to Josiah and the explicit parallels between Josiah and previous rulers, which stand out particularly when compared with the short and sketchy account of Hezekiah's reign.[42] Mayes himself is rather vague about the earlier edition and places more emphasis on Josiah.

38. G.E. Wright and R.G. Boling, *Joshua* (AB; Garden City: Doubleday, 1982).
39. H. Weippert, 'Die "deuteronomistischen" Beurteilungen', pp. 301-39.
40. Provan, *Hezekiah and Kings*, pp. 154-57.
41. Mayes, *The Story of Israel*, pp. 122-23.
42. Parallels have been pointed out by Cross and (especially) Nelson between Josiah and Joshua, as noted above in Chapter 1. On the other hand, Friedman makes the case for parallels between Josiah and Moses (pp. 1-43). Since the Dtr himself took care to draw parallels between Moses and his successor Joshua, the overlap should hardly be surprising.

Weinfeld also gives more attention to the Josianic era, although he posits an earlier document. The focus of his work, however, is on his theory that the DH has its origins in a wisdom school associated with the monarchy. While he is correct in his assumption that whoever wrote the pre-exilic DH had interests closely allied with the monarchy, there is little similarity between the passionately ideological tone of the Dtr's approach to national identity formation and the silence on the subject typically found in the wisdom literature. Politics, in the wisdom literature, usually means the interpersonal politics of getting along at the royal court, not the politics of nationalism.

3. *Alternatives*

M. O'Brien[43] offers an unusual blending of the Double Redaction (Cross) hypothesis and the Göttingen school. Like the Göttingen scholars, he believes that there is a prophetic stratum of editing in the DH, specifically a prophetic record of the monarchy which served as the basis of Samuel and Kings. Unlike them, however, he thinks that the prophetic stratum predates the exile and even underlies a redaction dating to the Josianic period. In his view, the document was subsequently re-edited more than once during the exile. However, his idea of a prophetic record places too much emphasis on the (supposed) coherence of the prophetic material, as noted by S. McKenzie, since often the different parts of the material bear little resemblence to each other. Also, the prophetic critiques of the monarchy can usually be explained as criticisms of specific leaders or situations. As Cross and Nelson have each pointed out, these criticisms serve to enhance the image of Josiah by contrast.

J. Van Seters[44] hearkens back to Noth's idea of a history composed during the exile. His work constitutes a challenge to those who posit a pre-exilic edition of the DH. Unlike the Göttingen scholars, who also place the composition in the exilic period but who focus on the differences between redactional layers, Van Seters stresses the unity of the DH (as did Noth). As McKenzie points out, however, Van Seters does not explain the pre-exilic themes and concerns which form a prominent part of the DH. Hardly anyone is denying the presence of exilic or post-exilic material in the DH. What is different about Van Seters is his

43. M.A. O'Brien, *The Deuteronomistic History Hypothesis: A Reassessment* (Göttingen: Vandenhoeck & Ruprecht, 1989).

44. J. Van Seters, *In Search of History: Historiography in the Ancient World and the Origins of Biblical History* (New Haven: Yale University Press, 1983).

insistence (like the Göttingen school) that the entire composition is exilic. He even goes so far as to deny the use of earlier sources in the composition.

As McKenzie says, the divine promise to David that he would always have a descendant on the throne and dominion in Jerusalem indicates a date in the era of the monarchy. That theme reaches its climax in the account of Josiah's reign as the culmination of the history, as Cross and Nelson mention as well. McKenzie also notes the sharp contrast between the account from Josiah's death onward and the previous material in Kings. The blame on Manasseh for the people's fate appears to him to be added on:

> Judah survived through previous evil kings because of David's faithfulness. The account of Josiah's reign leaves one with an optimistic outlook for the future. It makes no sense for Dtr to present such a positive picture of Josiah correcting all of Manasseh's wrongs and then to blame Manasseh for the exile. One expects Dtr to explain either that Josiah's efforts were ineffective in curbing the practices begun by Manasseh or that the sins of the people following Josiah brought on the exile. He does neither.[45]

McKenzie concludes that the efforts to explain away the Davidic and Manasseh themes have not been convincing and that the compositon of the DH belongs to the Josianic era. McKenzie agrees with Van Seters, however, on certain issues: the use of earlier sources or even the existence of a possibly earlier edition of the DH have been over-emphasised by previous scholars (such as O'Brien, with his concept of a prophetic document); also, McKenzie agrees with some of the observations of Van Seters regarding history writing. The purpose of the DH, according to Van Seters, was to provide an account of Israel's national traditions, and he compares the composition of the DH with Greek history writing. McKenzie concurs that 'Dtr may have been motivated by a contemporary search for national identity on the heels of the demise of the Northern kingdom'.[46] Both Van Seters and McKenzie, however, neglect to deal with the inherently idealogical aspect of history writing in sufficient depth.

The discussion of the date of the DH is inevitably intertwined with the question of the purpose of its composition. Therefore the following

---

45. McKenzie, *The Trouble with Kings*, p. 149.
46. McKenzie, *The Trouble with Kings*, p. 150.

section, while continuing to address the issue of dating, will deal explicitly with the issue of purpose.

C. *Purpose: the Deuteronomistic History as an Ideological Document Dating to the Reign of King Josiah*

In his recent monograph (cited above), McKenzie concedes that a work of history motivated by a quest for national identity and written during Josiah's reign would contain 'propagandistic elements favourable to him'.[47] He denies that the DH was designed as a piece of propaganda, however, on the grounds that such a composition would focus only on the monarchy. Why, he asks, would it contain the books of Deuteronomy through Judges at all? This question will be addressed not only in the present section, but in my own analysis of the Book of Joshua (especially in my Chapters 7 and 8), in which I discuss the ideological statement that the Dtr was making with his rendition of the conquest narrative. For the moment, however, the approaches of Cross, Nelson and the Cootes are the focus of my discussion because each of them has addressed some aspect of the issue (before McKenzie asked the question in the conclusion to his monograph).

The idea that the DH was written as propaganda for Josiah's reform was put forth earlier by F.M. Cross.[48] He notes that the exilic editor's additions (written sometime around 560 BCE) reinterpret the theological thrust of the original in order to bring the History up to date and make theological sense of the exilic experience. Both Cross and R.D. Nelson[49] see evidence of two layers of redaction (one Josianic, one exilic), on the basis of stylistic distinctions and a divergence in attitudes toward the Davidic promise (see below), which they say was always unconditional in the pre-exilic edition of the History. Nelson, like Cross, accepts the idea of a DH written (using sources) during the time of Josiah's reform and subsequently re-edited during the exile. He calls Cross's contention that the history was intended as propaganda for Josiah's policies a 'perfectly reasonable one', because such propaganda would have fulfilled a need in overcoming opposition to Josiah's policies from many different quarters:

> ...the newly unemployed provincial clergy (2 Kings 23.9), who presumably would still have had an influence upon their former parishioners,

47. McKenzie, *The Trouble with Kings*, p. 150.
48. F.M. Cross, *Myth*.
49. R.D. Nelson, *Double Redaction*.

...the average peasant, whose religious orientation and comfortable local rituals were being overturned...municipal officials who saw the prestige of their localities being destroyed along with their sanctuaries...the more extreme reformers who felt that Josiah had not gone far enough, among them perhaps Jeremiah...pro-Assyrian elements who had supported Manasseh and Amon, loyalists to the old pagan cults, and perhaps even paid Egyptian agents, and...possibly also die-hard Northern nationalists who refused to accept a Davidic king.[50]

The original history was intended to meet exactly this sort of opposition by emphasizing that the Deuteronomic law was of great authority and antiquity, that centralization was a feature of the earliest worship, and that Jerusalem was the place chosen by Yahweh for the centralization. Jeroboam's 'sin' of non-central worship had brought destruction to the Northern Kingdom. The great centralizer Josiah, by way of contrast, was pictured as a paragon of virtue.[51]

The exilic edition, in Nelson's view, is a 'doxology of judgment' (a phrase borrowed from von Rad) on the people for their refusal to heed the warnings of Yahweh's messengers; Nelson cites Judg. 2.2, 6.10; 2 Kings 17.14, 40; 21.9 to support his point.[52] Nelson primarily uses data from the Books of Kings rather than Joshua to advance his arguments, but one of the stylistic differences to which he draws attention is the rigidity of the exilic editor's stereotyped phrases. Although his examples come from the regnal formulae in Kings, his observation about the exilic editor's stereotyped expressions could apply with equal appropriateness to the excursus on the law which interrupts the war oracle in Joshua 1 (see detailed discussion on war oracle language in the subsequent chapter).

Cross and Nelson both argue that the two main themes of the History, the 'sin of Jeroboam' and the 'promise to David', climax in Josiah's reform with the reunification of the monarchy. They each go on to argue that the subtheme of inevitable punishment for Manasseh's sins must be an exilic addition because it is 'out of tune' with the historian's two central themes.[53] Although I agree with their separation of sources (for the most part) and their dating (for different reasons), I think that they have missed part of the point regarding the 'sin' and the 'promise'.

50. Nelson, *Double Redaction*, pp. 121-22.
51. Nelson, *Double Redaction*, pp. 121-22.
52. Nelson, *Double Redaction*, p. 123.
53. Nelson, *Double Redaction*, p. 128.

The Dtr's concern with the 'sin' of a leader by causing the people to 'sin' is related to the issue of centralization of religious and political power. The word 'sin' in the text of the DH, especially in the regnal formulae in Kings (which are the focus of Nelson's book), is narrowly defined, and for good reason. 'Sin' refers to religious variation because religious diversity threatens the centralization of power.

The crucial aspect of the 'promise' to the monarchy is also the centralization of political and religious power identified (in hierarchical arrangement) with a singular national deity. Loyalty to the leader can therefore be ideologically equated with loyalty to the god: one leader, one god, one place of worship, one unified community. A singular leader, set in place (through any socio-political institution) by the deity, can then be presented as the embodiment of the community. The power is consolidated with the consent, and perhaps even enthusiasm, of the people. Any diffusion of power and control could then be portrayed as bad, a transgression against divine will. A highly centralized government can be presented as having divine sanction, regardless of the nature of the institution (monarchy, judgeship, etc.) in order to subsume all of history under one ideology of leadership: whether the leader is charismatic or dynastic, the important point is the central embodiment of national identity. The emphasis on the mediatorial role gives divine legitimacy to this consolidation of control.

Dissenters to any aspect of the system can be accused of sin, since 'sin' is defined in DH as disloyalty to Yahweh (religious fragmentation). The 'sin' of a king (such as Jeroboam) is, therefore, a particularly heinous wrongdoing because he is supposed to be the embodiment of the national unity. Such a 'sin' would be an extremely dangerous threat in the ideology of the Dtr; national identity is at stake. Therefore, when a king is judged on the basis of whether or not he 'caused the people to sin' (jeopardizing the community's religious cohesiveness), he is being judged by the Dtr on whether or not his practices are conducive to centralized power.

Nelson acknowledges that the reign of Josiah was a time of great centralization, and he offers sound reasons for favouring a Josianic date. According to Nelson:

> Judah under Josiah was expanding geographically to fill the vacuum left by the decay of Assyrian power...In conjunction with this policy of national expansion came a radical religious and economic centralization...
> (a) pervasive sense of retrospection and nostalgia for the past permeated

the literary and intellectual life of the nation. In general, it was a period
marked by nationalism, reunification, centralization... dynastic pride, and
a desire to retûrn to the sources of the national life.[54]

There is no reason, however, to assume that the Dtr's (or King Josiah's)
version of the past was necessarily accurate or objective.

Robert and Mary Coote are more suspicious of the monarch's
motives, particularly with regard to the rural or regional powers among
Josiah's subjects who might have challenged his supremacy:

> The stories of the judges, in the book of Judges, represented the exploits
> of local and tribal strongmen of just the sort on whom Josiah strove to
> impose his law.[55]

According to the Cootes, the DH was a full scale history of the house of
David, undertaken by Josiah's scribes, starting with the original docu-
ments justifying David's usurpation of Israelite lands. The Cootes, like
Cross and Nelson, hold the opinion that Joshua is a thinly disguised King
Josiah: like Josiah, Joshua led the nation as one cohesive entity. Like
Josiah, he led a series of military rampages. Like Josiah, Joshua also
allotted conquered land to his followers.[56]

The last point is significant in the Cootes' analysis. The DH, according
to the Cootes, was read aloud to 'preempted magnates' who were
invited to do battle for new land under Josiah's 'Joshua-like banner':

> As Assyrian power waned... Josiah began a series of military rampages
> that left registers, whose tenure of land traced to Jeroboam or his succes-
> sors or Assyria, dead, and joiners... with part of their lands
> confirmed... Thus much land fell to Josiah, who, wanting not just to
> demote the magnates of Judah but to make them join his movement,
> offered them liberated lands in Israel...[57]

The DH may have been read aloud at public assemblies, as the Cootes
suggest, but its length indicates that perhaps the scribes intended it primarily as a written document. The great houses of the powerful rural
gentry would have included literate members necessary for record-
keeping and correspondence. Certainly the regional bureaucrats under
Assyrian imperial rule were among the literate classes.[58] The priestly

---

54. Nelson, *Double Redaction*, p. 121.
55. Coote and Coote, *Power*, p. 64.
56. Coote and Coote, *Power*, pp. 63-64.
57. Coote and Coote, *Power*, p. 60.
58. A.L. Oppenheim, *Ancient Mesopotamia: Portrait of a Dead Civilization*

functionaries would also have been literate. Probably the intended audience of the DH was more diverse than the Cootes suggest, including cultic personnel, influential householders, petty bureaucrats and former bureaucrats.

The DH appears to be aimed at an audience who would have been among the leadership in diverse areas of life; hence the emphasis on leaders who cause their followers to 'sin' by tolerating religious diversity. Not only do the judgment formulae highlight the virtues of King Josiah by contrast, but the formulae also indicate to leaders and potential leaders at subsidiary levels the importance of joining with the national enterprise headed by the monarchy and its national deity Yahweh.

The 'vacuum left by the decay of Assyrian power' to which Nelson refers may have plunged the region into greater chaos than biblical scholars have heretofore recognized.[59] The various factions, cultic personnel, regional leaders and other small-scale power-brokers may have provided King Josiah with serious competition, particularly from rural areas. Personal and communal identity was probably an open question for much of the population. Should they find their identity in the larger entity 'Israel', in their tribal affiliation, or in their adherence to a particular local cult? These are questions that King Josiah was trying to answer for his subjects, to his personal and political advantage.

(Chicago: University of Chicago Press, 1977 [1964]), pp. 228-35.

59. The view that the Assyrians had left as early as Nelson supposed has been challenged by Na'aman. However, Assyrian power would certainly have been in decline even before they had completely withdrawn. N. Na'aman, 'The Kingdom of Judah under Josiah', *Tel Aviv* 18 (1991), pp. 3-71.

Chapter 4

DIVINE WARFARE

I. *Introduction*

In the previous Chapter, I summarized the most prominent contemporary views concerning the historical and political context which produced the first edition of the DH, including the bulk of the Book of Joshua, in order to establish its relationship to King Josiah's political concerns. In the two Chapters subsequent to the present one, I intend to analyze the conventional language of war in the ancient Near East and in the Hebrew Bible, respectively, in order to demonstrate how Josiah and those around him were using well-known conventions for political purposes. In order to lay the groundwork, however, a brief look at some of the previous research on divine participation in warfare in the Hebrew Bible and the relevant ancient Near Eastern parallels is needed. While the present chapter is not intended to be a thorough survey, I shall attempt to present a reasonably representative picture of the scholarly debate. I believe that such a discussion is essential to understanding how the rhetoric of violence functions in the Book of Joshua because the Assyrian influence which is central to my thesis has not always been noticed or acknowledged by other scholars, nor has the connection between the rhetoric of violence and the monarchy.

Many scholars have addressed the issue of warfare in the Bible, but the majority of them have focused their research on an attempt to uncover a real-life institution of sacral warfare in Israel's early history. Several have focused on ancient Near Eastern parallels in order to determine whether or not there is anything unique about the Hebrew conception of divine participation in battle when compared with neighbouring cultures (a useful approach, although, as I point out below, most attempts have been too limited to yield definitive results). Still other scholars have attempted to deduce a theological message in the material, in order to place the biblical text into either a 'just war' theory or a defence of pacificism, but a theology of warfare is not my primary purpose here. In the present chapter, I focus specifically on the current scholarly debate concerning warfare in the Hebrew Bible.

II. *Divine Intervention in History*

B. Albrektson[1] addresses the question whether the Biblical 'idea of historical events as divine manifestations is quite as distinctive as is commonly claimed'. Although his study is not limited to warfare, many of his comments are relevant since one of the primary ways that a god acts 'in history' is through military victories and defeats. He laments the 'trend' in theology and biblical studies of contrasting the Bible's revelation through 'history' to the Mesopotamian emphasis on the 'eternal cyclical processes of nature' as the sphere of divine activity. He observes that such statements have been made by scholars of many different schools of thought, including Mowinckel, Noth, and Vriezen. For example, Noth claimed that the religions of the ancient Near East traced the divine powers in the recurring interplay of the forces of nature, whereas the Old Testament finds God revealed in unrepeatable acts of history.[2] Vriezen said that 'Israel did not derive its knowledge of God first and foremost from nature, as the ancient oriental peoples did, but from the acts of God in the history of the people...'[3] Albrektson examines primarily the comparative materials from other ancient Near Eastern cultures and concludes that while the gods of the various cultures may have been associated with forces of nature, they were not merely nature gods. Their sphere of activity extended into other areas of life, including battles, just as Yahweh's did. Divine participation in 'history', including warfare, is therefore not unique, but is part of the 'common heritage of ancient Near Eastern religions'.[4]

---

1. B. Albrektson, *History and the Gods: An Essay on the Idea of Historical Events as Divine Manifestations in the Ancient Near East and in Israel* (Lund: C.W.K. Gleerup, 1967).

2. M. Noth, *Gesammelte Studien zum Alten Testament* (München: Kaiser, 1957), p. 249.

3. T.C. Vriezen, *An Outline of Old Testament Theology* (Oxford: Oxford Unversity Press, 1958), p. 187.

4. Albrektson, *History of the Gods*, p. 122.

III. *Holy War, Yahweh War and Divine War*

Friedrich Schwally[5] was one of the first modern scholars to write about the concept of 'holy war'. He wrote at the beginning of the twentieth century. In his work, he compared the biblical text with other ancient Near Eastern martial literature and found that all of the cultures in the region claimed their gods' assistance in battle. Only Israel, according to Schwally, expressed the belief that it was unnecessary for the warriors to fight because Yahweh would do their fighting for them. Some scholars still maintain this distinction (see section below).

Much of the discussion concerning warfare in the Bible has dealt with whether or not the term 'holy war' is appropriate. Schwally used the term 'holy war', but many scholars since Schwally's time have pointed out that the type of warfare depicted in the Bible bears little resemblence to true 'holy war' in the sense that the ancient Greeks used the term, nor is it exactly like the Islamic *jihad*.

Gerhard von Rad sparked the debate over nomenclature when he published his *Heilige Krieg*,[6] which is now regarded as a classic, even though most scholars disagree with at least some of his conclusions. Other scholars, as detailed below, have suggested substituting the term 'Yahweh war', or (more recently) the general term 'divine war'.

Gerhard von Rad's study of 'holy war' bears the stamp of form-critical concerns, which dominated much of the scholarly debate during the time it was written. Much of his work was based on the use of formulaic language in the text. He engaged in an attempt to uncover the evidence for a real-life institution of sacral warfare associated with the 'tribal amphictyony' in the pre-monarchical period. The features he identified were: 1. the blast on the ram's horn to muster the tribes; an even earlier way of mustering consisted of sending out pieces of flesh; 2. the men were consecrated; 3. they made sacrifices and sought a divine oracle; 4. Yahweh moved out ahead of the army; 5. the enemies lost courage; 6. the highpoint and conclusion of the holy war was the *herem*; 7. at the end, the militia was dismissed with the cry 'To your tents, O Israel!'

Although he failed to accomplish his purpose, delineating an ancient social institution, he succeeded admirably in describing the kind of

5. F. Schwally, *Semitische Kriegsaltertumer I: Der heilige Krieg im alten Israel* (Leipzig: Dieterich, 1901).

6. G. von Rad, *Der heilige Krieg im alten Israel* (Göttingen: Vandenhoeck & Ruprecht, 1962).

rhetoric associated with warfare in the biblical text. His study therefore provides a good starting point for further discussion of the language of warfare.

Other scholars have taken issue with his choice of the term 'holy war' and recommend replacing it with the term 'Yahweh war', shifting the focus from the search for a cultic institution to the search for the roots of warfare conducted in Yahweh's name, with or without formal cultic involvement. R. Smend's work on Yahweh war[7] has many of the same short-comings as von Rad's on 'holy war', and for the same reasons, which are essentially methodological. Smend was attempting to discover whether the concept of Yahweh war originated among the Rachel tribes or the Leah tribes. Again, he was seeking the roots of a real-life socio-political and religious institution or practice by reading texts composed many centuries later. He not only overlooked the ideological function of the DH itself when he wrote his book on Yahweh war, but he also seemed oblivious to the fact, accepted by many anthropologists studying the Middle East at the present time, that tribal geneologies (such as those of the partriarchs and matriarchs) are more ideological than historical.[8] Therefore his focus on the distinction between the Rachel tribes and the Leah tribes may be a fruitless exercise.

Gwilym H. Jones[9] responded to the debate over terminology by proposing that the term 'Yahweh war' be used for old traditions of Yahweh's participation in warfare, while the term 'holy war' be used to describe the later formalization of these traditions in subsequent layers of redaction. He does not believe in an early Israelite cultic institution of 'Yahweh war'.

Fritz Stolz[10] also denies that there was such a pre-monarchical institution. He even denies the existence of a tribal federation. He argues that there was no common cultic or political setting which could be linked to the practice of 'Yahweh war'; there was no uniform ancient institution. There were only diverse experiences of tribal warfare, in which the belief was that Yahweh gave his people victory. He very sensibly credited the

---

7. R. Smend, *Jahwekrieg und Stämmebund* (Göttingen: Vandenhoeck and Ruprecht, 1963).

8. M.E. Meeker, *Literature and Violence in North Arabia* (Cambridge: Cambridge University Press, 1979).

9. G.H. Jones, 'Holy War or YHWH War?' *VT* 25 (1975), pp. 642-58.

10. F. Stolz, *Jahwes und Israels Kriege: Kriegstheorien und Kriegserfahrungen im Glauben des alten Israel* (Zürich: Zwingli Verlag, 1972).

Dtr with creating the appearance of an institution of 'Yahweh war' by reworking earlier traditions, using their own distinctive deuteronomistic perspective.

Some of the debate over biblical warfare stems from a tendency on the part of scholars to over-emphasize divine action over human military action. M.C. Lind[11] (discussed in more detail below), for example, sees a tension between the 'prophetic structure' of Israel and its warfare, on the one hand, and the 'kingship structures' of her neighbors, on the other. He links the origins of dependence on Yahweh rather than on military superiority to the exodus event, which was led by a prophetic figure, Moses. There was indeed human activity, says Lind, but it was the action of a prophet, not a warrior.

Stolz also thought that one of the sources of Israel's war traditions was the experience of the tribes with superior Canaanite forces. Part of the reason that scholars draw such conclusions is because of the Bible's emphasis on reliance upon divine power rather than human might, but M. Weippert[12] and others have demonstrated that this motif is found in other ancient Near Eastern war texts as well (see below), and there the motif is associated with the monarchy, not opposed to it. Also, some scholars tend to see the 'holy war' or 'Yahweh war' as something which was associated with popular movements and with 'charismatic' leadership, against the great military and political power of the vast empires or the strong city-states. For example, P. Weimar[13] cites the strong link between Yahweh and various prophetic figures such as Deborah and Samuel as well as Moses. Weimar posits a northern origin for the war narratives, which he says were brought to Jerusalem during David's time. These narratives were directed against the royal court and its ideology. He sees 'holy war' as a part of the opposition between the prophetic leadership and the monarchy and says that the 'holy war' traditions were used to criticize the kings. The implication is that the prophetic faction was criticizing the kings for placing the emphasis on earthly power, such as the monarchy and its institutions, rather than on

11. M.C. Lind, *Yahweh is a Warrior: The Theology of Warfare in Ancient Israel* (Scottsdale: Herald Press, 1980).

12. M. Weippert, '"Heiliger Krieg" in Israel und Assyrien: Kritische Anmerkungen zu Gerhard von Rads Konzept des "Heiligen Krieges im alten Israel"', *ZAW* 84 (1972), pp. 460-93.

13. P. Weimar, 'Die Jahwekriegserzählungen in Exodus 14, Josua 10, Richter 4 und 1 Samuel 7', *Bib* 57 (1976), pp. 38-73.

the sovereignty of Yahweh. The monarchy, however, was usually criticized in the DH when the king was allied with foreign governments (and the attendant deities) as vassals, which undercut the Davidic monarchy's power.

Those who see the biblical war traditions as anti-monarchy are not being sufficiently sensitive to the ideology of the DH, in which some kings are praised and others are criticized for their failure to live up to the leadership position entrusted to them by Yahweh. They have also ignored the patterns of leadership in the DH, which emphasize that Yahweh raises up one leader at a time as an embodiment of national identity. This pattern has been misinterpreted as pro-charismatic (prophetic) and anti-monarchy at times, and as pro-monarchy at other times. The confusion results from a misundertanding of the Dtr's attitude toward kingship, partly as a result of the Dtr's condemnation of those rulers who 'lead the people into sin' (idolatry). Nevertheless, I argue throughout my study of the Book of Joshua that the Dtr seems to believe in a hierarchical society with the king, or someone standing in his place, as the leader chosen by Yahweh (Moses, Joshua, Deborah, Samuel, etc.), functioning as a necessary hinge in the divine-human relationship.

Therefore, the modesty of a ruler in giving the deity credit for his military successes should not necessarily be taken as evidence of superior piety but should be read in the context of a work (the DH) which culminates in the reconstitution of monarchical power in the deity's name.

Weippert pointed out that other ancient Near Eastern texts also reflect the belief that the gods and goddesses, not superior military might, are what win wars. For example, Weippert quotes Assurbanipal:

> Not by my own might,
> not by the strength of my bow-by the might of my gods,
> by the strength of my goddesses,
> I subjected the lands... to the yoke of Assur.[14]

The evidence from Mari proves that this same motif goes back well into the second millennium BCE in Mesopotamia. The following oracle is from a Mesopotamian seer associated with the court of Zimri-Lim:

> A battle will not be fought. Right on arriving, his (Iéme-Dagan's) auxiliary troops will be scattered; furthermore, they will cut off the head of Iéme-Dagan and put it under the foot of my lord. Thus (my lord will say):

14. M. Weippert, '"Heiliger Krieg" in Israel', p. 483.

'The army of Iéme-Dagan is large, and if I arrive, will his auxiliary troops be scattered from his? They have hemmed in my auxiliary troops'. It is Dagan, Adad, Itér-Mer and Bélat-ekallim—and Adad indeed is the lord of decision!—who march at my lord's side. Heaven forbid that my lord should say this, saying: 'By means of arms I must lay them low'... Before my lord his army will be scattered.[15]

In his article on the Mari materials, W.L. Moran points out that the objection concerning the superior size of Iéme-Dagan's army and the difficult situation of Zimri-Lim's auxiliary forces is denied any validity by the seer on the ground that divine assistance will more than compensate for lack of numbers. The seer expresses the hope that the king will not be so lacking in faith as to suggest that wars are won with weapons. 'These lines', says Moran, 'will evoke in the minds of Old Testament scholars many a biblical passage'.[16]

Moran also calls attention to an oracle in which Zimri-Lim is told not to go to battle: 'Stay in Mari and then I alone will take responsibility'.[17] Moran comments that the 'quietism' of the oracle which would keep the king home and reserve all real action to divine intervention, anticipates by centuries the similar advice given to Assurbanipal. 'Of course', he says, 'it also recalls the silent, passive ranks of Exod. 14 and the extreme position of Isa. 30, 15'.[18] The biblical text can no longer be considered unique because of the emphasis on divine rather than human action in warfare. Also, in these oracles from Mesopotamia, the motif of divine power rather than military might winning battles is associated with the royalist ideologies of Assurbanipal and Zimri-Lim, respectively, not with any sort of anti-royalist position.

In his article on 'holy war' in Israel and Assyria, Weippert disputes several commonly-held assumptions concerning biblical accounts of warfare and related socio-political institutions, including 1. the uniqueness of Israel's attribution of victory to divine intervention; 2. the distinction (a false distinction, according to Weippert) between sacred and profane warfare in the ancient Near East; and 3. differences in presentation of offensive and defensive wars. Much of the article concerns von Rad's concept of 'holy war' as a set of military practices combined with

15. W.L. Moran, 'New Evidence from Mari on the History of Prophecy', *Bib* 50 (1969), pp. 15-56.
16. Moran, 'New Evidence', pp. 48-49.
17. Moran, 'New Evidence', p. 39.
18. Moran, 'New Evidence', p. 40.

religious rites and beliefs, which von Rad traces to the pre-monarchical days of the tribal amphictyony. By comparing the language and conventions found in Assyrian inscriptions with biblical texts, Weippert domonstrates that most of the elements which von Rad had identified as stemming from a specifically Israelite institution of 'holy war' are common to other ancient Near Eastern cultures as well. Weippert makes the same point concerning Smend's term 'Yahweh war'. 'He who would speak of "Yahweh war"', writes Weippert, 'must also speak of "Assur war" or "Ishtar war"'.

While his analysis of the Assyrian materials is complete, he refers only briefly to the Mari war oracles and a few other ancient Near Eastern (mostly Hittite) materials. This limitation of scope is understandable, given the topic of the article, but there are numerous examples from Egyptian literature which would have further supported his assertion that all warfare in the ancient Near East had a sacral aspect and that the terminology, ideology and practices of warfare had certain similarities throughout the region. Weippert's article includes an excellent section on the rhetorical function of the Assyrian inscriptions as a legitimation for the wars of the Assyrian kings, presented as a fulfilment of the divine will. Weippert observes that the inscriptions can also be interpreted as propaganda akin to the 'Siegesstelen', intended to intimidate those who dare to challenge Assyria's claims to territory and power.

M. Weinfeld[19] observes that scholars have recently begun to realize that the image of the fighting god aiding his people in warfare was not limited to Israel but was widespread in the ancient Near East. According to Weinfeld, descriptions of manifestations such as those found in Ps. 18.11-18 are rooted in the 'tradition of the storm god (Adad/Hadad), lord of thunder, lightning and rain'. Weinfeld also ascribes to this 'tradition' the passages in Canaanite, Egyptian and Greek literature which contain accounts of the changes of nature which follow or accompany the appearance of the god. He states that the language in which the change of nature is formulated is 'identical' in all of these sources. Although 'identical' is too strong a word, his examples from Akkadian, Ugaritic, Egyptian and Greek, as well as Hebrew, texts exhibit a remarkable consistency in their descriptions of the voice of the deity

---

19. M. Weinfeld, 'Divine Intervention in War in Ancient Israel and in the Ancient Near East', M. Weinfeld and H. Tadmor (eds.), *History, Historiography and Interpretation. Studies in Biblical and Cuneiform Literatures*, (Jerusalem: Magnes Press, 1983), pp. 121-47.

causing the earth (or sometimes heaven and earth) to tremble, shake, quake or reel. However, several of his examples have nothing to do with divine intervention in human warfare, which is ostensibly the subject of his article. The Ugaritic text cited, for instance, concerns mythological cosmic battle only, rather than intervention in human battle, while one of the biblical examples, Psalm 29, concerns the glory and magnificence of God in general, without mention of military affairs.

Weinfeld's article catalogues some valid examples from various ancient Near Eastern sources of descriptions of divine intervention in human warfare by means of stars, meteors, hailstones, pillars of fire and cloud, but his case is weakened by a tendency to strain to make the evidence fit the hypothesis, or to find correspondences which are simply not there. For example he claims to see three motifs common to the Song of Deborah (Judg. 5) and Exod. 14.18-22: 1. the heavenly 'factors' which wage war with the enemy; 2. a torrent which sweeps away the enemy; and 3. the destruction of the enemy chariotry. The first problem with his theory is that he has chosen to compare the Song of Deborah with the prose battle report of Exodus 14 rather than the poetic Song of the Sea (Exod. 15), in order to tie in the motif of the pillar of fire and cloud as a phenomenon comparable to the war-waging heavenly bodies of Judg. 5.20. Although there is no reason why poetry and prose cannot be compared, one might have expected a comparison of poetry with poetry and prose with prose in this unique case of two rare and probably very ancient Yahwistic war hymns, each accompanied by a prose battle report. A second problem with Weinfeld's comparison is the third element, the destruction of the enemy chariotry. Where the MT refers to the beating or stamping of the galloping horses' hooves (v. 22), Weinfeld appeals to the LXX to find a reading of Jud. 5.22 which implies that the horses were somehow interfered with: 'the horses' hooves were cut off (ἀπεκόπησαν)', version A, or 'were fettered (ἐνεποδίσθησαν)', version B, both of which make less sense than the MT and, anyhow, are not comparable to the total destruction of horses and riders in the sea. The reason for his straining to bring elements 1 and 3 together is apparently so that he can compare the two biblical passages with the Gebel Barkal stela of Thutmose III, which contains the following speech of the King:

> 'Hear you, O people of the South who are at the holy mount...so that you may know the wonderful deed (of Amon-Ra)...(the guards) were about to take up (their watchposts) in order to meet at night and carry out the

> watch command. It was in the second hour (= in the second watch) and a
> star came from the south of them. Never had the like occurred. It flashed
> against them from its position... Not one withstood before it... with fire
> for their faces, no one among them found his hand nor looked back. Their
> chariotry/horses were no more...'[20]

A more candid and straightforward comparison would have been to
point out the shooting star motif in the Gebel Barkal stela and in Judg.
5.20 and to point out separately the destruction of the enemies' horses
by divine intervention in both the stela and in the Song of the Sea.

His discussion of Resheph, Deber and Qeteb suffers from a similar
stretching of the evidence to find correspondences which add little to his
point. After a discussion of some genuine parallels to the imagery in
Judg. 5.20 of heavenly bodies taking part in human warfare, Weinfeld
states that the descriptions of stars which assail the warriors' camp
might be understood against the background of ancient Near Eastern
mythology in which pestilence and plague are sent forth as deadly
arrows. The connection is extremely tenuous: Weinfeld sees a similarity
between the concept of a shooting star and the concept of an arrow. He
cites a number of passages which mention bows, arrows, and quivers,
sometimes in connection with gods such as Apollo or the Mesopotamian
god Nergal. Then he mentions passages in which plague and pestilence
are 'sent forth' (שלח) as an arrow, as though the connection with meteors were obvious. Many of his examples have nothing to do with divine
intervention in battle, such as Ps. 91.5-6, which contains the line 'the
arrow that flies by day, or the pestilence that ravages at noon' (Deber
and Qeteb), or, worse, Song of Songs 8.6, in which רשפה רשפי אש 'its
darts are darts of flame', is an image for jealousy. The latter example
seems to be included for the sole purpose of forging a link between
arrows and fire, so that comets can be connected with arrows. The
image of a god intervening in human affairs by sending a plague on the
enemy is a valid object for scholarly examination, as is the image of a
shooting star intervening in battle. There is no reason to amalgamate the
two, since they are not combined in any of the martial literature cited.

Despite the disorderly presentation of material and the tenuous connections between examples in some cases, the article by Weinfeld
contains some striking parallels between biblical passages and other literatures in the ancient Near East. His strongest examples are drawn from

---

20. W. Helck, *Urkunden der 18. Dynastie* (Berlin: Akademie Verlag, 1955),
pp. 5-12.

concrete descriptions of weather phenomena, such as hailstones, clouds and fire, with which the gods intervene in warfare. He mentions a few passages in which the gods intervene in battle by causing fear, confusion or panic in the opposing army, but there are many more examples which could have been cited, particularly in the Egyptian materials. In most cases, Weinfeld categorizes the passages in which fear or panic is a major factor according to the type of weather phenomenon mentioned therein; for example, if a cloud is used to create confusion or panic, the passage is placed with other cloud stories, in which the cloud may serve other functions. Since the concept of divinely-induced fear as a decisive factor in battle is common throughout the ancient Near East, it deserves more thorough discussion as a literary convention.

P.D. Miller's[21] research is focused on the mythological background of divine warfare in ancient Israel, using parallels to the biblical motifs from the Ugaritic materials found at Ras Shamra, some of which depict cosmic battles for the establishment of order. Miller considers the concept of Yahweh as warrior to be a very early part of Israel's understanding of deity but acknowledges that the language of Yahweh as warrior dominated Israel's faith throughout its course. An earlier scholar, H. Fredriksson,[22] had investigated the biblical depiction of Yahweh as a warrior, looking both at those situations in which Yahweh was presented as a divine commander and those in which he was said to be fighting alone, either against human enemies or cosmic forces of chaos. One of the conclusions Fredriksson had drawn was that the image of Yahweh fighting the forces of chaos could be traced to Neo-Babylonian influence,[23] but Miller has been able to demonstrate conclusively that the motif can instead be traced to a much earlier period.

Miller discusses the parallels to the Hebrew Bible (especially Psalms 68, 74, and 89) in the Ugaritic myths, especially Baal's battles with the forces of chaos, represented by Sea, River, and Death. Nevertheless, he concludes that:

> Basic to the other religions of the Near East in one form or another was the mythological battle to preserve order... The gods acted to save men, but at the center of the religious concern was the battle for order over

21. P.D. Miller, *The Divine Warrior in Early Israel* (Cambridge, MA: Harvard University Press, 1973).

22. H. Fredriksson, *Jahwe als Krieger* (Lund: C.W.K. Gleerup, 1945).

23. Fredriksson, *Jahwe als Krieger*, pp. 78, 110.

> chaos, life over death, fertility over sterility. At the center of Israel's faith, however, lay the battle for Israel's deliverance...[24]

Like Lind, Miller sees the exodus event, particularly Exodus 15, as the nucleus of the 'epic tradition'.[25] Regrettably, he gives very little attention to the relationship between kingship and divine war. Since the Ugaritic materials are conspicuously lacking substantial stories of divine intervention in historical battles,[26] they make a poor case for comparison with the biblical stories of Yahweh's involvement in human events. His conclusions would have been very different if he had concentrated his attention on the Assyrian materials, as Weippert did, which have a more analogous ideological purpose. Nevertheless, his parallels to some of the poetic imagery are striking.

The three most recent studies of divine participation in war, those of Sa-Moon·Kang,[27] A. Van der Lingen[28] and K.L. Younger,[29] exhibit much more willingness than most earlier scholarship (excepting Weinfeld and Weippert) to acknowledge the similarity between the Bible and other ancient Near Eastern texts. Van der Lingen argues that the terminology of divine warfare is a literary phenomenon which is by nature a-historical and which has undergone a series of developments over time. Many of the occurrences of divine-war language in the Bible to which previous scholars have pointed as examples of very ancient 'Yahweh war' or 'holy war' traditions (e.g. von Rad, Smend), Van der Lingen views as the result of theological reflection *a posteriori* on historical events. He observes that there is no set Yahweh war schema in the earliest layers of redaction. Instead, there is a large amount of variation, although one or more of the terms and elements identified by von Rad may be present. Rather than finding a set structure which constitutes a divine-war story, Van der Lingen finds that it is impossible to recover a schema which is valid for all the stories relating the 'wars of Yahweh'.

24. Miller, *The Divine Warrior*, p. 164.

25. Miller, *The Divine Warrior*, pp. 167-68.

26. The exception is the Anat passage mentioned in my next Chapter.

27. Sa-Moon Kang, *Divine War in the Old Testament and in the Ancient Near East* (Berlin: de Gruyter, 1989).

28. A. Van der Lingen, *Les Guerres de Yahvé: L'implicaion de YHWH dans les guerres d'Israël selon les livres historiques de l'Ancien Testament* (LD, 139; Paris: Cerf, 1990).

29. K.L. Younger, *Ancient Conquest Accounts: A Study in Ancient Near Eastern and Biblical History Writing* (Sheffield: Sheffield Academic Press, 1990).

He draws the conclusion that usually the element of Yahweh causing the victory is a theological reinterpretation of a 'profane' battle.[30]

Furthermore, he points out, very few of the Yahweh war expressions are unique to the terminology of the 'wars of Yahweh'; some occur in other types of situations within the biblical text and some occur in other ancient Near Eastern literatures.[31] He therefore concludes that the Yahweh war terminology does not correspond to an isolated theme or institution but is reattached to many other themes of historiography and theology. The terminology cannot be traced to an amphictyony (von Rad, Smend) nor to the period when the tribes were integrated into a nation with imperial ambitions (Kang, see below) but is instead recurring words and phrases used in many different periods. Ultimately, Van der Lingen sees a similarity between the terminology of Yahweh war and the vocabulary of the 'post-exilic prophets'. The terminology, he argues, results from a theological idea which permitted Israel to survive during the period most dangerous to its existence, and which gave to Israel its definitive religious identity.[32]

Several problems with Van der Lingen's theories can be identified. First, his distinction between sacred and profane warfare (in the ancient world) is an anachronism. Although he discusses other ancient Near Eastern literatures in his book, he does not seem willing to admit the full implication of his work: all warfare in the ancient Near East was sacral warfare to some extent (see Chapter 5). Second, his emphasis on the post-exilic period obscures the fact that much of the vocabulary that he points out in the post-exilic writers consists of (apparently deliberate) allusions to military stories from the DH (see Chapter 6).

On the other hand, Van der Lingen is certainly correct in his assertion that there is no set schema of divine warfare which can be identified in the biblical text. There is, however, a repertory of typically military words and phrases. His emphasis on the terminology as a literary phenomenon is valid. He is wise to abandon von Rad's project of looking for an ancient and reconstructable institution of 'holy war' in ancient Israel. He is also correct in his argument that the same words and phrases may be adapted to different situations in different periods. What should be added to Van der Lingen's analysis is a recognition of the post-exilic tendency to spiritualize the combat imagery from other periods.

30. Van der Lingen, *Les Guerres*, p. 215.
31. Van der Lingen, *Les Guerres*, pp. 213-15.
32. Van der Lingen, *Les Guerres*, p. 258.

Sa-Moon Kang's book on divine war is one of the most complete books ever to discuss ancient Near Eastern parallels to warfare in the Hebrew Bible. His conclusion is that the motifs of divine war were formulated in the Davidic Kingdom in the light of those of divine war in the ancient Near East. He says that the idea of Yahweh's help and intervention in battle began to appear in the 'rising period of the Davidic Kingdom'.[33] He points out that Yahweh as warrior parallels the divine warriors who appeared in the 'rising time' of each empire of the ancient Near East.[34] His Mesopotamian examples include Inanna/Ishtar as a war goddess under the Sargonic empire of Akkad, Marduk the war god under the first Babylonian Dynasty, and Ashur the divine warrior under the Neo-Assyrian empire. In the same way, he says, Teshub was recognized as the divine warrior in the Hittite New Kingdom, and Amun-Re became a powerful divine warrior under the Egyptian New Kingdom. His connection of the divine warrior motif to times of imperial expansion is a major contribution to the discussion.

However, there is no way we can know whether the passages he cites reflect the historical reality of Davidic imperial ascendancy because nearly all of the material in the Bible pertaining to David is filtered through the lens of the Dtr's interpretation of events. In the absence of further archaeological findings dating to such an early period as that of King David, scholars may eventually have to accept the limitations of the Dtr's version of events and that of the Chronicler, who used the Dtr as a source. Other than through the DH, there is very little access to the Davidic kingdom. Therefore, the most that can be said about Kang's theory is that the Dtr presented the 'rising time' of the Davidic kingdom using motifs of divine war attested to by other ancient Near Eastern literatures and that these motifs do seem to be associated with the ascension of empires.

Therefore, I think that Kang is correct in linking the divine warrior motifs to imperial ideology, even though I do not think that he can substantiate tracing any passage from DH all the way back to actual Davidic times. Furthermore, I would say that the divine warrior motif seems to be associated not only with the ascension of new empires, but also with the defence, reorganization or expansion of existing political boundaries.

I would even go so far as to say that the divine warrior motif plays a part almost anytime the consolidation of power is at issue. After all, the

33. Kang, *Divine War*, p. 224.
34. Kang, *Divine War*, p. 203.

'rising period' of each great empire in the ancient world would also be (by definition) a time of attempted centralization of power by the would-be empire-builder. When viewed in the light of power centralization, all of Kang's examples fit my theory that a rhetoric of violence may be used to reconstitute and consolidate power (whether or not an empire is in its original period of ascendancy). The time of King Josiah was exactly the sort of period when one would expect to see a tendency to use the imagery of Yahweh the warrior in developing a Josianic ideology of social control as well as imperial expansion.

Kang came close to my own theory of an ideology of social control when he pointed out that the idea of Yahweh as a warrior becomes a particularly prominent theme in the prophets of Josiah's time and later,[35] such as Zeph. 3.17, who were specifically associated with Josiah's centralization of power. Since the divine warrior motif is extremely ancient throughout the Mesopotamian region, seeking the 'origins' of its use in Israel-Judah, as Kang wishes to do, is a fruitless quest. The question should not be framed in terms of origins. Instead, any changes in the rhetorical usage of the motif over time, as well as geographical or cultural variations in its usage, should receive more attention than scholars have previously been willing to grant. Therefore, the focus of research concerning the divine warrior motif in the Bible should be on the DH, which is its primary literary context, and on the Dtr's historical/political context to discern his distinctive usage of a well-worn motif, not on a search for origins. Numerous parallels are found, but no 'originary moment' (to use Greenblatt's terminology).

Younger compares the Biblical and ancient Near Eastern modes of writing 'history' and concludes that there is a great deal of commonality in the conquest accounts throughout the region. Although he is more concerned than I am with what actually happened when the land under discussion in the Book of Joshua came under the control of the people who eventually came to be identified as Israelites/Judahites, he wisely steers his argument in a different direction and avoids making a definite claim concerning the trustworthiness of the conquest story as 'history'. His approach, instead, centres on semiotics.

However, while I admire his work and agree with many of his points, I would argue that Younger pays insufficient attention to the historical context of the composition. His book includes a lengthy chapter on the

---

35. Kang, *Divine War*, pp. 203-204.

concept of 'ideology', but without tying the text to a particular socio-political situation, the word 'ideology' rings strangely hollow. After discussing several definitions of ideology, he eventually sides with Geertz, in what Younger calls a 'neutral sense' of the word ideology. In Geertz's view, ideology is 'a schematic image of social order...a pattern of beliefs and concepts (both factual and normative) which purport to explain complex social phenomena'.[36] Younger argues that it is hardly scientific to define ideology merely as distortion and selectivity (as other theorists have tried to do), because distortion and selectivity are secondary and empirical questions.[37]

When Younger applies Geertz's definition of ideology to the conquest accounts in Joshua, however, he does not say to which 'social order' he is referring since he skirts the issue of authorship. For example, he concludes that:

> Israelite ideology had certain similarities with the 'Imperialistic' ideologies
> of the ancient Near East—Assyrian, Hittite, Egyptian. In the previous
> chapter we described the areas of similarity: a similar view of the enemy,
> calculated terror, the high use of hyperbole, a jural aspect, and the use of
> stereotyped syntagms to transmit the high-redundance message of the
> ideology. It would seem that a similar ideology is underlying both the
> ancient Near Eastern and biblical texts.[38]

Although he admits the similarity of the Joshua text and ancient Near Eastern ideologies of imperialism, he quickly changes direction, backing away from the logical conclusion that the Book of Joshua must have some relationship with imperial expansion and consolidation of power. Instead of discussing the ideology of whoever might have produced the text, he looks in the other direction, toward the distant past. He immediately begins writing in the next paragraph about the various theories regarding the settlement of the land, beginning with Gottwald's notion of a peasants' revolt, in order to place the ideology of the conquest into that period depicted within it, rather than looking at the context which produced the text.

His comparison of ancient Near Eastern and biblical literature provides a helpful contribution to the scholarly debate on divine war because of the clarity of his parallel examples. His book, along with

36. C. Geertz, 'Ideology as a Cultural System', in *The Interpretation of Cultures* (New York: Basic Books, 1973), pp. 193-233.
37. Younger, *Ancient Conquest Accounts*, pp. 26-31.
38. Younger, *Ancient Conquest Accounts*, p. 230.

Kang's, has sounded the final death-knell for the older belief that there is something unique about the way the Bible presents divine participation in 'history' (through warfare). They also both recognize that there is a relationship between imperial ideology and the language of divine participation in war, a subject to which I return in the next Chapter and those which follow.

IV. *Theological Approaches*

M. Lind adopts a theological approach. As a member of one of the traditionally pacifist denominations, he seeks to harmonize the idea of Yahweh as a warrior with the Mennonite ideal of non-violence. He does so by placing the emphasis on divine action rather than human military feats as the decisive factor in victory for Yahweh's people, as mentioned earlier. For example, regarding the command to go up and take possession of the land in Deut. 1.21, Lind says that the command was not primarily an order to fight but rather to trust and have confidence in Yahweh 'who goes before you' and who 'will himself fight for you' (Deut. 1.30).[39] However, the whole point of the passage in Deuteronomy 1 is that the people are being given orders to go up and fight, orders which they are punished for ignoring. The orders to go up and take possession are a call to military action (which the people do not obey). The promise of divine assistance is to be the basis of their courage in battle, not a substitute for battle.

D.J. McCarthy makes an argument similar to Lind's, although his point of view is Roman Catholic, rather than Mennonite or Quaker. According to McCarthy, the first nine chapters of Joshua express the 'familiar lesson of the holy war': total trust in Yahweh, with added emphasis on the element of leadership. 'Yahweh accomplishes his designs through a leader he chooses and sustains'.[40] McCarthy's otherwise sensitive reading of the spies story (Joshua 2) is marred by his conclusion that:

> The behavior of the spies is an excellent example of man's part in the holy war. They are saved and their mission accomplished because of Rahab's intervention inspired by faith in Yahweh. They are entirely passive, the classic situation illustrating that Yahweh and not men win wars.[41]

39. Lind, *Yahweh is a Warrior*, p. 160.
40. D.J. McCarthy, 'The Theology of Leadership in Joshua 1–9', *Bib* 52 (1971), pp. 165-75.
41. McCarthy, 'The Theology of Leadership', p. 173.

Although the men are 'entirely passive' in the Rahab story, passivity can hardly be described as 'man's part in the holy war' in the rest of the Book of Joshua. For example, violent military action initiated by a war oracle occurs in Josh. 11.6-9:

> Then Yahweh said to Joshua, 'Do not be afraid because of them. At this time tomorrow I will deliver all of them slain before Israel. You shall hamstring their horses and burn their chariots with fire'. So Joshua and all the men of war with him came upon them suddenly by the waters of Merom, and attacked them. And Yahweh delivered them into the hand of Israel, so that they defeated them, and pursued them... and they struck them until no survivor was left to them. And Joshua did to them as Yahweh had told him. He hamstrung their horses and burned their chariots with fire.

This story (like other examples below) depicts what P. Miller has called a 'fusion' of divine and human action. Although victory was attributed to divine forces, the narrative presents Joshua and his warriors as actively involved in military endeavors. Even in Joshua 6, an idealization of the battle of Jericho in which little emphasis is placed upon actual fighting, the people still play a 'major and active role'.[42] I would add that they played an extremely violent role, destroying the population by sword (v. 21) and then burning the city with fire (v. 24). Therefore, even in a passage like Joshua 6 which concentrates on the ritual aspect of the 'holy war' stories, the human role is hardly passive.

Likewise, when 'Yahweh fought for Israel' by pelting the Amorites with stones from the sky, the army nonetheless used their swords against their opponents (Josh. 10.8-14). Also, after Yahweh told Joshua to stretch out his javelin toward Ai, the Israelites captured and burned the city. Then Joshua and his warriors 'turned back and slew the men of Ai' (Josh. 8.18-22).

Although victory in battle is sometimes brought about by marvellous events or objects, such as the stones from the sky or the trumpets at Jericho, Joshua is depicted as a ruthless military commander, fighting battles and wreaking total destruction in compliance with the ban (for example, Josh. 10.28-43; 11.10-12). The fact that the ban, like the conquest itself, is divinely ordained, only makes a moral point more difficult to extract (because of the violent and destructive nature of the ban). The narrator does not shrink from describing the carnage, and he passes no negative judgment upon Joshua for participating in it.

42. Miller, *The Divine Warrior*, pp. 156-59.

Placing the emphasis on divine action in the conquest stories only serves to make a pacifist interpretation more difficult because the deity is then involved in complicity with violence. Obviously a theological point would be easier to discern if all of the military victories in the narrative were brought about by marvellous divine intervention making the human warrior role unnecessary, but difficulties would still remain. Why would a deity who commands pacifism for his people engage himself in the slaughter of thousands of other people? Is there not also something problematic, from a pacifist point of view, about a deity, who supposedly possesses providential control over the entire earth, choosing to pick on mere human beings? An omnipotent being waging war against limited, frail living beings (Canaanites or not) comes across as a bit of a bully. No matter how much Lind and McCarthy try to play down the violence by insisting that the emphasis in the narrative is on divine action, not on human military feats, their theological reading does not hold up under scrutiny.

Certainly an obstacle to extracting a pacifist message from the portrait of Joshua and his deity in the DH is the unblinking violence of the behaviour in most of the war stories. By depicting Yahweh's providential control as occurring primarily by means of violent military action, by delivering the opponents into the hands of the warriors to be killed, the ethical and theological picture which emerges from the Joshua stories is inescapably problematic, at least from a pacifist point of view: Yahweh instigates violent actions; his instrument, Joshua, is judged by the thoroughness with which he carries out the often violent divine initiatives.

The issue of violence deserves further scrutiny because the pacifist argument fails to solve it. Nowhere in the historical books of the Hebrew Bible does an unequivocal censure appear regarding the violence of warfare. Michael Fishbane thinks that the Chronicler's interpretation of 1 Kgs 5.3-5 (in 1 Chron. 22.8-9; 28.3) involves a moral censure of David for his violence, which disqualified him from building the temple.[43] The implication in the Kings passage, according to Fishbane, is that David's time and energy were preoccupied with warfare and, therefore, he was unable to do the deed, but the Chronicler reinterprets the passage differently. However, H.G.M. Williamson has pointed out that 'the Chronicler is second to none in the Old Testament in his portrayal of God's activity in warfare on behalf of Israel in conjunction with religious ceremonial

---

43. M. Fishbane, *Biblical Interpretation in Ancient Israel* (New York: Clarendon Press, 1985), pp. 396-97.

and in answer to prayer', so that, rather than ethical culpability, the Chronicler had in mind a ritual uncleanness (indicated by the words 'before me upon the earth' in v. 8) which barred David from the particular task of temple-building, 'just as in the Levitical and priestly laws many conditions and functions which can in no way be deemed ethically culpable similarly lead to periods of ritual uncleanness and hence exclusion for a while from the cult'.[44]

T.R. Hobbs[45] observed that the warlike nature of much of the material in the 'Old Testament is an embarrassment' and a 'stumbling block' to many devout readers.[46] He takes his fellow-scholar, the late Peter Craigie, to task for failing to deal critically enough with 'the question begged by the title' of his book, *The Problem of War in the Old Testament*.[47] 'For whom', asks Hobbs rhetorically, 'is warfare in the Old Testament a problem?' He answers himself by demonstrating that war was clearly not treated as a problem by the ancient 'Israelites'. 'It is taken for granted as a part of life', he says. Therefore Hobbs turns his attention to the historical context of the ancient Israelites in order to understand their cultural view of warfare:

> The culture of ancient Israel was dominated by concepts of kinship/belonging, and intimately bound up with kinship is the religious ideology of the people. After all, is not the God of Israel the God of the 'fathers, Abraham, Isaac and Jacob'? Is not Israel itself called a 'family' (Amos 3.2) and do not familial terms predominate in descriptions of the people's relationship to God? If then God is seen in some way as a 'father-figure' of the people, and the members of the group or nation are seen as kin, either real, as in the exposition of the tribal system in Israel, or imagined (fictive), as in the designation 'children of Israel' for the whole body, does this not lead to a rather closed view of the group?

He goes on to say that a threat to any one member of the group is a threat to all, and any threat to 'the limits the group has established for itself' is a threat to the individual members. In such an understanding of society, Hobbs points out, 'religion' in the sense that Craigie uses the

---

44. H.G.M. Williamson, *1 and 2 Chronicles* (NCB; Grand Rapids: Eerdmans, 1982), pp. 154-5.

45. T.R. Hobbs, *A Time for War: A Study of Warfare in the Old Testament* (Wilmington: Michael Glazier, 1989).

46. Hobbs, *A Time for War*, pp. 14-15.

47. P. Craigie, *The Problem of War in the Old Testament* (Grand Rapids: W.B. Eerdmans Publishing, 1978).

word, would be unthinkable. 'If there be any "religion" it is the ideology which gives the group its founding stories, identifies members of the group, and perpetuates the "sense" of the group'.[48]

Although the remainder of his book veers off in a different direction from my own work, his introductory chapter raises several points which deserve emphasis. First, Hobbs is one of the few scholars to concern himself with the relationship between violence and 'the limits the group has established for itself', which I call boundaries of inclusion and exclusion. Second, Hobbs recognizes the importance of the group's sense of itself, which I call its identity (set over against the various 'Others'). Third, he indicates in the above passage a recognition that religion and political ideology are inseparable in the ancient world. Fourth, he indicates an understanding of the importance of a group's 'founding stories' in its identity, including the role of warfare as part of the community's collective experience. Throughout all of my subsequent chapters, I will repeatedly return to these four issues in my discussion of violence.

Although I have attempted to be fairly representative in surveying the voluminous previous research on divine participation in warfare, I have deliberately left out those works which focus entirely on attempts to describe what actually happened and how the warfare was conducted, such as the work of Yadin,[49] Liver[50] and others, because my focus is on the text as a production of Josiah's time. I also consider a review of the various versions of the 'just war' theological argument to be far beyond the scope of the present study.

V. *Conclusion*

I find myself ultimately forced to conclude that none of the research done by previous scholars on 'holy war', 'Yahweh war' or 'divine war' suffices to deal successfully with the violence in the Book of Joshua. Much of the work on ancient Near Eastern parallels is little more than a catalogue of terminology, which is primarily of antiquarian interest, while most theological solutions to the 'problem' of divine participation in warfare raise more questions than they answer.

48. Hobbs, *A Time for War*, pp. 21-22.
49. Y. Yadin, *The Art of Warfare in Biblical Lands* (New York: McGraw–Hill, 1962).
50. J. Liver (ed.), *The Military History of the Land of Israel in Biblical Times* (Jerusalem: Magnes Press 1964).

Perhaps a more fruitful approach would be to redefine the issue. Instead of looking for either an ancient institution or a theology of war in the DH, the relationships between violence, political power and rhetoric in the text should be examined. In later chapters, I wish to address the uses of violence in the text as they apply to the seventh-century BCE context, specifically Josiah's assertion of power. In order to do so, I will examine how the Dtr's tale of death and destruction illuminates the relationships between power, socio-political institutions, and the construction of identity. As a first step towards this goal, it will be necessary in the next chapter to study the rhetoric of violence in other ancient Near Eastern martial literatures as a point of comparison.

Chapter 5

THE CONVENTIONAL LANGUAGE OF WAR
IN THE ANCIENT NEAR EAST

I. *Introduction*

As several recent studies (reviewed in Chapter 4) have demonstrated, the conventional language of war in the Hebrew Bible shows a similarity to other ancient Near Eastern martial documents. One of the flaws, however, of many previous studies has been that scholars tend to ignore the processes of change over time, particularly when considering the Mesopotamian materials. They have also tended in the past to show insufficient sensitivity to the political uses of martial literature as internal and external propaganda by whoever produced the text or inscription. In the present chapter, I attempt to remedy some of these oversights by demonstrating that while there are many features in common throughout the region in the way war is presented in texts, some similarities are more striking than others. After showing how certain common ideas and motifs run through the Egyptian, Hittite, Moabite, Ugaritic, Mesopotamian and other martial literatures, my discussion culminates in an examination of the Neo-Assyrian war oracles, which I consider to be remarkably similar in form, content and even ideological usage to the biblical language of warfare found in the DH. By examining the evidence of Assyrian literary influence on the conventional language of war in the DH, I shall endeavour to demonstrate that the centuries of Assyrian hegemony left an indelible mark on smaller countries under its dominion, such as Judah.

II. *Divine Intervention in Warfare in the Ancient Near East*

A. *Ugarit*
The best place to begin comparing the biblical text with other literatures in the region is probably the Ras Shamra materials since they are close

linguistically and culturally as well as geographically. However, the Ugaritic epics contain only brief examples of divine intervention in human battles. Ordinarily, the Ugaritic gods fight among themselves in purely cosmic battles. The Baal Epic includes a brief episode in which the goddess Anat is said to be involving herself in human warfare, but the text is vague regarding who is fighting whom:

> ...And lo Anat is fighting violently
> Battling between the two cities
> She smites the people of the seashore
> Destroys mankind of the sunrise.
> Beside her are heads like grasshoppers,
> By her are hands like locusts,
>   Like thorns of *grmn*, the hands of troops.
> She piles up heads on her back
> She ties up hands in her bundle.
> Knees she plunges in the blood of soldiery
> Thighs in the gore of troops.
> With a stick she drives out foes
> Against the flank she draws her bow (CTA 3.2 [KTU 1.3 II].3-30).[1]

The text goes on to describe Anat's pleasure in bloodshed but does not return to the scene of the human military engagement. M.S. Smith[2] views the battle as 'universal' in scope. He says that 'peoples' are collectively the deity's enemies (cf. Isa. 59.15-19), described as populations to the east (rising of the sun) and west (toward the coast). Oddly, Gordon's translation of *ʾadm* as 'mankind' makes Smith's case better than Smith's translation of the word as 'populace' (of the east). Nevertheless, the word *ʾadm* is in parallelism with the word *pim* (people) and both may refer to particular enemy populations. The Ugaritic text is not clear regarding who the human enemies of Anat are, nor exactly why she is fighting them. Therefore statements about the 'universality' of her battles are excessively speculative and must be rejected in the interest of caution.

Smith observes that while Anat does not appear as a goddess in the Hebrew Bible, the martial imagery associated with her has many points of contact with the imagery of Yahweh as a warrior.[3] For example,

1.   C.H. Gordon, *Ugaritic Literature: A Comprehensive Translation of the Poetic and Prose Texts* (Rome: Pontifical Biblical Institute, 1949), pp. 17-18.
2.   M.S. Smith, *The Early History of God: Yahweh and the Other Dieties in Ancient Israel* (San Francisco: Harper & Row, 1990), pp. 60-64.
3.   Smith, *The Early History*, p. 62, makes a point of the location of the battle at

the deity's warfare produces gruesome human carnage (cf. Isa. 34.2; Deut. 32.43; Pss. 58.11; 68.24; 110.6). The language of the Ugaritic passage, however, resembles stylistically the poetic passages (listed in the sentence above) rather than the prose of the Joshua accounts.

Although there are no war oracles or battle reports in the Ras Shamra texts resembling the biblical accounts of warfare in the DH, the Anat passage demonstrates that the phenomenon of divine intervention in human battle at least existed as a Ugaritic concept. Kang also pointed out an example of Baal's intervention in human warfare in a newly discovered text:[4]

> If a strong one attacks your gate, a warrior your walls, raise your eyes to Baal (praying), O Baal, please drive away the strong one from our gate, the warrior from our walls... And Baal will hear your prayer. He will drive away the strong one from your gate, the warrior from your walls... (RS 24, 266).

Miller's book (see Chapter 4 for further discussion) on the divine warrior also contains many examples of imagery found in the Hebrew Bible (especially in the Psalms) which resemble the Ugaritic poetry, but for direct parallels to the language found in the war oracles and battle reports of the DH, we must look elsewhere.

B. *Moab*

Another close neighbour and rival of the Hebrew people was Moab. The two groups shared a similar worldview.[5] Therefore it is not surprising that the Moabite stone offers evidence of a belief in divine intervention in human warfare:

> I... Mesha, son of Chemosh-[...], king of Moab, the Dibonite... made this high place for Chemosh in Qarhoh [...] because he saved me from all the kings and caused me to triumph over all my adversaries... Now the

---

the mountain of the deity (cf. Pss. 2.1-2; 48.5-8; Joel 4.9-14; Zech. 12.3-4; 14.2). However, Anat may be said to come down to the foot of the mountain and fight in the valley.

4. Kang, *Divine War*, p. 74.

5. P.D. Stern, *The Biblical Herem: A Window on Israel's Religious Experience* (Atlanta: Scholars Press, 1991). My intention is not to discuss in any detail the voluminous secondary material on the *herem* in the ancient world. Instead, I would like to point out that the *herem* is only one of the ways that the motif of destruction may appear in an ancient text. I mention Stern's book on the *herem* because of its focus on the Mesha inscription.

men of Gad had always dwelt in the land of Ataroth...but I fought against the town and took it and slew all the people of the town as a satiation for Chemosh and Moab... (*ANET*, pp. 320-21).

The Moabite stone exhibits the close connection between the national divine warrior (Chemosh, in this case) and the monarchy. (The connection is even more explicitly developed in the Akkadian texts discussed below.) As J. Drinkard points out in an article confirming the theories of J.M. Miller,[6] the Moabite stone is a memorial inscription, listing the accomplishments of a king near the end of his reign but not necessarily in chronological order.[7] Some inscriptions of the memorial genre, according to Drinkard, make reference to the present king's success compared with the lack of success of his predecessors: 'Now deliverance and prosperity are coming for Moab under Mesha's leadership and, by inference, due to Kemosh's blessing'.[8] The idea that it is the presence or blessing of the deity which brings about the ruler's success is not unlike the Dtr's presentation of Joshua (not to mention Josiah).

Furthermore, some of the language in the Mesha inscription resembles the language of war in the DH. For example, the tendency to issue war oracle commands using pairs of terse imperative verbs (biblical examples are discussed in detail in the next chapter) is typical of the Dtr. 'Go, take possession' is a common phrase in the DH, resembling the words of Chemosh to Mesha, 'Go, take Nebo from Israel!' Similarly, the words 'Go down, fight against Hauronen', spoken by Chemosh, resemble the many imperative verbs of motion which occur in biblical war oracles. Another similarity is the tendency to follow the war oracle immediately with a battle report, which demonstrates the king's place in a hierarchical relationship with the deity by showing him following the god's commands without hesitation:[9]

6.   J.M. Miller, 'The Mesha Stela as a Memorial Inscription', *PEQ* 106 (1974), pp. 9-18.

7.   J. Drinkard, 'The Literary Genre of the Mesha Inscription' in J.A. Dearman (ed.), *Studies in the Mesha Inscription and Moab* (Atlanta: Scholars Press, 1989), pp. 131-54; cf. J.A. Dearman, 'Historical Reconstruction and the Mesha Inscription' (pp. 155-210 of the same volume): Dearman's article places more of the focus on the historical events surrounding Mesha's reign but likewise takes literary factors into account. He also stresses that such inscriptions do not lend themselves to the retrieval of chronological historical information.

8.   Drinkard, 'Genre', p. 154.

9.   An exaggerated example exists in the Assyrian annals of Esarhaddon:...they sent me the (following) trustworthy oracle (received by) extispicy: 'Go (ahead), do

And as for Hauronen, there dwelt in it [...And] Chemosh said to me, 'Go down, fight against Hauronen,' And I went down [and I fought against the town and I took it], and Chemosh dwelt there in my time...

And Chemosh said to me, 'Go, take Nebo from Israel!' So I went by night and fought against it from the break of dawn until noon, taking it and slaying all, seven thousand men, boys, women, girls and maid-servants, for I had devoted them to destruction for (the god) Ashtar-Chemosh... And the king of Israel had built Jahaz, and he dwelt there while he was fighting against me, but Chemosh drove him out before me... (*ANET*, pp. 320-21).

The devotion to destruction is an even more striking parallel, as Stern emphasized. The emphasis on total destruction is also found in Hittite[10] and Akkadian[11] materials (see below). According to Stern, the *herem* represented an attempt to bring moral and physical order to the universe of the group that used it by eradicating chaos. Central to this idea is the attitude in which warfare itself is viewed as a battle between order (represented by the people who perpetrated the *herem*) and chaos (represented by other national entities, the Others). In Stern's view, the Moabites and Israelites were trying to achieve a 'world order (literally creating sacred space) in which they could live and thrive'.[12] The problem with Stern's analysis, thorough as it is in many ways, is his lack of concern with the propagandistic value of ancient Near Eastern inscriptions.[13] His argument that ancient warfare was often perceived as a clash

not tarry! We will march with you, kill your enemies!' I did not even wait for the next day, nor for my army, did not turn back (for a moment), did not muster contingents of horses broken to the yoke or the battle equipment, I did not even pile up provisions for my expedition, I was not afraid of the snow and the cold of the month of Shabatu (in which) the winter is (at its) hard (est)—but I spread my wings like the (swift-)flying (storm)bird to overwhelm my enemies (*ANET*, p. 289).

10. Whether or not the Hittite examples of destruction qualify as the *herem* is discussed by Stern (pp. 72-77), but would be beside the point of the present discussion. Stern also finds examples of what he perceives to be the *herem* in Greek and Roman materials (pp. 58-65).

11. A. Malamat, 'The Ban in Mari and the Bible', *Biblical Essays 1966: Proceedings of the Ninth Meeting of Die Ou-Testament Werkgemeenskap in Suid-Afrika* (Pretoria: Stellenbosch, 1967), pp. 40-49; Malamat's concern, like Stern's, is primarily with the *herem*.

12. Stern, *Herem*, p. 219.

13. H.W.F. Saggs, 'Assyrian Warfare in the Sargonid Period', *Iraq* 25 (1963), pp. 145-60; M. Weippert, 'Heiliger Krieg', esp. pp.492-3.

between order and chaos is certainly not unfounded,[14] but it does not take adequate account of the role of martial texts in intimidation and political control.

The idea of destruction is extremely important because of its centrality to the Jericho story (especially Rahab's role) and the Achan incident, as well as the battle reports of Joshua 10 and 11, all of which are discussed in a later chapter (see Chapter 7 below) in the context of Otherness. Another reason that the idea of destruction is important is because it is one of the most ubiquitous motifs in martial texts throughout the ancient Near East. As I point out below, however, the emphasis on destruction in the Assyrian battle reports and in the DH appear to serve a deterrent purpose (cf. Saggs), whether or not the *ḥerem* is a feature of any given passage. One of the most striking points of comparison is the reason given for the original defeat of Moab: the deity's anger at his own people, a feature sometimes cited as unique to the Bible. The Ai incident in Joshua 7 is remarkably similar.

Although there are some important similarities between the Moabite stone and the conventional language of warfare in the DH, there are also some noteworthy differences. An important feature absent in the Moabite inscription is the standard promise of divine presence, 'and ___ your god will be with you', even though the presence of Chemosh with the king in battle is implied in other words and phrases. Particularly worthy of attention is the phrase, '(the god) drove him (or them) out before me', which appears often in the DH as a way of expressing divine help in warfare. However, the Moabite stone lacks some of the most prominent terminology found in the biblical text, such as the admonition to 'Fear not!' and the assurance that the god will 'deliver the enemy into your hand'.

C. *Egypt*

The literature of ancient Egypt contains many examples of divine intervention in warfare which resemble the biblical battle narratives and poetry. Some of the features which the Hebrew literature shares with the Egyptian include:

---

14. cf. Miller's view of the divine warrior motif; cf. also the Egyptian 'Repulsing of the Dragon' (ANET, pp.6-7), in which the analogy between the god Horus's defeat of the mythic dragon of darkness and chaos, Apophis, and the king's defeat of his earthly enemies is made explicit in the words of the magic spell.

1. Divine initiative in warfare, in the form of a command from the god to the human leader to go to war;

2. Encouragement from the god to be brave in the face of battle;

3. A statement of divine presence and assistance in battle, such as, the god is 'with you', gives 'strength' to the warrior, helps to fight, or provides protection as a 'shield';

4. An assurance that the foe will be delivered 'into your hand';

5. Creation of a state of fearfulness within the enemy, such as, 'god ____ has put the fear and dread of you into their hearts'.

There are two clear examples of a deity directly addressing a king who is about to go into battle. In the first of these, a prose bulletin describing a battle, including events leading up to it, the head of the Memphite pantheon, Ptah, visits the king, Merneptah, in a dream to initiate warfare by commanding the king to take a weapon he (Ptah) is extending to him. The god's exhortation to bravery in battle is similar to the many exhortations to 'fear not' or to 'be strong and bold' in the Bible:

> Then his majesty saw in a dream as if a statue of Ptah were standing before Pharaoh... He spake to him: 'Take thou (it)', while he extended to him the sword, 'and banish thou the fearful heart from thee'.[15]

Immediately prior to this oracle, the warriors are depicted marching into battle with divine accompaniment:

> ...the leaders of the bowmen in front thereof to overthrow the land of Libya. When they went forth, the hand of the god was with them; (even) Amon was with them as their shield...[16]

This text includes both the statement of divine presence with the human warriors, using the uniquely Egyptian expression 'the hand of the god is with them', and the image of the god as shield.

The second example of divine address to a warrior is found in the Kadesh Battle Poem, in which the king, Ramses II, is depicted as fighting alone, without his troops or chariots. In hyperbolic lament language, he calls out to his god:

> I call to you, my father Amun,
> I am among a host of strangers;
> All countries are arrayed against me,

15. J.H. Breasted, *Ancient Records of Egypt* (Chicago: University of Chicago Press, 1906), p. 245, no. 582.

16. Breasted, *Records*, p. 245, no. 581.

I am alone, there's none with me!
My numerous troops have deserted me,
Not one of my chariotry looks for me;
I keep on shouting for them,
But none of them heeds my call.
I know Amun helps me more than a million troops...
Amun is more helpful than they;
I came here at the command of your mouth,
O Amun, I have not transgressed your command![17]

The king claims to have entered into battle as a result of a divine command (cf. the annals of Thutmose III). The voice of the god Amun answers him with an assurance of divine presence and help:

Forward, I am with you,
I, your father, my hand is with you,
I prevail over a hundred thousand men,
I am lord of victory, lover of valor![18]

The result of the divine presence with pharaoh is described in vivid detail, first from the king's point of view:

I found my heart stout, my breast in joy,
All I did succeeded, I was like Mont...
Not one of them found his hand to fight,
Their hearts failed in their bodies through fear of me.
Their arms all slackened, they could not shoot,
They had no heart to grasp their spears...[19]

Then the poet shifts to the viewpoint of the enemy warriors:

The enemy warriors call out to one another, saying:
'No man is he who is among us,
It is Seth great-of-strength, Baal in person;
They are of one who is unique,
Who fights a hundred thousand without soldiers and chariots...
For he who attempts to get close to him,
His hands, all his limbs grow limp,
One cannot hold either bow or spears...'[20]

17. M. Lichtheim, *Ancient Egyptian Literature*, II (Berkeley: University of California Press, 1976), pp. 65-66.

18. Lichtheim, *Ancient Egyptian Literature*, II, p. 66.

19. Lichtheim, *Ancient Egyptian Literature*, II, p. 66.

20. Lichtheim, *Ancient Egyptian Literature*, II, p. 67.

In the course of battle, the king shouts to his army a battle-cry which includes two elements familiar from Old Testament war narratives, the exhortation to bravery, and the assurance of divine presence and help:

> Steady your hearts, my soldiers;
> Behold me victorious, me alone,
> For Amun is my helper, his hand is with me...[21]

Shortly thereafter, the king credits the god Amun with giving him 'strength', which was sufficient to defeat all the enemy troops single-handedly:

> Behold, Amun gave me his strength,
> When I had no soldiers, no chariotry...[22]

Some of the king's words of exhortation to the soldiers are repeated later to his shield-bearer, Menena, who, when he saw the enemy chariotry surrounding the king, 'became weak and faint-hearted': 'Stand firm, steady your heart, my shield-bearer!' Later, the soldiers and charioteers return to the camp, after seeing 'that my father Amun was with me' (the pronoun 'me' refers to the king, speaking in the first person), where they greet the king as 'O good warrior, firm of heart'. The many references to 'firm-heartedness', 'stout-heartedness' and the like are extremely important in Egyptian battle literature (see below), and are usually found in connection with references to divine presence and help:

> At dawn I marshaled the ranks for battle,
> I was ready to fight like an eager bull;
> I arose against them in the likeness of Mont,
> Equipped with my weapons of victory.
> I charged their ranks fighting as a falcon pounces,
> The serpent on my brow felled my foes,
> Cast her fiery breath in my enemies' faces,
> I was like Re when he rises at dawn.
> My rays, they burned the rebels' bodies,
> They called out to one another:
> 'Beware, take care, don't approach him,
> Sakhmet the Great is she who is with him,
> She's with him on his horses, her hand is with him;
> Anyone who goes to approach him,
> Fire's breath comes to burn his body!'[23]

21. Lichtheim, *Ancient Egyptian Literature*, II, p. 67.
22. Lichtheim, *Ancient Egyptian Literature*, II, p. 68.
23. Lichtheim, *Ancient Egyptian Literature*, II, p. 70.

However, the lines which conclude the poem give credit for the victory to the king's prowess as a warrior, which demonstrates that Egyptian martial literature assumed a 'synergism' of divine and human action, like the biblical battle narratives:

> My majesty overpowered them,
> I slew them without sparing them;
> They sprawled before my horses,
> And lay slain in heaps in their blood.[24]

There seems to be no pretense in this last section that the king was fighting alone; he mentions his troops and horses in the plural.

A prose section following the poem describes the Egyptians' return home under divine protection:

> ... His majesty returned in peace to Egypt with his infantry
> and his chariotry, all life, stability and dominion being
> with him, and the gods and goddesses protecting his body.
> He had crushed all lands through fear of him...[25]

In the poetic account of Merneptah's victory over the Libyans who had invaded Egypt, the poet describes the return of the defeated Libyan chief Merey to his own country, where the people speak the following lines, ascribing their defeat to divine control of human warfare:

> He is in the power of the gods, the lords of Memphis,
> The Lord of Egypt has made his name accursed;
> Merey is the abomination of Memphis...
> Merneptah... is given him as fate...[26]

The Lord of Egypt in this passage refers to the king, not the god, which indicates that although the gods are responsible for the outcome of military affairs, the king's prowess as a warrior is seen as an important factor also.[27]

Immediately after this speech, the poet again gives divine activity credit for the outcome. The god Seth was viewed as the protector of the foreign peoples to the east and west of Egypt, but here Seth has turned his back on his people, the Libyans:

24. Lichtheim, *Ancient Egyptian Literature*, II, p. 70.

25. Lichtheim, *Ancient Egyptian Literature*, II, p. 71.

26. Lichtheim, *Ancient Egyptian Literature*, II, p. 75.

27. Since kings in ancient Egypt were regarded as descendants of the sun god, the divine and human (royal) spheres of activity are not entirely separable.

Woe to Libyans, they have ceased to live...
Seth turned his back upon their chief,
By his word their villages were ruined...[28]

The poem also contains a quotation of a war oracle, which the poet attributes to soothsayers who tell the outcome of battles by reading the stars and winds:

As for Egypt, 'Since the gods', they say,
'She is the only daughter of Pre;
His son is he who's on the throne of Shu,
None who attacks her people will succeed.
The eye of every god is after her despoiler,
It will make an end of all her foes',
So say they who gaze toward their stars,
And know all their spells by looking to the winds.[29]

This passage is particularly noteworthy in the light of the Mari correspondence, in which prophets deliver oracles predicting military outcomes. A similar phenomenon is attested in Numbers 21–24, the Oracles of Baalam. Even if the Egyptian passage is a creation of the poet rather than an authentic quotation from an oracular source, it nevertheless demonstrates that war oracles predicting military outcomes were not unknown in Egypt.

The continuation of the poem contains the statement that the enemy was placed captive in Egypt's hand, an expression like the one common to biblical war language and Assyrian battle inscriptions, 'the ___ have been (or will be) delivered into your hand':

A great wonder has occurred for Egypt,
Her attacker was placed captive in her hand...
Merey, who stealthily did evil
To all the gods who are in Memphis,
He was contended with in On,
The Ennead found him guilty of his crimes.
Said the Lord-of-all: 'Give the sword to my son,
The right-hearted, kind, gracious Banere-meramun,
Who cared for Memphis, who avenged On...'[30]

After a detailed list of the king's just deeds, the gods say in unison:

28. Lichtheim, *Ancient Egyptian Literature*, II, p. 75.
29. Lichtheim, *Ancient Egyptian Literature*, II, p. 75.
30. Lichtheim, *Ancient Egyptian Literature*, II, p. 75.

> Grant him a lifetime like that of Re,
> To avenge those injured by any land;
> Egypt has been assigned him as portion,
> He owns it forever to protect its people.[31]

The Ennead is a divine council, shown here meeting in a court session at Heliopolis (On). The Lord-of-all is the sun-god Re or Pre, in all his manifestations, which include Re-Harakhti, Atum and Khepri.[32] The sword in this context refers to the sword of victory, awarded by the gods to the Egyptian king (Banere-meramun is another name for Merneptah). The reason that the Libyan foe was 'placed captive' in Egypt's hand is given in terms of justice: the king is presented as avenger of both the gods and the people against injustice and protector of Egypt from the unjust practices of other nations. The depiction of the divine council assigning Egypt to Merneptah (a son of the gods, as well as human king) as his 'portion' is reminiscent of Deut. 32.8-9. In this Egyptian poem, it is divine intervention in warfare on behalf of the just Egyptian king against an unjust nation which has determined the assignment.

The poem continues in the same vein, with Ptah, the chief god of Memphis, commanding that the enemy be given 'into the hand of' the Egyptian king:

> Then said Ptah concerning the vile Libyan foe:
> 'His crimes are all gathered upon his head.
> Give him into the hand of Merneptah, Content with Maat...
> It is Amun who curbs him with his hand,
> He will deliver him to his ka[33] in Southern On...'[34]

In addition to the formulae associated with battle literature, the Egyptian materials contribute to the discussion of martial poetry and prose a clear illustration of the literary conventions which give to ancient Near Eastern martial literature its characteristic flavour. Most of the narrative is structured around concepts of fear and courage: a fearful inner state in the foe brings about his defeat. Often the god is said to be

31. Lichtheim, *Ancient Egyptian Literature*, II, p. 76.
32. Lichtheim, *Ancient Egyptian Literature*, II, p. 223.
33. In Egyptian belief, the *ka* (often translated as 'personality' or 'vital force') is the part of the human soul with which a person is reunited at death. On is the place where supernatural beings dwell. To deliver someone to his *ka* is to cause his death; cf. H. Frankfort, *Kingship and the Gods: A Study of Ancient Near Eastern Religion as the Integration of Society and Nature* (Chicago: University of Chicago Press, 1948), pp. 61-78.
34. Lichtheim, *Ancient Egyptian Literature*, II, p. 76.

directly responsible for inducing the state of fearfulness, but sometimes the king's bravery and might inspire fear in enemy troops. However, in ancient Egypt, there was considerable overlap between the two concepts since the king was regarded as the son of the gods. In either case, the fearful inner state of the enemy, which contrasts with the firm-hearted bravery of the Egyptian warriors and their king, is the decisive factor in the victory.

In the prologue of the poetical stela of Thutmose III, the following speech of the god Amen-Re to the king abounds in exemplary descriptions of divine intervention in war:

> I gave you valor and victory over all lands.
> I set your might, your fear in every country,
> The dread of you as far as heaven's four supports,
> I magnified your awe in every body...
> I made your person's fame traverse the Nine Bows.
> The princes of all lands are gathered in your grasp,
> I stretched my own hands out and bound them for you.
> I fettered Nubia's Bowmen by tenthousand thousands,
> The northerners a hundred thousand captives.
> I made your enemies succumb beneath your soles,
> So that you crushed the rebels and the traitors.
> For I bestowed on you the earth, its length and breadth,
> Westerners and easterners are under your command.
>
> You trod all foreign lands with joyful heart,
> None could approach your majesty's vicinity,
> But you, with me your guide, attained them.
> You crossed the water of Nahrin's Euphrates,
> In might and victory ordained by me,
> Hearing your battle-cry they hid in holes.
> I robbed their nostrils of the breath of life,
> And made the dread of you pervade their hearts...
> My serpent on your brow consumed them...
> The lowlanders she swallowed by her flame,
> Asiatic heads she severed, none escaped,
> The foes were tottering before her might.
> I let your valor course through every land,
> The gleaming diadem protected you,
> In all that heaven circles, none can defy you...
> The foes who came before you I made weak,
> Their hearts aflame, their bodies trembled.[35]

35. Lichtheim, *Ancient Egyptian Literature*, II, p. 36.

The god Amun-Re is presented as controlling the outcome of the king's wars by means of 1. giving the king valor; 2. causing fear in the enemies (the word-pair fear and dread appears in this poem in parallelism, as it does in Ugaritic and Hebrew poetry, and in other Egyptian poetry as well); 3. stretching out his (the god's) own hands and binding the enemies; 4. making the enemies succumb beneath the feet of the king (an image found in the Akkadian materials also); 5. divine accompaniment (here, acting as the king's 'guide' in warfare); 6. consuming the enemy troops with flames (as Weinfeld pointed out, fire is one of the most common means of divine intervention in warfare); 7. severing enemy heads; and 8. 'protecting' the king (in this case, by means of the diadem, rather than the more usual 'shield'). All of these phenomena except for number 3 appear in other ancient Near Eastern literatures also. In this poem, numbers 1 and 2 clearly dominate. As this passage demonstrates, Egyptian war poetry describes in vivid detail the inner state of the combatants. Perhaps the Egyptian influence can partially explain the frequent references to fear, dread, terror and dismay as decisive factors in victory in biblical war poems and narratives.

In the triumphal poem which follows the prologue, the god continues to address the king. Each quatrain begins with the anaphora 'I came to let you tread on...' followed by a second anaphora, 'I let them see your majesty as...' Particularly interesting, because of the appearance of the same type of imagery in early Yahwistic war poetry, is an example pointed out by Weinfeld: 'I let them see your majesty as shooting star, that scatters fire as it sheds its flame'. Also noteworthy is the following line, because of the reference to firm-heartedness: 'I let them see your majesty as youthful bull, firm-hearted, sharp of horns, invincible'.

This poetical stela, found in the Karnak Temple, depicts Amun-Re welcoming Thutmose III and recounting the victories he (the deity) gave to the king throughout his reign; therefore it does not depict the god intervening in a particular battle. There are, however, examples of both poetry and prose in which the gods intervene in specific battles or campaigns. A monumental inscription from the annals in the Karnak Temple of the same king, Thutmose III, describes in prose the Battle of Megiddo, using recurring stylized phrases, many of which ascribe victory to divine help. Following a list of divine epithets, the account begins as follows:

> His majesty commanded to record [the victories his father Amun had given him] by an inscription in the temple... [to record] each campaign together with the booty which [his majesty] had brought [from it and the tribute of every foreign land] that his father Re had given him...

The campaign was undertaken at the command of Amun:

> ...first month of summer, day 5, departure from this place in valor, [strength], might, and right, to overthrow that wretched enemy, to extend the borders of Egypt, his father, mighty and victorious Amun, having commanded that he conquer...

> ...day 19, awakening in life in the royal tent at the town of Aruna. Northward journey by my majesty with my father Amen-Re, Lord of Thrones-of-the-Two-Lands, [that he might open the ways] before me, Harakhti fortifying [the heart of my valiant army], my father Amun strengthening [my majesty's] arm and...protecting my majesty...

> ...day 21...His majesty set out on a chariot of fine gold, decked in his shining armor like strong-armed Horus, lord of action, like Mont of Thebes, his father Amun strengthening his arm. The southern wing of his majesty's army was at a hill south of the Qina [brook], and the northern wing to the northwest of Megiddo, while his majesty was in their center, Amun protecting his person [in] the melee and the strength of [Seth pervading] his limbs...

> ...fear of his majesty had entered [their bodies], and their arms sank as his diadem overwhelmed them...

> Then the entire army jubilated and gave praise to Amun [for the victory] he had given to his son on [that day]...

> Then his majesty commanded his army, saying: 'Grasp well, grasp well, [my] valiant [army]! Lo, [all the foreign lands] are placed [in this town by the will of] Re on this day...'[36]

The phrase 'not one of them will be able to stand before you' is not uncommon in biblical war exhortations in which divine presence and help are promised, usually in connection with a formula of encouragement, such as 'fear not'.

Similar phrases are found in the Kadesh battle inscriptions of Ramses II, in which victory is ascribed to pharaoh fighting singlehandedly, deserted by his troops, but aided by the god Amun (the words of the god to the king have been quoted in full above). In both poetry and prose versions, enemy troops are unable to stand before the king because of his stout-heartedness in combat. The prose battle bulletin has the following words:

> His majesty was mighty, his heart stout, one could not stand before him.[37]

36. Lichtheim, *Ancient Egyptian Literature*, II, pp. 29-34.
37. Lichtheim, *Ancient Egyptian Literature*, II, p. 62.

Some of the same words are repeated in the poem:

> His (the king's) arms mighty, his heart stout,
> His strength like Mont in his hour...
> Head on he charges a multitude,
> His heart trusting his strength;
> Stout-hearted in the hour of combat,
> Like a flame when it consumes.
> Firm-hearted like a bull ready for battle,
> He heeds not all the lands combined;
> A thousand men cannot withstand him,
> A hundred thousand fail at his sight.
> Lord of fear, great of fame.
> In the hearts of all the lands...
> [Casting fear] in foreigners' hearts...
> Who goes forth in valor, returns in triumph...[38]

A similar phrase is used when pharaoh describes how he found himself fighting alone, which demonstrates a more general use of the phrase in military literature:

> My infantry, my chariotry, yielded before them,
> Not one of them stood firm to fight with them.[39]

The influence of both terminology and literary conventions from ancient Egypt upon other literatures in the region is not surprising, considering the dominance of the Egyptian empire over an extended period of time. Along with military and political hegemony came cultural influence, particularly since Egypt had already developed a tradition of elegant and sophisticated literature. The similarity of the biblical wisdom writings to the wisdom literature of Egypt is well known, but there is reason to think that the similarity extended to other types of poetry and prose also, including battle bulletins and martial poems, as I have attempted to demonstrate in the foregoing discussion.

However, there are also some important differences: 1. the divine status of the pharaoh in Egypt is unique when compared with concepts of kingship in other parts of the ancient Near East; 2. the Egyptian martial literature lacks some of the characteristic phrases which are prominent in both the DH and the Assyrian materials (such as the admonition to 'Fear not!'); and 3. the ideological purpose of the text is different. In Egypt, many of the inscriptions seem to have been created primarily to

---

38. Lichtheim, *Ancient Egyptian Literature*, II, pp. 62-63.
39. Lichtheim, *Ancient Egyptian Literature*, II, p. 65.

flatter the pharoah and his family by praising his supernatural courage. The ideological purpose of the martial literature in the DH bears a much closer resemblence to that of the Assyrian materials, as will be demonstrated below.

D. *Anatolia*

Since the Hittite empire at one time included most of the Syro-Palestine region, one would expect that there might be some similarity between Anatolian martial literature and texts from within the Syro-Palestine region. Indeed there is. The annals of Muršili II[40] demonstrate that the Hittite monarchs connected divine help in battle with the spread of their empire.

At the beginning of the Ten Year Annals of Muršili II, a new king had just suceeded his father as ruler. Humiliated by neighbouring enemies who thought him weak and who attempted to take advantage of the turmoil of transition, he fought back. His foes encroached upon his territorial holdings and taunted him, calling him a 'child'.[41] He prayed to the sungoddess, 'they have begun to seek to take your boundaries' (the 'your' refers to the goddess). As in the Bible and other ancient Near Eastern texts, the Hittite text identified the national territory with a deity (a goddess, in this case) as 'her' land and 'her' boundaries. Therefore, a transgression against the realm is a transgression against the deity.

To show his piety, the king put worship to the deity before military activity. The act of worship also served the purpose of consecrating the army, the weaponry and the battle itself to the deity (cf. Deut. 20.3). The Hittite text indicates that the ritual was a routine pre-battle procedure: before going out to war to avenge the enemies' transgressions, the king first performed the 'established festivals' for the goddess. The deity then accompanied him into battle, and caused him to have victory:

> Oh, sungoddess of Arinna, my lady—stand beside me, and defeat the aforementioned neighboring enemy countries before me. And the sungoddess of Arinna heard my word, and she stood beside me. And when I had sat down on the throne of my father, I conquered these enemy countries in ten years; and defeated them...

40. A. Goetze, *Die Annalen des Muršilis: Hethitische Texte in Umschrift, mit übersetzung und Eräuterungen* (vol.6; MVAG, 38; Leipzig: Hinrichs, 1933), pp. 14-137; H. Otten, 'Neue Fragmente zu den Annalen des Muršili', *MIO* 3 (1955), pp. 161-65; Younger, *Ancient Conquest Accounts*, pp. 143-59.

41. Younger, *Ancient Conquest Accounts*, pp. 141-44.

In the conclusion of the annals, he claims that the warfare was 'assigned' to him by the national goddess:

> But what the sungoddess of Arinna, my lady, assigns to me, that I will carry out, and I will accomplish...

This passage provides an example of divine instigation of warfare, like the war oracle in Joshua 1, and the many 'fear not' oracles throughout the DH.

The emphasis in the Hittite materials is on imperial control of vassal rulers and subject populations. However, rather than the destruction of human life depicted in Assyrian materials and in the Book of Joshua, the Hittite materials present an orderly picture of live captives taken from the destroyed areas after a defeat. The primary emphasis is still on divine action. As Kang pointed out,[42] there are even a few Hittite examples of the phrase (so central to the Assyrian oracles below) 'god gives X into my hand':

> When at that time I, the king, came to Lawazzantiya, Lahhas was hostile to me, and incited Lawazzantiyas to rebellion. And the god delivered it into my hand (I 20-21).[43]

In the above example, the connection with imperial ideology is especially prominent, as demonstrated by the reference to a rebellious vassal (Lahhas). As in the Assyrian examples in the section below, the implication is that the gods' desire is for the king of the empire to control the territory or city in question. It is not merely the king's desire, according to the ideology, but is a divine imperative. Likewise, the enemies of the king are the enemies of the god or goddess, which gives divine sanction to the total destruction:

> Envious enemies My Lady Ishtar put into my hand; and I destroyed them utterly... (I 59, III 45).[44]

Although Kang asserts that the Hittite materials, of all the ancient Near Eastern texts, place the greatest emphasis on destruction,[45] I have found the motif of total destruction to be more common in Assyrian battle reports than anywhere else, particularly when the annihilation of

---

42. Kang, *Divine War*, p. 67.
43. Kang, *Divine War*, pp. 67-69.
44. Kang, *Divine War*, pp. 67-69.
45. Kang, *Divine War*, p. 69.

human life as well as property is meant. When the Hittite battle reports boast of the 'total destruction' of a city or area, they usually mean that the property was destroyed and the people were taken captive:

> I, my sun, went to it (the region),
> and I attacked Halila and Dudduska which were major cities
> of the Kaskaeans.
> I took out from them the inhabitants (as captives),
> cattle (and) sheep;
> and I brought them forth to Hattusa.
> I completely burned down Halila (and) Dudduska
> (*KBo* III.4 Vs I. 30-35).

> I attacked [the city of...]humessena.
> [I took out] from it the inhabitants (as captives),
> cattle (and) sheep;
> I brought them forth to Hattusa.
> I completely [burned] down the city
> (*KBo* III.4 Vs I.43-48).

> I, my sun, attacked the city of Kathaidduwa.
> And I brought out from it the inhabitants (as captives),
> cattle (and) sheep to Hattusa.
> [The city] I burn[ed down completely]
> (*KBo* III.4 Vs I.49-52).

> [and I], my sun, [attacked] the city of Kammaman.
> [and the sungoddess of Arinna], my lady; [the mighty
> stormgod, my lord; Me]zzull[a (and) [all] the gods [ran
> before me].
> And [I conquered the city of Kammanman].
> [And I took out from it the inhabitants (as captives)],
> cattle (and) sheep.
> [And I brought it] to [Hattusa].
> [I burned down the city completely]
> (*KBo* III.4 Vs I.53- II.24).

In some examples, the language is more ambiguous:

> And I fought (with) it.
> And the sungoddess of Arinna, my lady; the mighty stormgod,
> my lord;
> Mezzulla; (and) all the gods ran before me.
> And the enemy of Pishuru I defeated behind Palhuissa.
> Moreover, I burned down the city completely
> (*KBo* III.4 Vs II.1-6).

I fought against these Kaskaeans of Mt. Asharpaya.
And the sungoddess of Arinna, my lady; the mighty stormgod,
my lord;
Mezzulla (and) all of the gods ran before me.
And the Kaskaens who had continued to occupy Mt. Asharpaya I
conquered.
and I defeated.
I made Mt. Asharpaya empty (of humanity)
(*KBo* III.4 Rs III.39-46).

Then I, my sun, went;
and I attacked those Kaskaeans who had continually occupied
the mountains of Tarikarimu.
And the sungoddess of Arinna, my lady; the mighty stormgod,
my lord;
Mezzulla; (and) all the gods ran before me.
And I conquered the Kaskaeans of the mountains of
Tarikarimu.
And I defeated them.
I made the mountains of Tarikarimu empty (of humanity).
I completely burned down the land of Ziharriya
(*KBo* III.4 Rs III.57-66).

Whether the implication is that the people were all killed or that they were taken captive and relocated, there is certainly none of the grisly display of corpses that one finds in the Assyrian materials. There are a few examples in the Hittite materials of mass killing. Interestingly, they come not from first-person battle reports, but from the accounts composed by Muršili II in order to commemorate the victories of his father, Suppiluliuma:[46]

(But) the Kaska enemy, all of their tribal troops, he met in
[the country].
And the gods stood by him.
[the sun goddess of Arinna, the storm god of Hatti, the
storm god of the Army, and Istar of the Battlefield,
(so that) the en[emy] died in multitudes.
He also [took] many prisoners;
and brought them back to Samuha
(Fragment 10 D Col. i.2-10)[47]

---

46. H.G. Güterbock, 'The Deeds of Suppiluliuma as Told by His Son, Muršili II', *JCS* 10 (1956), pp. 41-130; Younger, *Ancient Conquest Accounts*, pp. 160-62.
    47. Güterbock, 'Deeds', pp. 62-63.

> (So) my father went against him.
> And the gods ran before my father:
> the Sun Goddess of Arinna, the Storm god of Hatti, the Storm
> god of the Army, and the Lady of the Battlefield.
> (Thus) he slew the aforementioned whole tribe,
> and the enemy troops died in multitudes
> (Fragment 15 F Col. iv—G Col. i.5-10)[48]

> [and] he fought [...]
> And the gods [ran before] my father:
> [The Sun Goddess of Ari]nna, the Storm God of Hatti, the
> Storm God of the Army, [the god X, the god Y], Istar of the
> Battlefield and Zababa,
> [(so that) the enemy troops] died in [multi]tudes
> (Fragment 50 *BoTU* Col. i.11-18)[49]

Although the passage above reports the destruction of an entire tribe, the implication in all of the above passages seems to be that only enemy troops, not civilians, were killed in multitudes. Nowhere in the Hittite materials do we get any reports of the mass murder of women and children.

In the above examples, the emphasis is on the gods and goddesses as divine helpers. Likewise, the battle reports below state repeatedly that the victories were made possible by the presence and assistance of the various national dieties, usually employing the phrase 'all the gods ran before me':

> Then I, my sun, went after the inhabitants to Mt. Arinnanda,
> and I fought (them) at Mt. Arinnnanda.
> The sungoddess of Arinna, my lady; the mighty stormgod, my
> lord;
> Mezzulla (and) all the gods ran before me.
> Thus, I conquered Mt. Arinnnanda
> (*KBo* III.4 Vs II.15-49).

> And I, my sun, fought against him;
> and the sungoddess of Arinna, my lady; the mighty stormgod,
> my lord;
> Mezzulla; and all the gods ran before me.
> And I conquered Tapalazunauli... together with his troops and
> his charioteers
> (*KBo* III.4 Vs II.57-65).

---

48. Güterbock,'Deeds', p. 75.
49. Güterbock, 'Deeds', pp. 117-18.

[. . .] I fought [against it].
And the sungoddess of Arinna, my lady; the mighty stormgod,
my lord;
Mezzulla; (and) all the gods ran before me.
And I conquered Puranda
(*KBo* III.4 Vs II.79-86).

Then I, my sun, went to the land of Arawanna.
And I attacked the land of Arawanna.
And the sungoddess of Arinna, my lady; the mighty stormgod,
my lord;
Mezzulla; (and) all the gods ran before me.
And I conquered all of the land of Arawanna
(*KBo* III.4 Rs III.47-56).

And the sungoddess of Arinna, my lady; the mighty stormgod,
my lord;
Mezzulla, (and) all the gods ran before me.
I took Aripsa (and) Dukkamma through battle
(*KBo* III.4 Rs IV.35-43).

The Hittite materials also provide a parallel to the incident in Josh.
10:11-14, in which divine intervention in battle takes the form of a god
helping the imperial enterprise by interfering with the phenomena of
nature, specifically the heavenly bodies:[50]

So I marched,
and as I arrived at Mt. Lawasa,
the mighty stormgod, my lord, showed his godly miracle.
He hurled a meteor.
My army saw the meteor.
(And) the land of Arzawa saw (it).
And the meteor went;
and struck the land of Arzawa.
It struck Apasa, the capital city of Uhhaziti.
Uhhaziti fell on (his) knees;
and became ill.
When Uhhaziti became ill;
so he did not come against me to fight. . .

And I, my sun, fought with him.
The sungoddess of Arinna, my lady; the mighty stormgod,
my lord;
Mezulla, (and) all the gods ran before me.

50. Weinfeld also classified this Hittite example with the other examples of divine
interference with nature for military purposes.

And I conquered Piyama-KA, the son of Uhhaziti, together
with his troops and charioteers.
And I defeated him.
Then I pursued him,
and I entered into the land of Arzawa.
I entered into Apasa, into the capital city of Uhhaziti;
and Uhhaziti could not withstand me.
He fled before me;
and went across the sea by ship.
And he remained there.
The whole country of Arzawa fled
(*KBo* III.4 Vs II.15-49).

The Hittite battle reports also provide two instructive parallels to the
treaty which Joshua made with the Gibeonites (Joshua 9):

On the next day: I marched towards the city of Taptina.
When I arrived at the city of Tarkuma,
I burned Tarkuma down completely.
Then the people of the cities of Taptina, Hursama, (and)
Pikurzi came before me.
And they bowed themselves down at (my) feet.
And they spoke thus:
    'Our lord Do not destroy us!
    Take us into servitude;
    and make us troops and charioteers.
    And we will go on the campaign'.
So I took them into servitude.
And I made them troops and charioteers.
(*KBo* IV.4 Rs III.43-51).

When the people of the city of Azzi saw that fighting
(their) strong cities I subjugated them:
—the people of Azzi, who have strong cities, rocky
mountains, (and) high difficult terrain—they were afraid!
And the elders of the land came before me,
and they bowed themselves down at (my) feet.
And they spoke:
    'Our lord! Do not destroy us!
    Lord, take us into servitude,
    and we will begin to provide to (your) lordship troops
    and charioteers.
    The Hittite fugitives which (are) with us, we will
provide these'.
Then I, my sun, did not destroy them.

I took them into servitude;
and I made them slaves
(*KBo* IV.4 Rs IV.28-37).

Although the Hittite king states that they were taken into slavery, the word 'slaves' is apparently not meant as literally as in the biblical story of the Gibeonites. The king evidently absorbed the conquered subjects into the imperial military forces as infantry troops and charioteers, rather than subject them to the humiliation of slavery (like the Gibeonites, who had to cut wood and draw water). Although military service is more dangerous, it is less degrading than the fate of the Gibeonites.[51] Joshua took away their dignity and gave them the lowliest place in the hierarchy of his centralized society, in order to emphasize obedience to his authority structure. However, the people of Taptina, Hursama, Pikurzi and Azzi were merely doing what was expected of a vassal ruler and his people under the control of an empire in the ancient Near East, serving in the imperial defense. Nevertheless, there are strong similarities to the Joshua passage, particularly in the way the subject people approach the ruler, and the military context. The language of the two Hittite passages is also strikingly similar to the covenant language in Joshua 9. As in Joshua 9, the conquered people submit voluntarily to the Hittite ruler because of his military prowess, and in return their lives are spared. However, the element of trickery so crucial to Joshua 9 is lacking.

The Hittite battle reports exhibit many of the same features as the terminology of divine intervention in warfare in the DH:

1. divine instigation to military action;

2. divine help and accompaniment in battle, even the deity or deities fighting for the conquerors;

3. divine intervention through natural phenomena by interfering with or manipulating the heavens, or other forces of nature (meteor, sun, moon);

4. the deity presented as the embodiment of national identity, and the king as the representative of the deity, making him also an embodiment of national identity;

5. taking people into servitude, because they (awed by the military successes of the conquerors) voluntarily submit to the conquerors in order to save themselves (like the Gibeonite situation, Joshua 9); however, they are only absorbed into the imperial military rather than put into a truly degrading occupation or social status.

---

51. The ideological meaning of the Gibeonite incident is covered in more detail in Chapter 7.

Although many elements are similar, particularly with regard to divine participation in battle, the Hittite materials also show some significant differences:

1. the language describing divine participation in battle is not particularly similar; there is no Hittite equivalent to the 'fear not' oracles;

2. there is none of the emphasis on fear/courage, so prominent in the Bible and in the Assyrian materials;

3. there are none of the terse imperative commands of the Moabite stone and the Bible, such as 'Go, take possession'.

Like Younger,[52] I have found that the main difference between the Hittite and Assyrian martial literatures lies in the greater Assyrian emphasis on inspiring terror. The Assyrians' descriptions of torture and execution of rebellious vassals are particularly graphic, which would certainly tend to deter the temptation to assert an independent national identity on the part of the smaller entities under Assyrian domination. When the Assyrians boasted of the total destruction they inflicted on the places they conquered, they referred to the destruction of human life and not merely property. Although the Hittites have a similar imperial ideology, the fierce Assyrians seem to have geared their texts much more to propagandistic purposes, aimed directly at intimidating potential rivals for power in the realm.

E. *Mesopotamia*

Although there are similarities in the ideologies, literary forms and terminologies of the literatures of warfare throughout the ancient Near East, the Assyrian martial literature bears the most striking resemblence to the DH, particularly the Book of Joshua (see below). The resemblence extends to the usage as well, since the Dtr apparently was using war oracles and battle reports for intimidation in a fashion which was much more closely related to the Assyrian style and purpose than that of any other ancient Near Eastern empire.

1. *Early Mesopotamia*. In the cone inscription of Entemena (ca. 2404-2375 BCE), when Ush, the ruler of Umma, invaded the boundary of Lagash, Ningirsu made war against Umma by the command of Enlil: 'Ningirsu, the warrior of Enlil, made war against Umma by his righteous

---

52. Younger, *Ancient Conquest Accounts*, p. 159.

command'.[53] The divine warrior motif, therefore, extends all the way back into the documents of the earliest civilization in Mesopotamia, playing a role in boundary disputes.

The Sumerian hymn to Ninurta as a god of wrath exalts the ability of the deity to suppress rebellion in the realm:

> My king, who vanquishes the houses of the rebellious lands, great lord of
>   Enlil,
> You, with power you are endowed.
> Lord Ninurta, who vanquishes the houses of the rebellious lands, great
>   lord of Enlil,
> You, with power you are endowed...
> My king, when you approached the enemy, you scattered him like rushes,
> You meted out to him...
> Lord Ninurta, when you approached the enemy, you scattered him like
>   rushes,
> You meted out to him... (*ANET*, p. 577).

Another Sumerian hymn praises Inanna as a supreme goddess in charge of cosmic order. Her military powers are presented as an extension of her control of the *me*, the destinies:

> Queen of all the *me*, radiant light...
> who grasps in her hand the seven *me*...
> In the van of battle, everything was struck down before you,
> My queen, you are all devouring in your power,
> You kept on attacking like an attacking storm...
>
> You burnt down its great gates,
> Its rivers ran with blood because of you, its people had nothing to drink,
> Its troops were led off willingly (into captivity) before you,
> Its forces disbanded themselves willingly before you,
> Its strong men paraded willingly before you,
> The amusement places of its cities were filled with turbulence,
> Its adult males were driven off as captives before you...
>   (*ANET*, pp. 579-80).

The letters from the Kingdom of Mari illustrate that the roots of Akkadian war oracle language go at least as far back as 1730–1700 BCE. The Mari correspondence contains a series of letters in the form of war oracles from prophets promising the king divine support in battle. Some of the letters contain an exhortation to have confidence, which is a prominent feature of the neo-Assyrian oracles to Esarhaddon and

---

53. Kang, *Divine War*, p. 13.

Ashurbanipal (discussed below) and the biblical DH. Furthermore, the exhortation to be confident is linked to the promise of divine presence and assistance in battle, using the *Übergabeformel*, 'I (the deity) will deliver X into your hand'. The following examples[54] depict a prophet speaking for a deity:

> O Zimri-Lim, with a revolt they would put you to the test. Guard your-self...And as for the men who would put you to the test, I shall deliver these men into your hand (*ARM* X 7).[55]

> Your enemies I shall deliver into your hand (*ARM* X 8).[56]

> O Zimri-Lim, the city Sarrakiya [I shall giv]e [to] its enemies and those who [en]circle it (*ARM* X 81).[57]

It is (the gods)...who march at my lord's side...before my lord his (the enemy's) army will be scattered (*ARM* X 4).[58]
Sometimes the horrors that are to be inflicted on the enemies of Zimri-Lim are described in more vivid language:

> ...your [ad]versaries will be [sl]it open. I alone have trampled them down (*ARM* X 53).[59]

> My lord will see what the god(dess) will do to this man. You will conquer him and over him you will stand. His days are short. He will not survive (*ARM* X 6).[60]

Although the presence of exhortations to be confident are undisputed in the Mari correspondence, a more complicated question is whether there are any specific equivalents in the Mari letters to the exhortation 'fear not'. Heinz cites two examples which he argues are parallels to the biblical texts:[61]
1) *la i-ḫa-aš* (*ARM* XIII 114), which Heinz translates as 'qu'il ne s'inquiète pas'. He argues that it is synonymous with 'ne crains point'.[62]

---

54. The following examples were translated by W.L. Moran in the article mentioned in Chapter 4, 'New Evidence from Mari on the History of Prophecy'.
55. Moran, 'New Evidence', pp. 29-30.
56. Moran, 'New Evidence', p. 31.
57. Moran, 'New Evidence', p. 33.
58. Moran, 'New Evidence', pp. 46-48.
59. Moran, 'New Evidence', p. 34.
60. Moran, 'New Evidence', p. 35.
61. J.-G. Heinz, 'Oracles prophétiques et 'geurre sainte' selon les archives royales de Mari et l'Ancien Testament', *VT* 17 (1969), pp. 112-35.
62. Heinz, 'Oracles', pp. 121-22.

2) *a-na ra-ma-ni-šu iš-ta-na-ar-r[a]-a[r]*
a-na ra-ma-ni-ka la ta-aš-t[a]-na-ar-ra-a[r] (*ARM* X 80), which he
translates as:

> 'Il est continuellement vacillant quant á sa personne...
> Quant á ta personne, ne sois pas vacillant'.[63]

Dion questions whether interpreting either of the two passages above as
equivalent to 'fear not' (or 'ne crains point') is actually supported by the
text.[64] The first, *la i-ha-aš* (from the verb *hâšu*), he argues, is better
translated as something like 'do not worry', which is close to 'fear not',
but it is not the verb used in the neo-Assyrian oracles (*palāhu*). Futher-
more, *hâšu* is never used as a synonym for *palāhu* in the Mari texts.
Dion goes on to point out that even if one concedes that *la i-ha-aš* can
be translated as 'fear not', an argument that it was part of the stereotyped language of war in the second millennium BCE cannot be supported, since *la i-ha-aš* as a war oracle phrase in *ARM* XIII 114 is a
unique occurrence. He believes that Heinz has strained the evidence to
make a case for the antiquity (second millennium) of the 'fear not'
exhortation. However, in answer to Dion, I would argue that *la i-ha-aš*
can still be included as an example of an exhortation to confidence in a
war oracle, even if it is not the exact equivalent of 'fear not' (*la ta-pal-
lah*).

The second example above is more questionable. Dion agrees with
Moran's translation of *šarâru* (to be 'moving about' by himself, as a
synonym of *alâku*), rather than Heinz's translation (to be wavering).
Whereas Heinz emphasizes the element of vacillation, with overtones of
anxiety, Moran emphasizes the warning aspect of the oracle: the king is
being cautioned against walking about unprotected.

The exhortation 'fear not' appears in two Akkadian texts which
apparently date back to the second millennium BCE. One is the
Gilgamesh Epic. The other is the Cuthean Legend of Naram Sin. Both
of these works exist in several different and fragmentary versions from
different periods.

Although most of the texts of the Gilgamesh Epic were found in the
library of Ashurbanipal and are written in Akkadian, there are versions

---

63. Heinz, 'Oracles', p. 123.

64. H.M. Dion, 'The "Fear Not" Formula and Holy War', *CBQ* 32 (1970),
pp. 565-70; and 'The Patriarchal Traditions and the Literary Form of the "Oracle of
Salvation"', *CBQ* 29 (1967), pp. 198-206.

or fragments in Sumerian, Hittite and Hurrian as well as fragments of an Old Babylonian text from the first half of the second millennium BCE.[65] In the Gilgamesh Epic, the phrase 'fear not' is used by Gilgamesh and Enkidu to encourage each other to be fearless when they are entering battle against the monster Ḫuwawa (Old Babylonian version, Tablet III, l.12; *ANET*, p. 79). Gilgamesh offers to enter the combat ahead of Enkidu and tells his friend to encourage him from behind with the words 'fear not'. Although the use of the exhortation in the Gilgamesh Epic does not qualify as a war oracle, nor is it an example of divine intervention in human warfare, it certainly involves combat (albeit mythological).[66]

The Cuthean Legend[67] is a fictitious royal inscription counselling future kings not to go out to war in an attempt to expand the boundaries of the realm. The writer of the inscription, pretending to be Naram Sin (at least in the Sultantepe version), goes into battle against a superhuman army. After a series of misadventures, he consecrates himself for the battle, according to an oracle from a deity. He defeats the frightening superhuman troops and then draws the conclusion that victory in warfare is a divine gift rather than something accomplished by human

65. Oppenheim, *ANET*, p.72; cf. A. Heidel, *The Gilgamesh Epic* (Chicago: University of Chicago Press, 1949), p. 36; and J.H. Tigay, *The Evolution of the Gilgamesh Epic* (Philadelphia: University of Pennsylvania Press, 1982), *passim*.

66. Dion argues that these exhortations cannot be taken as examples of the 'oracular style' (p. 200). However, no one disputes that a combat situation is involved.

67. The most complete version of the Cuthean Legend comes from Sultantepe. Previously, four fragments were known from the library of Asurbanipal, but it was the Sultantepe version which attached the name of Naram Sin to the legend and showed how the fragments fit together. Gurney published a neo-Assyrian version in 1955: O.R. Gurney, 'The Sultantepe Tablets IV: The Cuthean Legend of Naram Sin', *AS* 5 (1955), pp. 93-113. Then in 1957, Finkelstein published an Old Babylonian fragment, some parts of which closely resemble the neo-Assyrian version: J.J. Finkelstein, 'The So-called "Old Babylonian Kutha Legend"', *JCS* 11 (1957), pp. 83-88; cf. C.B.F. Walker, 'The Second Tablet of ṭupšenna pitema: An Old Babylonian Naram Sin Legend?', *JCS* 33 (1981), pp. 191-95. A third source consists of parts of two prisms found at Bogazköy, which also contain many parallels to the neo-Assyrian, according to T. Longman III, *Fictional Akkadian Autobiography: A Generic and Comparative Study* (Winona Lake: Eisenbrauns, 1991), pp. 103-17. A fourth source is a Hittite version that had been published earlier by H.G. Güterbock, 'Die historische Tradition und ihre literarische Gestaltung bei Babyloniern und Hethitern bis 1200', *ZA* 44 (1938), pp. 49-61.

might. His (following) words to future rulers contain the advice to stay at home rather than engaging in political adventurism:

> Be not bewildered, be not confused,
> Be not afraid (*la ta-pal-laḫ*), do not tremble... (vv. 154-55).[68]

The phrase *la ta-pal-laḫ*, which Gurney translates as 'be not afraid', is the same exhortation as that which appears in the neo-Assyrian war oracles to Esarhaddon and Ashurbanipal, below. Dion acknowledges that the so-called Cuthean Legend supplies a second-millennium example of the words *la ta-pal-laḫ*, but again points out (rightly) that the words do not appear in a war oracle until the neo-Assyrian period.

An additional feature worthy of notice in the tablet above is the two pairs of negative imperatives in the exhortation. The exhortations in Josh. 1.1-9 and Deut. 31.6-8 contain remarkably similar sets of words. The setting is different, however: in the Cuthean Legend, future rulers are being encouraged to stay home and tend to domestic affairs rather than going out to wars of territorial conquest. In the biblical passages, Joshua is being exhorted to undertake the conquest with Yahweh's help in battle.[69]

2. *Assyrian Battle Reports.* Van Seters observed that the form of the victory inscriptions of the Assyrian kings was essentially the same as that of the biblical battle reports.[70] He summarized the Assyrian accounts as follows:

> ...the king musters his forces at the command of a deity (or deities) and traverses the land to the battle site. The battle is engaged but there is no contest; the victory is immediately apparent. There is a great slaughter on the side of the enemy with cities taken and plundered and its kings captured. Those who take flight are pursued and slain...[71]

He goes on to point out the prominence of the divine element:

---

68. Gurney, 'The Sultantepe Tablets IV,' pp. 93-113.

69. Ironically, the Akkadian text is the one encouraging 'quietism', although scholars (especially Lind) often claim that a major difference between Mesopotamian and biblical war literature is the emphasis on divine rather than human action in the biblical text.

70. J. Van Seters, 'The Conquest of Sihon's Kingdom: a Literary Examination', *JBL* 91 (1972), pp. 182-97.

71. Van Seters, 'The Conquest of Sihon's Kingdom', p. 188.

> ...the king acts on divine command. He usually receives a confidence-inspiring oracle, either before he sets out or before the crucial battle, which is then fulfilled exactly as stated. The decisive cause of victory is the terrifying spendor which the gods (and secondarily the king) inspire in the enemy which causes them to flee. Finally much of the booty taken is dedicated to the deity.[72]

Although the focus of his article is not on the Book of Joshua, Van Seters has identified several important aspects of the Assyrian reports which are remarkably similar to the deuteronomistic battle reports in Deut. 2.24-3.11.[73] He traces the origin of the style used in both the Assyrian and deuteronomistic versions to 'a scribal convention of recording military campaigns', which he said would have been wide-spread 'during the late monarchy and exilic periods when the deuteronomistic literature was written'. By phrasing his sentence vaguely, he begs the question of whether the deuteronomistic accounts were written in pre-exilic times or during the exile.

Furthermore, he goes on to say that the literary conventions of the battle report in Mesopotamia underwent a process of change over time. The deuteronomistic accounts of the Sihon battle, he says, are reminiscent of the Assyrian annals, which are most frequently narrated in the first person. The Dtr depicts Moses speaking in the first person in the role of the leader of the people Israel. A little less frequently, the Assyrian annals are in the third person. They are similar in style and form and place the same emphasis on divine intervention. However, in the neo-Babylonian period, the style and form of the accounts change to 'a brief synopsis of the great deeds of former kings, very likely based on commemorative inscriptions, but recorded in the third person'.[74] His

---

72. Van Seters, 'The Conquest of Sihon's Kingdom', p. 188.

73. The battle reports he discusses in Deuteronomy would presumably have been composed by the same hand as those in Joshua (discussed in my next Chapter) if one subscribes to the theories of the DH examined in Chapter 3.

74. (pp. 188-89); Van Seters goes on to discuss in detail his theory that the Numbers account of the Sihon battle corresponds most closely to the Neo-Babylonian chronicle form. His discussion of Numbers need not detain us here, except to note that the difference between the DH version and the P-source document corresponds to the difference between Assyrian annalistic style and the Neo-Babylonian form, in his opinion. The most noteworthy difference in the Neo-Babylonian chronicles, according to him, is the virtual elimination of the element of divine intervention, which he says is 'very rare and in most accounts entirely lacking'. Kang, however, has demonstrated that Marduk is presented as a divine warrior

observations concerning the neo-Babylonian reports and the passages in
Numbers can be set aside. His essential point for my purposes is that the
Assyrian battle reports resemble the battle reports in the DH. Therefore
a close examination of the Assyrian annals and other documents is warranted to determine whether or not a resemblence exists.

The following early example from the foundation document of the
Anu Adad temple expresses the idea that King Tiglath-Pileser I (1114–
1076 BCE) lives and fights entirely under the command of the national
warrior-gods. The king claims that the gods gave him victory over his
enemies and that his ability to overthrow enemies is due to his trust in
the gods:

> ...the courageous hero who lives (guided) by the trust-inspiring oracles
> given (to him) by Ashur and Ninurta, the great gods and his lords, (and
> who thus) overthrew (all) his enemies; son of Ashurreshishi, king of the
> world, king of Assyria, (grand) son of Mutakkil-Nusku, also king of the
> world, king of Assyria... (*ANET*, p. 275).

Even in the early inscriptions from Tiglath-Pileser I and Shalmaneser III,
there are passages in which the imperialistic claim is made that the
king's conquests are undertaken at the instigation of the national god
Ashur and that the territories are conquered and ruled by Assyria
because it is the divine will:

> At the command of my lord Ashur I was a conqueror (lit.: my hand con-
> quered) from beyond the Lower Zab River to the Upper Sea which (lies
> towards) the West (*ANET*, p. 275).

> At the time [Ashur, the great lord...gave me scepter, staff]...necessary
> (to rule) the people, (and) I was acting (only) upon the trust-inspiring
> oracles given by Ashur, the great lord, my lord, who loves me to be his
> high priest and...all the countries and mountain regions to their full
> extent... I swept over Hatti in its full extent (making it look) like ruin-
> hills (left) by the flood...(thus) I spread my terror-inspiring glare over
> Hatti (*ANET*, p. 277).

The following examples from the reports of Shalmaneser III express
the idea that the god has the power to affect the outcome of the battle
by inspiring terror in the enemies and inspiring courage and 'trust' in
the king's Assyrian forces. They also express the idea that faith in the
deity (in this case Ashur) is more valuable in warfare than trust in a
numerically superior army or superior weaponry:[75]

at least during the ascendancy of the Neo-Babylonian empire.
    75. See the discussions in my fourth Chapter of scholars who insist that the

The terror and the glamor of Ashur, my lord, overwhelmed [them]... and they dispersed. I destroyed the town, tore down (its wall) and burnt (it) down. From La'la'ti I departed, I approached the town of Ki[.]qa, the royal residence] of Ahuni, man of Adini. Ahuni, man of Adini, [putting his trust] upon his numerous [army, ro]se for a decisive battle... I fought with him upon a trust(-inspiring) oracle of Ashur and the (other) great gods, my lords, (and) inflicted a... defeat upon him. I shut him up in his town. From the town Ki[.]qa I departed, the town Bur-mar'ana which (belongs to) Ahuni, man of Adini, [I approached]. I stormed and conquered (it). I slew with the sword 300 of their warriors. Pillars of skulls I erec[ted in front of the town] (*ANET*, p. 277).

Other elements common to the DH battle reports (particularly Joshua 10 and 11) are found in the above passage: the emphasis on destruction of property and the emphasis on slain enemy warriors. The pillars of skulls, a grisly demonstration of what happens to those who dare to rise up against Assyria, would be expected to serve a deterrent purpose, as would the many executions of rebellious vassals. In several cases, cited below, the bodies of executed kings are displayed in public, which calls to mind the incident in Josh. 10.18-26, in which Joshua executes the enemy kings with the sword and then leaves the corpses hanging on trees. H.W.F. Saggs[76] pointed out the value of intimidation in psychological warfare in order to minimize rebellion and guerilla warfare. In the absence of mass media, terror spreading from village to village was the only means of softening up an enemy in advance. Other examples of gruesome carnage appear in the following passages, also from Shalmaneser III:

Hani from Sam'al, Sapalulme from Hattina, Ahuni, man from Adini, Sangara from Carchemish put their trust on mutual assistance, prepared for battle and rose against me to resist. I fought with them (assisted) by the mighty power of Nergal, my leader, by the ferocious weapons which Ashur, my lord, has presented to me, (and) I inflicted a defeat upon them. I slew their warriors with the sword, descending upon them like Adad when he makes a rainstorm pour down. In the moat (of the town) I piled them up, I covered the wide plain with the corpses of their fighting men, I dyed the mountains with their blood like red wool... I erected pillars of skulls in front of his town, destroyed his (other) towns, tore down (their walls) and burnt (them) down (*ANET*, p. 277).

Hebrew Bible is unique in ascribing glory and victory to God by downplaying human effort and military superiority.

76. Saggs, 'Assyrian Warfare', pp. 145-60.

I departed from Argana and approached Karkara, his (text: my) royal residence... (all together) these were twelve kings. They rose against me [for a] decisive battle. I fought with them with (the support of) the mighty forces of Ashur, which Ashur, my lord, has given to me, and the strong weapons which Nergal, my leader, has presented to me, (and) I did inflict a defeat upon them between the towns Karkara and Gilzau. I slew 14,000 of their soldiers with the sword, descending upon them like Adad when he makes a rainstorm pour down. I spread their corpses (everywhere), filling the entire plain with their widely scattered (fleeing) soldiers. During the battle I made their blood flow down... the plain was too small to let (all) their (text: his) souls descend (into the nether world), the vast field gave out (when it came) to bury them. With their (text: sing.) corpses I spanned the Orontes before there was a bridge. Even during the battle I took from them their chariots, their horses broken to the yoke (*ANET*, p. 279).

...I departed and approached the city of Karkara. Hadadezer (Adad-id-ri) of Damascus... Irhuleni of Hamath with 12 kings from the seacoast, trusting their combined power, set out (to march) against me for a decisive battle. I fought with them. I slew in battle 25,000 of their experienced soldiers... (*ANET*, p. 279).

At that time Hadadezer [of] Damascus, Irhulina from Hamath, as well as the kings of Hatti and (of) the seashore put their trust in their mutual strength and rose against me to fight a decisive battle. Upon the (oracle-) command of Ashur, the great lord, my lord, I fought with them (and) inflicted a defeat upon them. I took away from them their chariots, their cavalry-horses and their battle equipment, slaying 20,500 of their battle-experienced soldiers (*ANET*, p. 279).

In the above examples, the carnage inflicted by the Assyrians is made possible by the assistance of a god or gods. Far from apologetic about the horrors of war, the Assyrians are almost gleeful in reporting the volume of blood and the number of corpses. Although these particular examples are from the annals of Shalmaneser III, the theme remains fairly consistent throughout the neo-Assyrian period (see further examples below).

As mentioned above, the emphasis in the preceding passages is also on trust in the deity's promise of divine assistance rather than superior numbers or strength. The divine promise, given through an oracle, is linked in these examples with the successful slaughter and humiliation of the enemy through divine help. Victory is attributed to '(the support of) the mighty forces of Ashur' (or Nergal) and 'strong weapons' presented to the king by Nergal (or Ashur). This is juxtaposed to their opponents' reliance on numerical strength through military alliances, usually indicated by the phrase '(they) put their trust in their mutual strength', or something similar.

Even as early as the reign of Ashurnasirpal II (883–859 BCE), the Assyrian annals emphasized the use of brutal destruction, including the destruction of human life as well as property, which is a prominent theme in the Book of Joshua (cf. Josh. 6.21; 10.28, 30, 32, 35, 37, 39, 40; 11.8, 11, 12, 14):

> I conquered the (other) towns of Luhuti, defeating their (inhabitants) in many bloody battles. I destroyed (them), tore down (the walls) and burned (the towns) with fire; I caught the survivors and impaled (them) on stakes in front of their towns (*ANET*, p. 276).

The above passage is noteworthy because it implies that civilian inhabitants were not distinguished from enemy soldiers. Often in the Assyrian annals, the text is ambiguous regarding the status of those who are killed. Ashurnasirpal II's son and successor Shalmaneser III (859–824 BCE) continues the theme and his annals provide numerous cases:

> ...[their/his army] I scattered, I stormed and conquered the town... I carried away as booty...his horses, broken to the yoke. I slew with the sword... During this battle I personally captured Bur-Anate from [Iasbuk]. I con[quered] the great cities (mahazu) of Hattina... I overthrew the...of the Upper [Sea] of Amurru and of the Western Sea (so that they became) like ruin-hills (left by) the flood (*ANET*, p. 278).

> I conquered 97 towns of Sangar, I conquered 100 towns of Arame, I destroyed (them), tore (their walls down) and burnt (them) down... I conquered the town Ashtamaku together with 90 (smaller) towns, I made a massacre (among) them and their booty I carried away. At that time, Hadadezer of Damascus, Irhuleni of Hamath together with 12 kings from the seacoast trusting their combined strength set out (to march) against me for a decisive battle. I fought with them and inflicted a defeat upon them (*ANET*, pp. 279-80).

In other cases, the text explicitly states that the slain were warriors. The rhetorical purpose appears to be to demonstrate the power of the Assyrians (often relying on divine help, see below) to defeat large numbers of worthy opponents, 'battle-experienced soldiers':

> I approached the town of Pakaruhbuni (and) the towns of Ahuni, man of Adini, on the other side of the Euphrates. I defeated (his) country, turning his towns into ruins. I covered the wide plain with the corpses of his warriors: 1,300 of their battle-experienced soldiers I slew with the sword (*ANET*, p. 277).

> Hazael of Damascus... put his trust upon his numerous army and called
> up his troops in great number... I fought with him and inflicted a defeat
> upon him, killing with the sword 16,000 of his experienced soldiers
> (*ANET*, p. 280).

In still other cases, the emphasis is on the total destruction of property,
and the fate of the people is unclear or unstated:

> The towns of the Hattineans, [those of] Ahuni, man of Adini, those
> (belonging) to the peoples of Carchemish, (and) to the MarGus[i. . .][(in
> short) all the to]wns on the other embankment of the Euphrates, I
> destroyed, tore down (the walls) and burnt (them) down (*ANET*, p. 278).

> I marched as far as the mountains of Hauran (Iade Ha-u-ra-ni), destroy-
> ing, tearing down and burning innumerable towns, carrying booty away
> from them which was beyond counting (*ANET*, p. 280).

In the eighth century BCE, the theme of intimidation as a factor in the
outcome becomes much more prominent and explicit, as in the following example from Tiglath-Pileser III (744–727 BCE):

> He heard [about the approach of the] massed [armies of] Ashur and was
> afraid... I tore down, destroyed and burnt [down... for Azri] all they had
> annexed, they (thus) had reinforced him (*ANET*, p. 282).

During the eighth century, texts more frequently state that the opponents were seized with fear, terror and pounding hearts (cf. Josh. 2.9-
11). Sometimes the terror which befalls the enemies of Assyria is
sufficient to make them surrender voluntarily (cf. Josh. 9.8, 24-25),
offering tribute, as in the following example from Sargon II (721–705
BCE):

> [and the seven ki]ngs of Ia', a district on [Cy]prus ([Ad]nana) which [lies
> a]midst the Western Sea... [lea]rned, far away in the midst of the sea, [the
> feats which I have achie]ved in Chaldea and in Hatti, and their hearts
> began to pound, [terror] fell upon them. They sent me, [to] Babylon,
> gold, silver, objects made of ebony and boxwood (which are the)
> treasures of their country, and kissed my feet (*ANET*, p. 284).

The annals of Sargon II give credit for his military success to the 'terror-
inspiring glamor' of the deity Ashur, an expression which goes back to
the reign of Shalmaneser III (see above):

> I installed an officer of mine as governor over his entire large country and
> its prosperous inhabitants, (thus) aggrandizing (again) the territory
> belonging to Ashur, the king of the gods. The terror (-inspiring) glamor
> of Ashur, my lord, overpowered (however) the king of Meluhha and he

threw him (i.e. Iamani) in fetters on hands and feet, and sent him to me, to Assyria. I conquered and sacked the towns Shinuhtu (and) Samaria,[77] and all Israel (lit.: 'Omri-Land' Bit Hu-um-ri-i) (*ANET*, p. 285).

Sargon II's annals also demonstrate several other themes prominent in the DH. The passage immediately above states that the territory conquered belongs to Ashur, not merely to the king. The emphasis on the relationship between deity and territory is reminiscent of the many passages in the DH pertaining to Yahweh and the land. The passages below emphasize again that it is the deity who sends Assyria into battle, using variations of a phrase which also dates back to Shalmaneser III:

I inflicted a defeat upon them (i.e. Hanno and Sib'e) upon an (oracle) order (given) by my lord Ashur, and Sib'e, like a *sipa* (i.e. shepherd) whose flock has been stolen, fled alone and disappeared. Hanno (however, I captured personally and brought him (with me) in fetters to my city Ashur. I destroyed Rapihu, tore down (its walls) and burned (it). I led away as prisoners 9,033 inhabitants with their numerous possessions (*ANET*, p.285).

Upon a trust (-inspiring oracle given by) my lord Ashur, I crushed the tribes of Tamud, Ibadidi, Marsimanu, and Haiapa, the Arabs who live, far away, in the desert (and) who know neither overseers nor official(s) and who had not (yet) brought their tribute to any king. I deported their survivors and settled (them) in Samaria (*ANET*, p. 286).

The Sargon II annals provide more examples than any of his predecessors of divinely-inspired terror overcoming the enemies of Assyria:

The king of Ethiopia who [lives] in [a distant country]...he did hear, even (that) far away, of the might of Ashur, Nebo (and) Marduk. The awe-inspiring glamor of my kingship blinded him and terror overcame him (*ANET*, p.286).

...the terror-inspiring glamor of Ashur, my lord, overwhelmed him and he brought as tamartu -present 12 fine (lit.: big) horses from Musri which have not their equals in this country (*ANET*, p.286).

But I, Sargon, the rightful ruler, devoted to the pronouncements (uttered by) Nebo and Marduk, (carefully) observing the orders of Ashur, led my

77. As B. Becking points out, there is dispute regarding whether the fall of Samaria should be credited to Sargon II or Shalmaneser V. Sargon claims to be the conquerer eight times in his inscriptions, but Bab Chron I ii.28 states that it was Shalmaneser, as does the Bible. The facts surrounding the historical events in Samaria are not germane to my point, however. B. Becking, *The Fall of Samaria: An Historical and Archaeological Study* (Leiden: Brill, 1992).

army over the Tigris and the Euphrates, at the peak of the(ir) flood, the spring flood, as (if it be) dry ground. This Greek, however, their king who had put his trust in his own power and (therefore) did not bow to my (divinely ordained) rulership, heard about the approach of my expedition (while I was still) far away, and the splendor of my lord Ashur over-whelmed him and...he fled... (*ANET*, p. 287).

Examples of destruction and torture also abound in Sargon II's reports:

I smash[ed] like a flood-storm the country of Hamath (A-ma-at-tu) in its entire [extent]. I br[ought its] ki[ng] Iaubi'di as well as his family (*ANET*, p. 284).

I conquered (it) and burnt (it). Himself I flayed; the rebels I killed in their cities and established (again) peace and harmony (*ANET*, p. 285).

The annals of Sennacherib (704–681 BCE) describing the Siege of Jerusalem continue the three themes of 'awe-inspiring' divine interven-tion, either making battle unnecessary or causing Assyria to prevail, by overwhelming the enemy with fear of the god, initiation of conquest through an oracle, and describing scenes of torture and death:

The awe-inspiring splendor of the 'Weapon' of Ashur, my lord, over-whelmed his strong cities (such as) Great Sidon, Little Sidon, Bit-Zitti, Zaribtu, Mahalliba...they bowed in submission to my feet (*ANET*, p. 287).

Upon a trust(-inspiring) oracle (given) by Ashur, my lord, I fought with them and inflicted a defeat upon them (*ANET*, p. 287).

I assaulted Ekron and killed the officials and patricians who had commit-ted the crime and hung their bodies on poles surrounding the city. The (common) citizens who were guilty of minor crimes, I considered prisoners of war (*ANET*, p. 288).

In many Assyrian documents, the monarch is said to be chosen by the diety, who gives him responsibility for 'shepherding' his subjects, as in the following text from a broken stone slab found at Calah pertaining to the expedition to Palestine of Adad-nirari (810–783 BCE):

Property of Adad-nirari, great king, legitimate king, king of the world, king of Assyria—a king whom Ashur, the king of the Igigi (i.e. the dei superi) had chosen (already) when he was a youngster, entrusting him with the position of a prince without rival, (a king) whose shepherding they made as agreeable to the people of Assyria as (is the smell of) the Plant of Life, (a king) whose throne they established firmly; the holy high priest (and) tireless caretaker of the temple e sar ra, who keeps up the rites of the sanctuary, who acts (only) upon the trust-inspiring oracles (given) by Ashur, his lord; who has made submit to his feet the princes within the four rims of the earth; conquering from the Siluna mountain of the Rising Sun, from the banks of the Euphrates, the country of the Hittites, Amurru-country in its full extent, Tyre, Sidon, Israel (Hu-um-ri), Edom, Palestine (Pa-la-as-tu), as far as the shore of the Great Sea of the Setting Sun, I made them submit all to my feet, imposing upon them tribute (*ANET*, p. 281).

Included in the ideology is the assumption that his 'subjects' include the conquered people who occupy the territories the deities give to the Assyrian king to rule over. The king not only rules his own people by divine right, but according to the Assyrian ideology of kingship, he also extends his empire according to the divine will and command. Esarhaddon, for example, claimed to be 'the true shepherd' placed on the throne by the national gods of Assyria, who pronounced him the legitimate king of Assyria since he was a child:

Property of Esarhaddon, great king, legitimate king, king of the world, king of Assyria, regent of Babylon, king of Sumer and Akkad, king of the four rims (of the earth), the true shepherd, favorite of the great gods, whom Ashur, Shamash, Bel and Nebo, the Ishtar of Nineveh (and) the Ishtar of Arbela have pronounced king of Assyria (ever) since he was a youngster (*ANET*, p. 289).

The reason he needed such elaborate justification for his accession becomes clear: Sennacherib had been murdered by his sons, and Esarhaddon was in a fight for the throne against his brothers. Furthermore, he was the youngest, not the eldest:

I was (indeed) the(ir) youngest brother among my elder brothers, (but) my own father, upon the command of Ashur, Sin, Shamash, Bel and Nebo, the Ishtar of Nineveh (and) the Ishtar of Arbela, has chosen me... (*ANET*, p. 289).

He goes on to explain how the gods protected him against the 'evil' attempts of his elder brothers at usurpation, which would have been a usurpation against the divine will, even though from another point of view, he himself would be regarded as the usurper.[78] Then the gods sent him into battle against the brothers by means of a war oracle promising divine presence and help in battle:

Go (ahead), do not tarry! We will march with you, kill your enemies! (*ANET*, p. 289).

78. A.L. Oppenheim, *Ancient Mesopotamia*, p. 169.

True to their word as expressed in the oracle, the gods gave Esarhaddon the military victory and the kingship, not because of his superiority, but because it was the divine will for him to rule:

> Ishtar, the Lady of Battle who likes me (to be) her high priest, stood at my side breaking their bows, scattering their orderly battle array. And then they spoke among themselves: 'This is our king!' Upon her lofty command they went over in masses to me and rallied behind me (*ANET*, p. 289).

Ishtar is depicted in the above text as though she were fighting alone, without human participation in the battle and without any actual bloodshed. Therefore, while statements like those of Lind that 'Yahweh as God of war fought for his people by miracle, not by sword and spear'[79] are true, Lind's argument, that there was something distinctive about Yahweh's intervention by means of miracle when compared with the other ancient Near Eastern literatures, is proven false. The DH must be read with the awareness of the Assyrian uses of rhetoric.

Furthermore, Solomon (like Esardaddon above) in 1 Kings 2 encounters similar internal threats to his enthronement and is exhorted by his father David to take military action against his internal political enemies. The Dtr depicts Solomon as Yahweh's choice over other potential rulers, although he was not the eldest son (like Esarhaddon in the passage above):

> as Yahweh lives who has established me and set me on the throne of David my father... (1 Kgs 2.24).

David had previously been chosen by Yahweh although he was the youngest of seven sons. Like Esarhaddon, the Dtr had to justify, with a rhetoric of divine choice, David's (and then Solomon's) accession to the throne over the elder sons, his brothers. Therefore, instead of reading the biblical passages pertaining to the Davidic monarchy solely as expressions of the Dtr's approval of David's (and his progeny's) piety, one should place them in the context of Assyrian rhetoric of kingship and divine will, which in turn is linked to an ideology of imperial control. The annals of Esarhaddon, for example, go on to describe, in language very similar to the battle reports in Joshua, Judges and throughout the DH, the victories given to Assyria by the gods over rebellious vassals:

---

79. Lind, *Yahweh is a Warrior*, p. 23.

> As for Sunduarri, king of Kundi and Sizu, an inveterate enemy, unwilling
> to recognize me as ruler (and) whom the gods (therefore) forsook...
> and...the king of Sidon, his ally...they put their trust upon their own
> force while I trusted Ashur, my lord,—I caught him like a bird in his
> mountains and (likewise) cut off his head (*ANET*, pp. 290-91).

The piety of Esarhaddon in putting his trust in divine rather than human
might is emphasized, as in the other battle reports cited above. Therefore, the 'piety' of King Josiah and of the Dtr himself should be
approached with an unsentimental assessment of the resemblence
between the rhetoric used by those connected with the monarchy in the
DH and those connected with the monarchy in Assyria. In both cases,
the rhetoric of divine participation in warfare is intertwined with the
rhetoric of an imperial ideology based on centralized control. In both
cases, a pious-sounding rhetoric of divine control is employed in the
service of a hierarchy that is simultaneously political and religious.

After Esarhaddon had taken over the throne, he worked to expand
his territory all the way to Egypt as well as deal with internal enemies.
He continued to use the stock elements of Assyrian battle reports against
external and internal enemies, including divine assistance and instigation
of the battles, 'marching (against the enemy) upon the trustworthy
oracles of my lord Ashur' (*ANET*, p. 293).

> But the terror(-inspiring sight) of the great gods, my lords, overwhelmed
> them and they turned into madmen when they saw the attack of my strong
> battle array. Ishtar, the Lady of Battle, who likes me (to be) her high
> priest, stood at my side breaking their bows, scattering their orderly battle
> array...I reached the embankment of the Tigris and upon the (oracle)
> command of Sin and Shamash, the (two) lords of the (celestial) embank-
> ment, I had all my troops jump over the Tigris as if it be a small ditch
> (*ANET*, pp. 289-90).

> (I am Esarhaddon), the conqueror of Sidon, which lies (on an island)
> amidst the sea...(he) who has leveled all its urban buildings—I even tore
> up and cast into the sea its wall and its foundation, destroying (thus)
> completely the (very) place it (i.e. Sidon) was built (upon). I caught out of
> the open sea, like a fish, Abdimilkutte, its king, who had fled before my
> attack into the high sea, and I cut off his head (*ANET*, p. 290).

> They put their trust upon their own force while I trusted Ashur, my
> lord,—I caught him like a bird in his mountains and (likewise) cut off his
> head. (Then) I hung the heads of Sanduarri and of Abdimilkutte around
> the neck of their nobles/chief-officials to demonstrate to the population the
> power of Ashur, my lord, and paraded (thus) through the wide main street
> of Nineveh with singers (playing on) sammu-harps (*ANET*, pp. 290-91).

> Abdimilkutte, king of Sidon, without respect for my position as lord, without listening to my personal orders, threw off the yoke of the god Ashur, trusting the heaving sea (to protect him). As to Sidon, his fortress town, which lies in the midst of the sea, I leveled it as (if) an abubu-storm (had passed over it), its walls and foundations I tore out and threw (them) into the sea destroying (thus) its emplacement completely. I caught Abdimilkutte, its king, who fled before my attack into the sea, upon an oracle-command of Ashur, my lord, like a fish on high sea and cut off his head (*ANET*, p. 291).

> I led siege to Memphis, his royal residence, and conquered it in half a day by means of mines, breaches and assault ladders; I destroyed (it), tore down (its walls) and burnt it down (*ANET*, p. 293).

Ashurbanipal followed Esarhaddon as ruler. Esarhaddon had appointed one of his sons, Ashurbanipal, to become king of the realm, and another, Sama-sum-ukin, to be king of Babylon. After a period of about sixteen years, Sama-sum-ukin formed an alliance of all enemies of Assyrian rule from Elam to Israel. It took Ashurbanipal four years to regain control over the rebels and subdue Babylon. Punitive campaigns followed against Elam, Susa, and the Arabs. His treatment of his enemies (internal and external) is particularly horrible and vindictive, but the most important aspect of the following passage from the annals of Ashurbanipal is the way he equates the political plotting against him, the 'god-fearing prince', with blasphemy against the national god of Assyria:

> I tore out the tongues of those whose slanderous mouths had uttered blasphemies against my god Ashur and had plotted against me, his god-fearing prince; I defeated them (completely). The others, I smashed alive with the very same statues of protective deities with which they had smashed my own grandfather Sennacherib—fed their corpses, cut into small pieces, to dogs, pigs, zibu-birds, vultures, the birds of the sky and (also) to the fish of the ocean (*ANET*, p. 288).

The same themes developed in the earlier annals continued unabated in the annals of Ashurbanipal. The folly of putting trust in merely human military might rather than depending on divine strength for victory in battle is joined with the idea that the gods help and intervene on Assyria's behalf. Sometimes the deities are said to march at the king's side in battle and fight for him. The gods often intervene by inspiring terror in the enemies, thus 'overwhelming' them, which may cause them to flee, lose or surrender. Closely related is the divine oracle which initiates the battle, inspiring trust by promising divine help:

Upon a trust(-inspiring) oracle (given) by Ashur, Bel, Nebo, the great gods, my lords, who (always) march at my side, I defeated the battle (-experienced) soldiers of his army in a great open battle. Tirhakah heard in Memphis of the defeat of his army (and) the (terror-inspiring) splendor of Ashur and Ishtar blinded (lit.: overwhelmed) him (thus) that he became like a madman. The glamor of my kingship with which the gods of heaven and nether world have endowed me, dazzled him and he left Memphis and fled, to save his life, in to the town Ni (Thebes). This town (too) I seized and led my army into it to repose (there) (*ANET*, p. 294).

This (same) Tirhakah forgot the might of Ashur, Ishtar and the (other) great gods, my lords, and put his trust upon his own power (*ANET*, p. 294).

The terror of the (sacred) weapon of Ashur, my lord, overcame Tirhakah where he had taken refuge and he was never heard of again (*ANET*, p. 295).

Upon a trust(-inspiring) oracle of Ashur and Ishtar I, myself, conquered this town completely (*ANET*, p. 295).

With the help of Ashur, Sin, Shamash, Adad, Bel, Nebo, the Ishtar of Nineveh—the Queen of Kidmuri—the Ishtar of Arbela, Ninurta, Nergal (and) Nusku and by pronouncing my name which Ashur has made powerful, Kamashaltu, king of Moab, a servant belonging to me, inflicted defeat in an open battle upon Ammuladi, king of Qedar who, like him (Abiate), had revolted and had continuously made razzias against the kings of the Westland (*ANET*, p. 298).

In several passages, the trust-inspiring oracle is followed by an emphasis on the destruction that resulted:

He (Urdamane) assembled his (armed) might; he made his weapons ready and marched on to deliver a decisive battle against my army. (But) upon a trustworthy oracle of Ashur, Sin and the great gods, my lords, they (my troops) defeated him in a great open battle and scattered his (armed) might. Urdamane fled alone and entered Thebes, his royal residence. They (i.e. my army) marched after him (covering) a distance of one month (in) 10 days on difficult roads as far as Thebes. They conquered this city completely, smashed (it as if by) a floodstorm (*ANET*, p. 297).

Upon the oracle-command of Ashur, and Ishtar (I called up) my army and defeated him in bloody battles, inflicted countless routs on him (to wit) in...the towns of Azaril (and) Hirata (-)kasaia, in Edom, in the pass of Iabrudu, in Beth-Ammon, in the district of Haurina, in Moab, in Sa'arri, in Harge, in the district of Zobah. In the(se) battles I smashed all the inhabitants of Arabia who had revolted with him, but he himself escaped before the powerful 'weapons' of Ashur to a distant region. I set fire to the tents in which they live and burnt them down (*ANET*, p. 298).

> Upon the oracle-command of Ashur and Ninlil, the great gods, my lords, who (thus) encouraged me, I defeated Iaute' who had put his trust upon (the assistance of) the Nabiati country and... I turned his cities into ruin-hills and heaps (of debris) (*ANET*, p. 300).

In other passages, the emphasis is on the public punishment, humiliation and torture of captives, especially rebellious vassals. In some cases, the captives were not executed:

> During the battle, according to the (oracle-)command (given) by Ashur and Ishtar, my lords, I myself caught Abiate' (and) Aammu, son of Te'ri, alive and fettered them with iron fetters on hands and feet (*ANET*, p. 299).

> Upon an oracle-command of Ashur and Ninlil I pierced his cheeks with the sharp-edged spear, my personal weapon, by laying the very hands on him which I had received to conquer opposition against me; I put the ring to his neck and made him guard the bar of the east gate of Nineveh... (Later) I had mercy upon him and granted him life in order to praise the glory of Ashur, Ishtar (and) the great gods, my lords.

In other cases, however, death remains the punishment for disobedience:

> On my return march, I conquered the town Ushu... I killed those inhabitants of Ushu who did not obey their governors by refusing to deliver the tribute which they had to pay annually. I took to task those among them who were not submissive (*ANET*, p. 300).

> I killed also those inhabitants of Accho who were not submissive, hanging their corpses on poles which I placed around the city (*ANET*, p. 300).

According to the logic of the Assyrian ideology, to rebel against Assyria is to defy the divine will and thus incur just punishment. The annals express the idea that the gods make vassals bow to the king's yoke. The king not only wins his battles because of divine will, but the gods are responsible for gving him his army. The logical corrollary is that he rules the territories by divine will—the gods have given him the land (cf. Josh. 1.3):

> They filled up completely and to its entire extent all my land(s) which Ashur has given me (*ANET*, p. 299).

> I lifted my hands, prayed to Ashur and to the Assyrian Ishtar. (Then) I called up my mighty armed forces which Ashur and Ishtar have entrusted to me... (*ANET*, p. 294).

The kings from East and West came and kissed my feet. (But) Tirhakah (Tarqu), against (the will of) the gods, planned to seize Egypt (and) to... He thought little of the might of Ashur, my lord, and put his trust in his own power (*ANET*, p. 296).

They (i.e. the great gods) made bo[w] to my yo[ke] all the countries from the Upper Sea to the Lower Sea... and they pulled the straps (absanu) (of) my (yoke). Upon their mighty command, quickly... I conquered Thebes (Ni) (*ANET*, p. 297)

he had cast away the yoke of my rule which Ashur (himself) has placed upon him... (*ANET*, p. 297)

The annals of Ashurbanipal also contain an extremely colourful description of divine assistance in battle:

And (verily) Ninlil, the lordly Wild-Cow, the most heroic among the goddesses who rivals in rank (only) with Anu and Enlil, was butting my enemies with her mighty horns; the Ishtar who dwells in Arbela, clad in (divine) fire (and) carrying the melammu -headwear, was raining flames upon Arabia; Irra, the Warrior, armed with anuntu, was crushing (underfoot) my foes; Ninurta, the Arrow, the great hero, the son of Ellil, was cutting the throats of my enemies with his sharp point; Nusku, the obedient messenger (of the gods) proclaimer of my lordship, who accompanied me upon the command of Ashur, (and) the courageous Ninlil, the Lady of [Arbela], who protected me as king, took the lead of my army and threw down my foes. (When) the troops of Uate' heard the approach of the(se) mighty 'weapons' of Ashur and Ishtar, the great gods, my lords, which during the battle had come to my assistance, they revolted against him. He became frightened and left the house (sanctuary) into which he had fled, so that I caught him personally according to the trustworthy oracle of Ashur, Sin, Shamash, Adad, Bel, Nebo, the Ishtar of Nineveh—the Queen of Kidmuri—the Ishtar of Arbela, Ninurta, Nergal (and) Nusku—and brought him to Assyria (*ANET*, p. 300).

The passage is important partially because it contains several of the themes mentioned previously, and partially for several relatively rare phrases which are closer in sentiment and terminology to some of the phrases in the DH, most notably the statement that the deity 'took the lead of my army and threw down my foes' or was 'crushing (underfoot) my foes' (cf. Deut. 1.30; Josh. 10.14; 11.6; 23.10). An even more striking parallel to the DH (cf. Josh. 2.24; 6.2, 16; 8.1, 18; 10.8, 19; Judg. 3.28; 4.7, 14; 7.9, 15; 18.10; 20.28; 1 Sam. 14.12; 17.46; 23.4; 24.4; 26.8; 1 Kgs. 20.28) is contained in the following passage:

> The kumirtu-priestess of the [goddess Dilbat who] had become angry with
> Hazail, king of Arabia...and had him delivered into the hands of
> Sennacherib, my own grandfather, by causing his defeat... (*ANET*,
> p. 301).

The following passage contains close parallels to the battle reports in
Joshua 10 and 11, saying that the officers put the inhabitants to death
with the sword and did not spare anyone among them (cf. Josh. 10.25-
28, 30, 32, 35, 37, 39, 40; 11.8, 11, 12, 14):

> And they (the officers) put to the sword the inhabitants, young and old, of
> the towns of Sais, Pindidi, Tanis and of all the other towns which had
> associated with them to plot, they did not spare anybody among (them).
> They hung their corpses from stakes, flayed their skins and covered (with
> them) the wall of the town(s) (*ANET*, p. 295).

3. *Assyrian War Oracles*. The closest parallels to the language and
ideology of the warfare in the DH are found in the war oracles
associated with Esarhaddon and Ashurbanipal. The oracles are usually
delivered by a prophetess with advice or exhortations concerning the
king's military endeavours. The exhortation to courage usually employs
the phrase 'fear not', which is common in the DH (cf. Deut. 20.3; 31.6,
8; Josh. 8.1; 10.8, 25; 11.6; 1 Sam. 23.16-17).[80] The basis for courage in
both the Assyrian and biblical oracles is usually divine presence and
assistance in battle. The terse example below looks remarkably like
many of the passages listed above, in which the exhortation to the leader
is followed by an assurance that the deity will deliver the enemy into his
power:

> (oracle) from the lips of the woman Ishtar-latashiat of Arbela: King of
> Assyria, fear not! The enemy of the King of Assyria I deliver to slaughter!
> (*ANET*, p. 449).

Some of the longer passages have the same basic structure: courage is
based on trust in the deity, who will destroy or frighten away the ruler's
enemies:

---

80. The expression 'fear not' also appears in an Aramean war oracle in the Zakir
inscription (*ANET*, p. 510) from the eighth century BCE. This provides further evidence that the exhortation was increasingly coming into use during the neo-Assyrian
imperial period, when the elements of fear and courage became a staple of Akkadian
martial texts. However, the oracles to Ashurbanipal and Esarhaddon provide evidence that 'fear not' became a stereotyped war oracle phrase primarily in the seventh
century texts, as far as we know.

> [Esarhad]don, king of the countries, fear not! [No]tice the wind which blows over you; I speak of it without... Your enemies, like a wild boar in the month of Sivan, from before your feet will flee away. I am the great divine lady, I am the goddess Ishtar of Arbela, who will destroy your enemies from before your feet. What are the words of mine, which I spoke to you that you did not rely upon? I am Ishtar of Arbela. I shall lie in wait for your enemies, I shall give them to you. I, Ishtar of Arbela, will go before you and behind you: fear not!... (*ANET*, p. 449).

In the above example, the goddess promises to deliver them (the enemies) over to the king, which is similar to the many occurrences of the phrase, mentioned above, that the deity will 'deliver them into your hand'. She also promises to accompany him into battle, going before and behind him (cf. Deut. 31.6-8; Josh. 1.9). Divine presence in battle is described even more vividly in the following oracle:

> Fear not, Esarhaddon! I, the god Bel, am speaking to you. I watch over your inner heart (lit.—the beams of your heart) as would your mother who brought you forth. Sixty great gods are standing with me and protect you. The god Sin is at your right, the god Shamash at your left. The sixty great gods are standing around you, ranged for battle. Do not trust human beings! Lift your eyes to me, look at me! I am Ishtar of Arbela; I have turned Ashur's favor to you. When you were small, I chose you. Fear not!... (This oracle is) from the woman Baia of Arbela (*ANET*, p. 450).

Another common element in both the DH and the Assyrian texts, already mentioned above in connection with the batle reports, is the statement that the deities choose the ruler:

> I am Ishtar of Arbela, O Esarhaddon, king of Assyria. In the cities Ashur, Nineveh, Calah, Arbela, I shall grant you many days, endless years. I am the great midwife (who helped at your birth), the one who gave you suck, who has established your rule under the wide heavens for many days, endless years... (*ANET*, pp. 605-606).

The same oracle continues, linking together the ideology of divine choice with divine protection in warfare:

> Fear not, O king! Because I have spoken to you (in an oracle), I will not abandon you. Because I have encouraged you, I will not let you come to shame. I will help you cross the river safely. O Esarhaddon, legitimate heir, son of the goddess Ninlil! I am... for you. With my own hands, your foes I shall annihilate. O Esarhaddon, in the city Ashur I shall grant you long days, endless years. O Esarhaddon, in Arbela, I am your good shield... (*ANET*, pp. 605-606).

Another noteworthy feature of the above passage is the parallelism of two of the lines:

> Because I have spoken to you...
>   I will not abandon you.
> Because I have encouraged you,
>   I will not let you come to shame.

The parallelism is reminiscent of the parallelism in the lines of Deut. 31.6, 8 and Josh. 1.5, 'I will not fail you or forsake you', which likewise occur in connection with exhortations to be brave in battle, especially the exhortation 'fear not'. The annihilation of foes is also consistent with 'fear not' oracles in the DH (cf. Josh. 8.1; 10.8).

The following oracle is less similar in terminology to those of the DH except for the exhortation 'fear not', but it contains the promise of divine protection, the overthrow of enemies and the granting of sovereignty over territory by the deity:

> The goddess Ninlil is highly regarded as a sybil. This is the word of Ninlil herself for the king, 'Fear not, O Ashurbanipal! Now, as I have spoken, it will come to pass: I shall grant (it) to you. Over the people of the four languages (and) over the armament of the princes you will exercise sovereignty'... [The kings] of the countries confer together (saying), 'Come (let us rise) against Ashurbanipal... The fate of our fathers and our grandfathers (the Assyrians) have fixed: [let not his might] cause divisions among us'. [Nin]lil answered saying, '[The kings] of lands [I shall over]throw, place under the yoke, bind their feet in [strong fetters]. For the second time I proclaim to you that as with the land of Elam and the Cimmerarians [I shall proceed]. I shall arise, break the thorns, open up widely my way through the briers. With blood shall I turn the land into a rain shower, (fill it with) lamentation and wailing'. You ask, 'What lamentation and wailing?' Lamentation enters Egypt, wailing comes out (from there)... Ninlil is his mother. Fear not! The mistress of Arbela bore him. Fear not! As she that bears for her child, (so) I care for you. I have placed you like an amulet on my breast. At night I place a spread over you, all day I keep a cover on you. In the early morning heed your supplication, heed your conduct. Fear not, my son, whom I have raised (*ANET*, pp. 450-51).

The final example is a negative oracle, in which the king, Ashurbanipal, is told to stay home and to 'fear not' because the goddess will do his fighting for him:

> The goddess Ishar heard my anxious sighs and said 'Fear not!' and gave me confidence, (saying), 'Since you have lifted your hands in prayer and

your eyes have filled with tears, I have had mercy'. During the night in which I appeared before her a sabru-priest lay down and had a dream. He awoke with a start and then Ishtar caused him to see a nocturnal vision. He reported to me as follows: 'The goddess Ishtar who dwells in Arbela came in. Right and left quivers were suspended from her. She was hold-ing a bow in her hand, and a sharp sword was drawn to do battle. You were standing in front of her and she spoke to you like a real mother. Ishtar called to you, she who is most exalted among the gods, giving you the following instructions: 'wait with the attack; (for) wherever you intend to go, I am also ready to go'. You said to her, 'Wherever you go I will go with you, O goddess of goddesses!' She repeated her command to you as follows: 'You shall stay here where you should be. Eat, drink wine, make merry, praise my divinity, while I go and accomplish that work to help you attain your heart's desire. Your face will not be pale, nor your feet shaky, and you need not wipe off your (cold) sweat in the height of battle'. She wrapped you in her lovely babysling, protecting your entire body. Her face shone like fire. Then she went out in a frightening way to defeat your enemies, agianst Teumman, king of Elam, with whom she was angry' (*ANET*, pp. 605-606).

III. *Conclusion*

Although several scholars (see discussion in the previous Chapter) have commented on the similarities in language between Assyrian battle reports and the battle reports in the DH, few have acknowledged the extent of the similarity in ideology. For example, when Van Seters wrote his series of articles comparing the battle reports' language and style, he did so without drawing any conclusions with regard to the imperial ide-ology of the DH and the implications concerning King Josiah's political ambitions.

As in the DH, much of the emphasis in the Assyrian battle reports is on inspiring terror in those who dare to rebel against the king. In some cases, the deities are said to inspire terror in the enemies directly (cf. Josh. 2.9-11), causing their defeat at the hands of Assyria. In other instances, the terror is caused by the gruesome tactics of flaying, torture and decapitation of rebellious vassals or enemy kings (cf. Josh. 10.25). In still other cases, the Assyrians attempt to intimidate by describing the total destruction that they are able to inflict on enemy populations (cf. Joshua 10–11).

Like Joshua, the Assyrian kings are presented as pious rulers acting on the 'trust-inspiring oracle' of their gods or goddesses when they enter battles of imperial conquest. As in the text of Joshua, the Assyrian rulers display a false humility in claiming that they are merely following divine commands initiating their battles.

Divine intervention in battle is common in the texts of the ancient Near East. However, the DH resembles none of the other martial literatures of these ancient cultures so much as that of the Assyrian empire. In the Assyrian annals, certain aspects of the battle reports are relatively stable, from the ninth century BCE until the neo-Babylonian conquest: the theme of putting faith in divine help rather than military might is prominent, as is the emphasis on total destruction of cities and the emphasis on the death count. The Assyrian reports also stress the public display of corpses or parts of corpses, especially those of humiliated rebellious vassals, as a deterrent to other potential rebels. Not only would the grisly sight discourage others from rebellion, but so would the reports of the horror which would be carried by word of mouth as well as being contained in the annals themselves. The emphasis (important also in the DH) on a deity's ability to affect the outcome of war by inspiring terror in enemies or potential rebels is a theme which becomes increasingly prominent in the eighth and seventh centuries BCE.

Exhortations to courage in battle on the basis of divine assistance in warfare are common throughout the ancient Near East until the rise of the neo-Babylonian empire. However, the phrase 'fear not' as a stylized element of war oracles seems to come into prominence with the Assyrian oracles to Ashurbanipal and Esarhaddon, who lived during the century after Hezekiah's death. The DH seems to show the influence of the Assyrian 'fear not' oracles current during the time period immediately prior to Josiah's reign. While the presence of the phrase 'fear not' provides insufficient evidence to prove anything about the dating of the DH, it does indicate a possible literary relationship.

Chapter 6

THE RHETORIC OF VIOLENCE IN JOSHUA 1.1-9

I. *Introduction*

The conquest narrative in the Book of Joshua begins with an oracle from Yahweh ordering Joshua, as military commander, to march into the land, crossing the symbolic boundary of the 'promised land', the Jordan, to take possession of the land by military victory. The use of war oracle language sets the tone for the narrative, which consistently maintains a military flavour, and also serves to establish the lines of authority in a heirarchical pattern. The passage also contains a thinly veiled threat to any who would oppose Joshua (explicit in v. 5), about which more will be said in later chapters. The next chapter is a New Historicist analysis examining the role of the key phrase חזק ואמץ elsewhere in the conquest narrative. A preliminary look at some of the issues surrounding Josh. 1.1-9 is therefore warranted in the present chapter. The methodology for the present chapter will be taken from the more traditional methods of biblical studies, in order to establish that the language of Josh. 1.1-9 belongs in the context of military terminology.

That the passage (Josh. 1.1-9) consists of war oracle language is not immediately apparent to some scholars, even though the phrase 'fear not' occurs in it. Some scholars have argued that Josh. 1.1-9 and the two parallel passages in Deuteronomy (Deut. 31.6-8, 23) are based on an old installation genre instead. Since almost the same words occur three times in the story of Joshua's succession to Moses, they must rate highly in significance. Therefore a discussion of whether the language is essentially a war oracle or another genre is an important issue. The issue is obscured somewhat by a portion of the passage which most scholars have argued (rightly) is an addition by the later editor of the DH. Since the passage begins the war of conquest, its relationship to other war oracle language is vitally important.

The present chapter will be a discussion of the scholarly debate regarding the nature and genre of the passage, including the arguments concerning sources and redaction where relevant. I shall endeavour to demonstrate that the passage (except for the excursus on the law, which I argue is a later addition) is a war oracle, similar in meaning, form and terminology to other war oracles.

II. *Installation Genre or War Oracle?*

The question has been raised whether the language of Josh.1.1-9 might be taken from an 'installation genre', used for the installation of a person into public office, rather than from the language of warfare. Some scholars have argued that there is a schema discernable in several instances in which a person is placed in an official role and charged with a specific task (or set of tasks) to carry out. The office may be civil or military depending upon the nature of the tasks involved, according to those scholars who hold the view that such a genre exists.

The 'installation genre' is said to consist of three elements: 1. an exhortation to be bold, usually some form of חזק ואמץ, although the second word may vary; 2. a statement of the task, introduced by כי אתה; and 3. an assurance of divine presence and support, such as עמך יהוה.[1]

Most of those who have written about the 'installation genre' have noticed that the terminology used within its elements bears at least some resemblence to the language associated with warfare. However, the point regarding the connection between the 'installation genre' and the biblical war narratives which has been given insufficient attention is that each time the schema (described above) occurs in the DH, it appears in a context of military action. Furthermore, in the DH, characteristic phrases from the schema sometimes appear in isolation (that is, without the other elements of the genre) in the context of war narratives as an exhortation and admonition addressed to those entering a military confrontation (as in 2 Sam. 10.12).

---

1. N. Lohfink, 'Die deuteronomistische Darstellung des Übergangs der Führung Israels von Moses auf Josue: Ein Beitrag zur alttestamentliche Theologie des Amtes', *Scholastik* 37 (1962), pp. 32-44; Lohfink identified the three elements of the schema as an 'Ermätigungsformel', usually חזק ואמץ (which I call exhortation), 'Nennung einer Aufgabe', beginning with כי אתה (which I call statement of task), and 'Beistandsformel' using the words עמך יהוה (which I call assurance of presence and help).

It has been generally acknowledged that the schema was used for military leaders, but some scholars think that its use extended to other kinds of public office as well. However, even in late texts, it is arguable whether there are any complete examples of the schema used for offices of an exclusively civilian nature. In the DH, the schema is always found in connection with military action or battle preparations, although in some situations, the commander's overall role may be a combination of military, civil and religious leadership. However, since there was no separation of religion from public life ('separation of church and state'in American legal terminology) in the ancient world, the literary context is probably a more reliable guide.

Therefore, it may be concluded that the three-element schema does not function primarily as an 'installation genre' for installing a person into public office. Rather, the schema, even as described by the 'installation genre' proponents themselves, finds its earliest and most complete expression as a war oracle. The warrior is commanded to be strong and bold (element 1) in carrying out the military task (element 2) because divine presence and help in battle are promised (element 3), thereby assuring a victorious outcome.

A. *The Argument for an Installation Genre*
N. Lohfink, D.J. McCarthy[2] and J.R. Porter[3] have all written articles arguing for the existence of the installation genre. Lohfink was one of the first to concern himself with the possibility that there might be an installation (*Amtseinsetzung*) genre. In his article, he identified the three-element schema described above. He discerned the three-element pattern in Josh. 1.1-9, Deut. 31.7-8, 23, but in his view, the 'old text' Deut. 31.23 is the prototype for the other two. Although the deuteronomistic author only used the schema three times, according to Lohfink, the Dtr seems to be working with a fixed form, which possibly has its roots in an old commissioning ceremony. In Lohfink's theory, the ceremony must have existed in real life, rather than merely as a literary convention of the Dtr, because of the many occurrences of the schema in postexilic texts. However, since the DH is generally acknowledged to have influenced the postexilic texts that he mentions, Lohfink's argument is

---

2.   D.J. McCarthy, 'An Installation Genre?', *JBL* 90 (1971), pp. 31-41.

3.   J.R. Porter, 'The Succession of Joshua', in J.I. Durham and J.R. Porter (eds.), *Proclamation and Presence: Old Testament Essays in Honour of Gwynne Henton Davies* (London: SCM Press, 1970), pp. 102-32.

problematic. Although Lohfink is certainly correct that the schema is most likely not an original literary creation of the Dtr, he (Lohfink) gives no convincing reason why the form could not be a literary convention which would have been generally familiar. Lohfink admits that the objection could be raised that the exhortation formula (חֲזַק וֶאֱמָץ) combined with a promise of divine presence and help is found in Deut. 31.6 and Josh. 10.25, outside an *Amtseinsetzung* (office installation); furthermore, in both cases, the exhortation functions as a summons to holy war. Lohfink answers the objection by saying that presumably the genre (*Gattung*) 'Speech of the Leader in Holy War' stands in the background of Deut. 31.6 and Josh. 10.25 and that the exhortation formulae of two different genres appear to have become confused.

There are two reasons why it is unlikely that these are two separate genres. First, the material upon which Lohfink's article is primarily focused, Deut. 31.23 and Josh. 1.1-6, 9, is just as closely related to a 'holy war' context as Deut. 31.6 and Josh. 10.25, which he identifies as 'holy war' speeches. In each case, the subject matter of the speech is the war of conquest, using war oracle terminology, in the case of the Joshua passage, even including the phrase 'fear not'.

Secondly, there is a strong resemblence between the content of these passages (Deut. 31.6-8, 23; Josh. 1.1-6, 9) and the content of the war oracles which play so prominent a role throughout Joshua 10 and 11 (including the aforementioned passage Josh. 10.25) and elsewhere in the DH. A section of the present chapter is a more thorough discussion of the form and terminology of war oracles with an examination of the ways in which this oracular form resembles the others. The importance of understanding this oracle and its usage stems from its centrality to the Moses–Joshua succession and its close association with the role of Joshua himself.

B. *The Argument Against an Installation Genre*

The conquest is inherently a military event, and the military language connected with the installation of Joshua is explicit: one of the reasons given in Deut. 31.1-2 for Joshua's commission as leader is that Moses, at the age of 120, can no longer lead the forces out (יָצָא) and bring them back in (בוֹא). The same idea is expressed in Num. 27.17-18, in which the same verbs are used, and Joshua is subsequently invested with the leadership office. Although Moses and (later) Joshua both perform various leadership functions, the focus in Deut. 31.1-8, 23 and Josh. 1.1-6, 9 (as in Num. 27.17-18) is the military role.

Lohfink, McCarthy and others who have written about the 'installation genre' have argued that Joshua is charged with a civil as well as a military duty in Josh. 1.1-6, 9 since in v. 6 he is given the responsibility for putting the people into possession of the promised land: תַּנְחִיל אֶת־הָעָם הַזֶּה אֶת־הָאָרֶץ. Lohfink's interpretation of the task articulated in v. 6 is: 'Jahweh betraut Josue also mit dem Amt, den Israeliten den Erbbesitz zu verteilen' ('Yahweh entrusted Joshua with the task of distributing the inheritance to the Israelites').[4] I take exception to his translation of נחל in the *hiphil* as 'verteilen', because the *hiphil* of נחל, strictly speaking, means 'put into possession' or 'cause to take possession' (see below), while the German 'verteilen' carries the meaning 'distribute'. Lohfink obviously has in mind the division of the land among the tribes, but the tribal divisions are not mentioned in Josh. 1.1-6, 9. Rather, the passage refers to the entire land of Canaan, from border to border as described in Josh. 1.2-4, as the possession of Israel collectively: 'Every place on which the sole of your foot treads, I have given to you' (v. 3). At this point in the narrative, the unity of the 'sons of Israel' as a people (or a fighting force, as discussed below) is emphasized: 'cross this Jordan, you and all this people, to the land which I am giving them, to the sons of Israel' (v. 2). Likewise in Deut. 31.1-9, Moses is said to be speaking to 'all Israel' when he gives the people and Joshua the charge to cross the Jordan and take possession:

> So Moses went and spoke these words to all Israel... (Deut. 31.1);

> then Moses called to Joshua and said to him in the sight of all Israel, 'Be strong and bold, for you shall lead this people into the land which Yahweh has sworn to their fathers to give them, and you shall put them into possession of it' (Deut. 31.7).

Putting 'all Israel' (collectively) into possession of the land is not the same as specifically assigning each tribe its own parcel. Joshua's non-military role of assigning individual sections of the land to the different tribes is not mentioned in the schema as it appears in Josh. 1.1-6, 9; only his military role of warrior, who will take possession of the territory he conquers as commanding officer, is mentioned in the task-assignment element of the formula. Joshua's other role does not become prominent until later in the narrative, and even then he shares the task of land distribution with Eleazar the priest and the heads of the households of the

---

4. Lohfink, 'Die deuteronomistische Darstellung', p.39.

tribes (Josh. 14.1; 19.51), which is expressed by the plural form of נחל in the *piel*.

The semantic distinction between 'put into possession' and 'distribute' may seem at first glance to be an overly fine one, but it is important in that much of Lohfink's argument hinges on his contention that Joshua is being installed into office and entrusted with his two tasks simultaneously: that of military command in the war of conquest and that of dividing the conquered land among the tribes (a civil office). In Lohfink's opinion, the passage (Josh. 1.1-6, 9) deals with more than Joshua's military role and, therefore, cannot be primarily a holy war narrative. One of his most important points is that the 'installation genre' is used for civilian as well as military office, and he uses v. 6 as an example of the assignment of a civilian task in part 2 of the schema.

A close examination of the uses of נחל in its various themes is in order because a clear distinction between the *piel* and *hiphil* usages of this verb emerges. The *piel* always refers to land distibution, while the *hiphil* (discused in detail below) seems to have a more general causative meaning (usually with a double accusative), 'to put someone into possesion of something', or 'to cause someone to inherit something'. The *piel* occurs only in that part of the narrative which concerns the apportionment of the land to the tribes:

> These are the inheritances which Moses apportioned in the plains of Moab... (Josh. 13.32).

> And these are the inheritances which the people of Israel received in the land of Canaan, which Eleazar the priest, and Joshua the Son of Nun, and the heads of the households of the tribes of the sons of Israel apportioned (נחל *piel*) to them for an inheritance... (Josh. 14.1).

> These are the inheritances which Eleazar the priest and Joshua the Son of Nun and the heads of the households of the tribes of the sons of Israel distributed by lot in Shiloh... (Josh. 19.51).

The only other occurrence of the *piel* of this root in the entire Bible is in Num. 34.29, where its use is exactly the same:

> These are those whom Yahweh commanded to apportion the inheritance to the sons of Israel in the land of Canaan.

This remarkable consistency in the usage of the *piel* indicates that נחל *piel* may be a technical term for land distribution. Without exception, it means 'to allot, distribute, apportion' parcels of land.

E. Jenni also makes a distinction between the *piel* and *hiphil* forms of this root. According to Jenni, the *piel* is factitive and means 'allot' or 'distribute' ('Besitz zuteilen', Josh. 19.51) or bring someone into possession ('jemand zu Besitz bringen', Num. 34.29; Josh. 13.32; 14.1, with accusative of person). He says that a causative meaning for the *piel* does not recommend itself here because a causative *hiphil* already exists alongside, meaning 'jemand etwas zum Besitz geben' (give someone something as a possession, give someone possession of something), or 'jemand etwas ererben lassen' (let someone inherit something). Jenni's hypothesis is that perhaps the meaning of the *piel* is derived from the relevant passive meaning of נחל: 'als Besitz erhalten' (receive as a possession), 'belehnt werden' (become invested). The *piel* then would be factitive to (zu) 'belehnen', so that the resultant meaning would be: 'jem. zum Besitzer machen', 'belehnt machen'.[5] However, even Jenni, with his careful attention to fine distinctions in meaning, has not sufficiently distinguished the differences in usage between the *hiphil* and *piel* of this root, which indicate that the *piel* is a specialized technical term.

On the other hand, Jenni's trenchant remarks on the meaning of the *qal* of נחל strengthen this argument that the *piel* has a technical meaning not shared by other forms of the root. The *qal*, he says, always has the meaning 'receive something as an inheritance', 'take possession', 'acquire'. Only in Num. 34.17-18 is the meaning 'distribute as an inheritance' found, and here it is usually corrected to *piel*.[6] Although the other scholars he cites also correct Josh. 19.49 to *piel*, Jenni thinks that this alteration is not necessary since the word in this verse can be translated 'take into possession' rather than 'distribute'. However, the context of land distribution makes the *piel* emendation more logical. The fact that these other scholars prefer the emendation in this passage indicates that although they do not identify the *piel* of this root as a technical term, they have noticed that the *piel* is at home in the context of land allotment.

G. Gerleman has also commented on the uses of נחל in its various themes but sees no difference between the *hiphil* and the *piel*. He ascribes a causative meaning to both.[7] However, although at first glance

5. E. Jenni, *Das Hebräische Piel* (Zurich: EVZ-Verlag, 1968), p. 213.

6. As in Num. 34.29, which I have translated above. As noted by Jenni (p. 213), this emendation is corroborated by KB as well as R. Kittel, *BH*(3), and Noth (p. 214). Not mentioned by Jenni is this same emendation by BDB, p. 635.

7. G. Gerleman, 'Nutzrecht und Wohnrecht: Zur Bedeutung von אחזה und

the meaning of the *piel* (allot, apportion, distribute) may appear to be similar to that of the *hiphil* (put into possession), its usage and distribution in the text are very distinctive.

1. *The Military Nature of the Task and the* Hiphil *of* נחל

The *hiphil* of נחל occurs far more frequently in the Book of Deuteronomy (seven times) than in any other single book in the Bible.[8] Three of these occurrences appear in connection with the phrase חזק ואמץ, in passages which concern Joshua's charge to lead the conquest:

> Charge Joshua and strengthen him (וחזקהו) and encourage him (ואמצהו), for he shall cross over (יעבר) before this people and he shall put them into possession (ינחיל) of the land which you will see (Deut. 3.28).

> Joshua the son of Nun, who stands before you, he shall enter (יבא) there; strengthen him (חזק) for he shall put Israel into possession of it (ינחלנה) (Deut. 1.38).

> Then Moses called to Joshua and said to him in the sight of all Israel, Be strong and bold (חזק ואמץ) for you shall enter (תבוא) with this people into the land which Yahweh has sworn to their fathers to give them, and you shall put them into possession of it (תנחילנה) (Deut. 31.7).

Like Josh. 1.1-6, 9, these three passages occur in a military context. In the last of the three (Deut. 31.7), there is evidence (given below) that תבוא את העם הזה (enter with this people) should be read תביא את העם הזה (lead this army in), as in Deut. 31.23. עם is sometimes used to refer to people bearing arms (a fighting force, or army),[9] as in 1 Sam. 11.11:

> . . . Saul put the עם into three companies, and they entered [ויבאו] into the midst of the camp at the morning watch and struck down the Ammonites until the heat of the day . . .

נחלה', *ZAW* 89 (1977), pp. 313-25.

8.   The *hiphil* of this root never appears anywhere in the first four books of the Bible. I have included in a later section a discussion of the verb ירש, which occurs in war oracles connected with Moses' military exploits (Deut. 1.8, 21; 2.24, 31) in order to demonstrate that 'take possession' is one of the stock imperatives in war oracles.

9.   R.M. Good makes the same point in his monograph, *The Sheep of His Pasture: A Study of the Hebrew Noun 'Am(m) and Its Semitic Cognates* (Chico, CA: Scholars Press, 1983). He demonstrates the military use of the term in several Semitic languages.

and in Josh. 8.13:

> They stationed the עַם, all the encampment which was on the north side of
> the city and its rear guard west of the city...
> (cf.1 Kgs 20.10, and the עם המלחמה in Josh. 8.1, 3, 11; 10.7; 11.7).

Both the *hiphil* תביא and the *qal* תבוא are common in war narratives,
meaning to 'lead' or 'bring' the troops in for the purpose of engaging in
battle (in the case of תביא) or to 'enter' with the troops to engage in battle
(in the case of תבוא). Although the MT has the *qal* תבוא את העם הזה (in
which את is translated as the preposition 'with': 'you shall enter with this
people'), there is considerable support for the argument that the MT
reflects a scribal error which resulted in ו instead of י. The *hiphil* תביא,
'you shall lead this people (or army) in...', with את as the accusative
particle, is found in the Samaritan text. Several ancient versions, including the Peshitta, the Vulgate, the Targum Neofiti 1, and one manuscript
of the Targum Onkelos understood the verb to have been a *hiphil*.[10]
This reading is adopted by Dillmann,[11] Oettli,[12] and Kuenen[13] (amongst
others) on the basis of the Samaritan, Peshitta and Vulgate evidence.
Von Rad also chooses to translate the verb as a *hiphil* in this passage.[14]
S.R. Driver agrees that the *hiphil* ('lead this people in') is preferable
because the *hiphil* better emphasizes the leadership aspect of Joshua's
role in this passage.[15] Perhaps more importantly, the two causative verbs
then complement each other: 'You shall lead this army into the
land...and you shall put them into possession of it.' This reading is not
only more pleasing aesthetically, but is also closer to the parallel passage
Deut. 31.23: 'You shall lead (תביא) the בני ישראל into the land...'

The *hiphil* of נחל is also found in Deut. 12.10, which once again concerns crossing the Jordan to take possession of the land of Canaan:
'When you cross the Jordan and dwell in the land which Yahweh your
God is putting into your possession (מנחיל) and he gives you rest from
all your enemies...' The speech is addressed to the people as a whole,

10. B. Grossfeld, 'Targum Neofiti 1 to Deut. 31.7', *JBL* 91 (1972), pp. 533-34.
11. A. Dillmann, *Numeri, Deuteronomium und Josua* (KEH; Leipzig, 1886).
12. S. Oettli, *Das Deuteronimum und die Bücher Josua und Richter* (München, 1893).
13. A. Kuenen, *The Hexateuch* (Leiden: Brill, 1885).
14. *Heilige Krieg*, p. 75; also *Deuteronomy* (London: SCM Press, 1966), p. 187.
15. S.R. Driver, *A Critical and Exegetical Commentary on Deuteronomy* (ICC; Edinburgh: T. & T. Clark, 1895), pp. 334-35.

and the subject matter is apparently the land in general, not the particular tribal divisions.

Similarly, in Deut. 19.1-3, the land referred to is the land of Canaan as a whole, of which the Israelites are being given possession by Yahweh:

> When Yahweh your God cuts off the nations whose land Yahweh your God is giving to you, and you dispossess them and settle in their cities and in their houses, you shall set aside three cities for yourself in the midst of your land, which Yahweh your God gives you to possess. You shall prepare the roads for yourself, and divide into three parts the territory of your land, which Yahweh your God will give you as a possession (ינחילך), so that any manslayer may flee there.

The clause 'which Yahweh your God will give you as a possession' refers to the land as a collective entity, with the verb נחל in the *hiphil* used in its usual causative sense. Therefore this passage from the deuteronomic law is consistent with other נחל passages we have examined thus far: the *piel* is reserved for a specialized usage, referring to land distribution, while the *hiphil* has the more general causative meaning.

One of the remaining occurrences of נחל in the *hiphil*, Deut. 21.16, makes no reference to the conquest literature at all, but is in a legal code describing the inheritance laws which apply to the sons in a family when one wife is favoured over another:

> And it shall be, in the day when he bequeaths (הנחילו) his possessions to his sons, he cannot make the son of the loved the first-born before the son of the unloved, who is the first-born.

The final occurrence in Deuteronomy of נחל in the *hiphil* is found in the Song of Moses, within a difficult passage which also contains the noun form נחלה (Deut. 32.8-9):

> When the Most High put the nations
> into posession of their inheritances (*hiphil* of נחל)
> When he separated the sons of man,
> He fixed the boundaries of the peoples
> According to the number of the sons of God.
> But Yahweh's portion is his people,
> Jacob his allotted heritage.

Attempts to determine the precise meaning of the *hiphil* of נחל in Deut. 32.8-9 are complicated by a textual problem in v. 9 which obscures the issue of who is receiving what from whom. The MT reading, 'sons of

Israel', is emended by most scholars to 'sons of God' on the basis of evidence from the LXX and, more recently, a fragment discovered at Qumran which has the phrase 'sons of El'. Patrick Skehan pointed out that the Qumran fragment breaks off too soon for certainty as to whether El was the entire word, or whether it may have been Elim (cf. Pss. 29.1; 89.7) or Elohim (cf. Job 38.7).[16] Any of the three could be translated 'sons of God', but 'sons of the gods' is a possibility also.

The Qumran fragment provides the first evidence in an ancient Hebrew manuscript for the reading 'sons of God', but it had been inferred from the LXX form of v. 8. For example, Steuernagel[17] had written, in a commentary which predated the Qumran discovery, that El is to be read with the LXX in place of Israel. Steuernagel took the 'sons of El' to be angelic beings, with each nation having its own divinely appointed guardian angel, except for Israel, which Yahweh himself would protect. Therefore, the text meant that the nations were parcelled out according to the number of guardian angels in existence, according to Steuernagel. Traditionally, the number seventy[18] is given, but the number need not detain us because the emphasis in the text is on the relationship between human beings, divine beings and territories, not on the number itself. The concept underlying this interpretation is that Elyon is another name for Yahweh, who is in control of assigning the angelic beings to the nations.

Examination of the Ugaritic materials has led to extensive discussions regarding the influence of the Canaanite concept of a divine council upon Hebrew thought.[19] Although there can be little doubt that the idea of a pantheon is reflected in certain Psalms (cf. Psalms 29 and 89), the biblical literature consistently identifies the head of the pantheon (El or Elyon) with Yahweh. As E.T. Mullen wrote concerning Deut. 32.8-9:

16. P.W. Skehan, 'A Fragment of the "Song of Moses" (Deut. 32) from Qumran', *BASOR* 136 (1954), pp. 12-15.

17. C. Steuernagel, *Übersetzung und Erklärung der Bücher Deuteronomium, Josua, und allgemeine Einleitung in den Hexateuch* (Göttingen: Vandenhoeck & Ruprecht, 1900).

18. W. F. Albright has pointed out that the number of the *banu* (sons of) 'Athirat (Asherah, the consort of El) in the Baal Epic is also seventy, and that the Table of Nations (Genesis 10) lists approximately seventy peoples. W.F. Albright, 'Some Remarks on the Song of Moses in Deuteronomy XXXII', *VT* 9 (1959), pp. 339-46.

19. F.M. Cross, *Canaanite Myth and Hebrew Epic*; P.D. Miller, *Divine Warrior*; E.T. Mullen, *The Divine Council in Canaanite and Early Hebrew Literature* (Chico, CA: Scholars Press, 1980).

> It is clear... that within biblical tradition, 'Elyon was regarded as a suitable appellative for Yahweh (cf. Num. 24.16, where 'Elyon parallels 'El and Sadday; Ps. 18.14 = 2 Sam. 22.14, where it parallels Yahweh; Gen. 14.22, where 'El 'Elyon is applied as an epithet of Yahweh; Ps. 47.3, where 'Elyon is an epithet of Yahweh, etc.). Traditions in Hebrew usage of the term make it most probable that the writer here equates 'Elyon and Yahweh.[20]

The resulting picture of Yahweh sitting at the head of a divine council (containing lesser deities) is therefore not so different from Steuernagel's concept of Yahweh presiding over an assembly of angelic beings. In both instances, the 'sons of God' are regarded as members of a heavenly assembly subordinate to Yahweh, but each possessing a special relationship with a particular nation assigned by Yahweh.

The idea, asserted by Mullen, that Elyon and Yahweh are meant to be equated in Deut. 32.8-9 had already been cited by Albright as an example of 'parallelism carried over groups of verses' (cf. vv. 21 and 30 for other examples). He sensibly goes on to say that in 'some earlier polytheistic form of this ethnographic myth', two separate gods may have been involved.[21] While there certainly may have been two separate gods originally, the word-pair Elyon and Yahweh is most likely intended to stand as a synonymous parallelism in the text of Deut. 32.8-9. One of the points being emphasized in the text is the special relationship between the Israelites and Yahweh/Elyon, who kept them back to be his own possession (v. 9) when he was making the assignments.

In this Song of Moses passage, the *hiphil* of נחל could be either the causative 'to put into possession', or the other meaning, 'to distribute' or 'parcel out', usually signified by the *piel*. Since both make sense, the Song of Moses sheds no light on the fine shades of meaning I am attempting to distinguish.

Other than in the חזק ואמץ passage of Josh. 1.6, the *hiphil* of נחל occurs only one time in the DH, outside of the Book of Deuteronomy, in the Song of Hannah:

> He raises the poor from the dust,
> He lifts the needy from the ash heap,
> To make them sit with nobles,
> To cause them to inherit a seat of honour (1 Sam. 2.8).

---

20. Mullen, *The Divine Council*, p. 204.

21. W.F. Albright, *Yahweh and the Gods of Canaan* (Garden City: Doubleday, 1968), p. 343.

There is no question that the *hiphil* verb נחל in this passage has a general causative meaning unrelated to the apportionment of the tribal lands. Scholars agree that the Song of Hannah is not an original composition of the Dtr, and most scholars date the poem to a much earlier period,[22] but the important point is that the *piel* was consistently reserved for specialized legal usage in connection with land distribution, while the *hiphil* was used more generally as a causative. The Song of Hannah passage therefore fits perfectly with this distinction.

Perhaps Lohfink was thinking of the noun form (נחלה), which is used in a variety of ways. In a few passages, the term נחלה is used theologically, referring to Israel (the people, the land, or both) as Yahweh's נחלה. Other passages, primarily concentrated in the Book of Deuteronomy, speak of Israel (as a whole) as having a נחלה. Only sometimes does it refer to the inherited possession of a tribe, a clan, or an individual.

H. Forshey,[23] in an article about the concept of Israel as Yahweh's נחלה, points out a shift in focus between those texts which seem to refer primarily to the territorial aspect of the נחלת יהוה (2 Sam. 20.19, 21.3) and those which refer primarily to the people as Yahweh's possession. His theory is that the latter usage belongs to a later (exilic) stage of the deuteronomic materials:

> In a context in which people and land are no longer coterminus, נחלה comes increasingly to refer to the community itself rather than to the land. Thus, Israel's relationship to Yahweh can continue to be affirmed despite her alienation from her land.

Forshey is probably correct about this shift in focus, but more important (for my purposes) is the distinction between the theological use of נחלה which concerns the three-way relationship among the divinity, the people and the land, and the more pragmatic, or even secular, use of נחלה as a matter of territorial boundaries. The distinction shows only when the root is used as a verb; then the difference between the *hiphil* and the *piel* emerges.

Other commentators on this passage have sometimes been too willing to accept Lohfink's interpretation of the task expressed in Josh. 1.6.

22. Albright, *Yahweh and the Gods of Canaan*, pp. 20-22; J.T. Willis, 'The Song of Hannah and Psalm 113', *CBQ* 35 (1973), pp. 139-54; P.K. McCarter, Jr, *I Samuel* (AB; Garden City: Doubleday, 1980), pp. 74-76. Each dates the poem somewhere between the 11th and 9th centuries.

23. H.O. Forshey, 'The Construct Chain naḥ\u1ealat YHWH/\u02bfelōhîm', *BASOR* 220 (1975), pp. 51-53.

G. Wenham implies in his article on the deuteronomistic theology of the Book of Joshua[24] that Joshua's two-fold office, that of military commander and that of distributor of the land, is bestowed on him all at once, and he is right in the general sense that elsewhere in the narrative Joshua is portrayed as Moses' successor in his civil and religious roles as well as his military role. However, the question is whether the civil task is mentioned in Josh. 1.1-6, 9 or not. Wenham says that Joshua's work as commander is denoted by the terms 'come' and 'cross over' (בוא and עבר), and his work as distributor of the land by 'cause to inherit' (נחל *hiphil*).[25] Wenham goes on to say that in Josh. 1.6, Joshua is 'confirmed in his second office as distributor of the land. But not until Josh. 13.7 is he told to start exercising his second office and actually to distribute the land.' Wenham is correct regarding the role of Joshua in Joshua 13 but not in his statement regarding the 'confirmation' of Joshua as distributor of the land in Josh. 1.6. There is no reason why the verb meaning 'put into possession' or 'cause to inherit' should be interpreted as anything other than a military task since a military commander's job is to lead his army in the taking of territory in battle.

A.D.H. Mayes also links the concept of 'putting the people in possession of the land' (נחל *hiphil*) with the concept of dividing the land.[26] Concerning 'those texts in Deuteronomy and Joshua relating to the transfer of leadership of Israel from Moses to Joshua (Deut. 3.28; 31.7-8, 23; Josh. 1.6, 9b)', Mayes says that 'the task for which Joshua is instituted has two aspects: he is to go over into the land at the head of the people, and he is to put the people into possession of the land. The first of these is a command to conquer the land, the second a command to divide the conquered land among the tribes...'[27]

Like Lohfink, D.J. McCarthy uses the allegedly non-military task as an argument that the schema need not necessarily be identified with holy war and its ideology. McCarthy says that 'even within the Joshua passages the task of allotting the land has no intrinsic connection with war'.[28] In my view, the task articulated in part 2 of the schema in Josh. 1.6 does have an intrinsic connection with war because in holy war

24. G. Wenham, 'The Deuteronomic Theology of the Book of Joshua', *JBL* 90 (1971), pp. 141-42.
25. Wenham, 'Deuteronomic Theology', p. 145.
26. A.D.H. Mayes, *The Story of Israel*, p. 45.
27. Mayes, *The Story of Israel*, p. 45.
28. McCarthy, 'An Installation Genre?', p. 38.

literature, as in real-life military engagement, the conquering army's commanding officer is said to put his nation (or whatever faction he represents) into 'possession' of the conquered territory.

2. *The 'New Task' Theory*

One scholar who has been influenced by the 'installation genre' theory without accepting it wholesale is E.W. Conrad. He acknowledges that חזק ואמץ is military language, but holds that the phrase occurs 'most frequently but not exclusively' at the appointment of a warrior to a new task.[29] However, the task given to 'all Israel' in Deut. 31.6 (with plural imperative verbs) is a repetition of the same military activity which defeated 'Sihon and Og, the kings of the Amorites' (v. 4). Furthermore, although Moses' words to the people in Deuteronomy 31 are employed on the occasion of the passing of leadership to Joshua, there is no evidence that the personnel being addressed with the exhortation חזקו ואמצו in v. 6 are being appointed to new offices; they are apparently the same army which vanquished the Amorites, and they are being called to a repeat performance in the same capacity.

In 2 Sam. 10.9-13, Joab's words are a general exhortation to bravery in battle (חזק ונתחזק). Since the exhortation נתחזק is in the first person, and Joab himself has taken on no new responsibilities, it is doubtful whether the exhortation has anything to do with the appointment of a warrior to a new task. The text gives no hint that there is anything new or unusual about Abishai's role in the battle either; he is performing the sort of task which would be expected of a military officer. The ordinary fighting men who have been picked to fight the Syrians rather than the Amorites (v. 9) have not been given new responsibilities either, except in the obvious sense that each new battle is a new task facing the army, which would entail specific commands tailored to that particular battle-plan. The exhortation in 2 Sam. 10.9-13 is a pre-battle word of encouragement to do what warriors are always supposed to do in combat: fight bravely.

Conrad's theory that חזק ואמץ is used when a warrior is given a new task or new responsibilities was probably unduly influenced by Lohfink's installation genre theory and by McCarthy's theory (see below) that the phrase (along with the schema of which it is a part) is an exhortation, rooted in cultic ritual, used to encourage those facing new

---

29. E.W. Conrad, *Fear Not Warrior: A Study of 'al tira' Pericopes in the Hebrew Scriptures* (Chico, CA: Scholars Press, 1985), pp. 26-27.

and difficult situations. Although Conrad correctly traces the phrase to the conventional language of war, rather than to the cult, as McCarthy does, Conrad overemphasizes the newness of the tasks associated with חזק ואמץ. Since most military directives are, by definition, statements of a new task (each battle is, in some sense, a 'new and difficult situation'), a weakness in Conrad's argument is that almost every war oracle he examines from the DH could be said to contain a statement of a 'new' task. This is inevitable because of the function and position of war oracles in the narrative: they are positioned immediately prior to battles so that the deity can command the army (or leader) and assure them of the outcome, in accordance with 'holy war' literary convention.

In Josh. 10.25, the phrase חזקו ואמצו appears in another context unrelated to either the installation of a leader (as in Lohfink's argument) or the assignment of a new task (as in Conrad's argument). The imperatives are in the second person plural, which is common in war oracles addressed to the entire army or its officers. The context in Josh. 10.25 is undoubtedly a military situation, in which Israel defeated the Amorites, described in conventional 'holy war' terminology: 'for Yahweh has delivered them into your hand' (v. 19); '...for Yahweh fought for Israel' (v. 14). The oracle of v. 25 is somewhat unusual in that it occurs after the battle rather than prior to it; another 'fear not' oracle precedes the battle in v. 8. However, the oracle of v. 25 is followed by the execution of the enemy kings, a military-related activity, and it functions, like other 'fear not' oracles, as an assurance that Yahweh is on the Israelites' side in battle: '...for thus Yahweh will do to all your enemies with whom you fight' (v. 25b).

Most importantly, the combination of אל תיראו ואל תחת with חזק ואמץ helps to forge the link of חזק ואמץ with typical war oracle terminology. The same combination of terms occurs in Deut. 31.8, but the use of חזק ואמץ is especially significant in Josh. 10.25, where it is attached exclusively to holy war, far removed from the installation of Joshua (and where there are no traces of elements 2 and 3 of the 'installation genre' identified by Lohfink). As mentioned previously, the activity in Josh. 10.24-26 is unusual because it precedes a military-related execution of captured enemy kings rather than a battle. The army chiefs are told to put their feet on the necks of the captive kings before the execution, but there is no hint that this action has anything to do with the assignment of new responsibilities to the chiefs. Their role as war leaders remains unchanged.

Conrad stresses that the phrase חזק ואמץ is connected with the 'secular or mundane practice of war' as well as holy war,[30] but the passage he chooses to illustrate his point ends with the admonition, 'Be of good courage (חזק) and let us take courage (ונתחזק), for our people, and for the cities of our God; and may Yahweh do what seems good to him' (2 Sam. 10.12). Clearly the last part of the passage reflects the belief, generally found in 'holy war' narratives, that the outcome of the battle is under Yahweh's control. Also, the idea that their cities (for which they were fighting) were somehow connected with 'their' God gives the battle a religious dimension.

III. *Interruption of the Oracle: The Excursus on the Law*

The war oracle language in Joshua 1 is interrupted by a brief excursus on obedience to the law (vv. 7-8), which is considered by most scholars to be a secondary addition. The repetition of the phrase חזק ואמץ in v. 7 involves a reinterpretation of the meaning of the words. In v. 6 Joshua is commanded to be brave in the battle over the promised land in the light of Yahweh's firm promise of help and accompaniment. In vv. 7-8, the promise of success suddenly becomes conditional; this marks an abrupt change, not only from the rest of Josh. 1.1-9, but also from the promise of divine help explicitly stated in Deut. 31.1-8. As R. Smend has pointed out, the difference is made more apparent by the repetition of חזק ואמץ in Josh. 1.7, where the phrase is twisted around to an entirely different meaning: in v. 6, the words mean (as usual) courage and fearlessness in battle, but in v. 7, they are reinterpreted to mean 'make every effort, do everything possible'.[31] The theme of the law receives further emphasis in v. 8, in which Joshua is not just to obey the law, but is to meditate upon a book of the law day and night. Smend was struck by the inappropriateness of v. 8 in the context of battle preparations: 'Joshua had his hands full undertaking the conquest of Canaan; he had no time to meditate on the law book day and night'.[32]

T.W. Mann also noticed the deuteronomistic reinterpretation of the concept of divine presence and guidance, in which the Torah, as a form of divine guidance, leads the people in the 'way'. The 'way' is no longer

---

30. Conrad, *Fear Not Warrior*, p. 26.
31. R. Smend, 'Das Gesetz', pp. 494-509.
32. Smend, 'Das Gesetz', p. 496.

a geographical reference but has become a metaphor, 'not an actual path from which Joshua is not to turn, but the Way of Torah'. Israel's keeping of the commandments becomes, in vv. 7-8, a condition of divine presence, constituting a 'synergism for the protective guidance of the divine messenger'.[33] No such synergism exists in Deut. 31.1-8, in which Yahweh's accompaniment in war is unconditionally assured, hence the exhortation to be fearless; the implication is that one can be fearless precisely because of Yahweh's unconditional promise of help.

Lohfink also sees a break between v. 6 and v. 7, but he thinks that v. 9a, the rhetorical question, 'Have I not told you to be strong and bold?', is part of the insertion. 9b is then a continuation of v. 6.[34] Mayes agrees that the insertion begins with v. 7 and ends in v. 9a, forming a passage concluding with the same words with which it began, 'be strong and bold'.[35] He is in agreement with Lohfink, Smend, Mann and Noth that the reinterpretation of the words in v. 7 marks a clear break with the sense of v. 6: in v. 6, the phrase is 'properly and exactly used' to encourage Israel in the face of the forthcoming battle; in v. 7 the vocabulary has been applied in a quite different way which is 'not wholly suitable', to mean doing one's best to obey the law. Mayes also points out that a different interpretation of the divine promise is involved. In v. 6, the basis for Israel's success in taking the land is the divine promise, while in v. 7, her success is dependent upon obedience to the law. He thinks that the basic text takes up again at v. 9b.

However, while Lohfink, Smend, Mann, Noth and Mayes are certainly correct in identifying vv. 7-8 as an insertion, Lohfink and Mayes are mistaken in assigning v. 9a to a secondary hand. Rhetorical questions such as that of v. 9a (הלוא צויתיך) are not unusual in military exhortations. A very similar rhetorical question appears in Deborah's war oracle to Barak in Jud. 4.6: הלא צוה יהוה אלהי ישראל, and in Judg. 6.14, Yahweh says to Gideon, הלא שלחתיך. Josh. 8.8 uses language similar to that of Josh. 1.9a in the form of a rhetorical reiteration: 'See, I have commanded you' (ראו צויתי אתכם). Therefore, the rhetorical question in v. 9a would not be out of place in a battle context such as the commencement of the conquest.

---

33. T.W. Mann, *Divine Presence and Guidance in Israelite Traditions* (Baltimore: The Johns Hopkins University Press, 1977), pp. 201-202.

34. Lohfink, 'Die deuteronomistische Darstellung', pp. 36-38.

35. Mayes, *Story of Israel*, pp. 46-47.

Noth, on the other hand, thinks that v. 9b, with Yahweh in the third person, is certainly secondary.[36] Lohfink and Mayes consider 9b to be an element in the installation genre, upon which they both believe this passage to be based, although Mayes concedes that the change to third person poses problems. He suggests that the switch in person may be accounted for by the close relationship between this passage and Deut. 31.7-8, where the deity is referred to in the third person, in a phrase which is almost identical.[37] Although I cannot accept the 'installation genre' theory, I suspect that Mayes is correct in his assumption that the phrase in Josh. 1.9b is based on the Deut. 31.7 passage. If my theory is correct that Deut. 31.7-8 is the original war oracle upon which the parallel passages (Deut. 31.5-6, 23; Josh. 1.1-6, 9) were based (see section above), then it is likely that the phrase 'Yahweh will be with you' was borrowed without alteration from the oracular language of the original when the various early sources were woven together by the Dtr to create a chronological narrative. I am not suggesting that Josh. 1.1-6, 9, Deut. 31.5-6 and 23 are later additions to the text; they were certainly included when the first edition of the DH was composed. Only vv. 7-8 are a secondary (exilic) insertion.

J.A. Soggin thinks that part of v. 7 belongs to the original form of the text, which probably spoke only of 'doing according to all that Moses my servant commanded you', but that a later gloss understood this to mean the Torah. Soggin ascribes v. 8 to a 'later adaptation' which transforms Moses' command not just into the Torah but into a book of the law.[38] Smend also raised the possiblity that v. 8 was added, at a time later than v. 7, as a further expansion of the thoughts expressed by the nomistic editor who had added v. 7, but Smend left the question open.[39] Smend does not, in any case, agree with Soggin that the first part of v. 7, with its reinterpretation of the exhortation to be strong and bold, is original to the passage. I agree with Smend, along with Lohfink, Mayes, Noth, Mann and Fishbane (discussed below) that the end of v. 6 marks a radical break, both in tone and subject matter, which is not resumed until v. 9.

---

36. M. Noth, *Das Buch Josua*, (HAT; Tübingen: J.C.B. Mohr, 1953), pp. 28-29.

37. Mayes, *The Story of Israel*, p. 158.

38. J.A. Soggin, *Joshua* (trans. R.A. Wilson; OTL; Philadelphia: Westminster Press, 1972).

39. Smend, 'Das Gesetz', pp. 495-96.

Fishbane says that an 'entirely new dimension' has been added to the 'old military exhortation formula' in Joshua 1.[40] According to Fishbane, vv. 7-8 are 'aggadic theologizing' in which Joshua is told to be strong and of good courage in obeying the Torah since only in this manner will he succeed in his venture. Not only is there a new emphasis on the value of the Torah, says Fishbane, but the intrusion also transforms the exhortation to physical prowess into an exhortation to spiritual fortitude. Furthermore, the intrusion makes the divine support of the venture (the conquest) conditional, whereas in other cases the exhortatory formula is used to assure Yahweh's unconditional support. (These are the same issues raised by Mayes and others above.) Fishbane accurately identifies the intrusion in vv. 7-8 as a radical and thorough transformation of the meaning of the passage.

The few scholars who believe that vv. 7-8 are part of the original composition do not advance any arguments which counteract the allegation that v. 7 departs significantly from the meaning of v. 6. T. Butler argues that only in v. 8 do we have reason to suspect a later literary hand, representing a later strand of legalistic piety.[41] He insists that v. 7 is consistent with the emphasis upon the law throughout the DH and cites a number of key passages which support his contention.[42] However, many of these are passages which have been identified by Smend, Fishbane and others as secondary additions, by the same editor who added vv. 7-8 of Joshua 1, on the basis of similarity in vocabulary and theological attitude.

R. Boling also thinks that vv. 7-8 are original to the passage, forming a framing device in which the exhortation to be strong and bold is repeated three times, with the reference to the law as the centerpiece of the frame. To subtract the verses concerning the law would 'blunt the rhetorical structure' of the passage.[43] However, his contention that the rhetorical structure would be blunted depends entirely upon his decision as to what the rhetorical structure is: if one assumes that Joshua 1 is primarily a nomistic homiletic passage, then Boling's argument would have some merit, but if the passage is part of a military narrative, as its

40. M. Fishbane, *Biblical Interpretation*, pp. 384-85.

41. T.C. Butler, *Joshua* (WBC; Waco: Word Books, 1983), pp. 8-9.

42. Deut. 1.5; 4.44; 28.69; 31.9; Josh. 22.2,4, 5; 23.6; Jud. 2.20; 1 Sam.12.14-15; 2 Sam. 8.10-12; 1 Kgs 2.3-4; 8.24-25, 56-57; 9.4-7; 11.9-13, 31-39; 14.7-11; 2 Kgs 17.7-20; 18.6-7; 21.2-15; 22.11-20.

43. Boling, *Joshua*.

place in the literary context of the surrounding conquest narrative indicates that it is, then the excursus on the law is an intrusion.

IV. *Other* חזק ואמץ *Passages*

The phrase חזק ואמץ or something very similar appears in several biblical passages not mentioned above. Therefore, a close look at the other occurrences of the phrase חזק ואמץ is warranted in order to shed further light on how the exhortation is used.

A. *Psalms*
Unlike Lohfink, who thinks the setting for the schema of the installation genre was originally a commissioning ceremony, McCarthy traces the schema to the cult.[44] Citing the appearance of the phrase חזק ואמץ in the concluding verses of Psalms 27 and 31, McCarthy suggests that the schema is an exhortation used on the occasion of a difficult encounter, expressing a firm trust in Yahweh, and formalized in cult ritual to meet a recurring situation. In Psalms 27 and 31, חזק ואמץ occurs as a response to lamentation and gratitude, according to McCarthy:

> Whatever the circumstances, one must rely on Yahweh. This is the message of these verses, whether they are oracles of priests or cult-prophets responding to the preceding prayers, or a kind of concluding meditation in which the psalmist encourages himself.[45]

McCarthy does not claim that Psalms 27 and 31 are themselves old enough to be the sources of the installation genre but rather that the attitudes embodied therein (fidelity to duty, trust in Yahweh because of his assured help) are 'as old as Israelite religious poetry' and that the matrix in which the genre was formed was the concrete expression of these attitudes 'in the cult as carried on in the royal temple'.[46]

However, if the genre were truly at home in a cultic context, then one would expect to see the schema more fully expressed in the Psalms. The lines cited in Psalms 27 and 31 are extremely fragmentary examples of the schema—only the two words חזק ואמץ link the Psalms to the genre:

> Wait for Yahweh. Be strong and let your heart take courage (חזק ואמץ לבב); Wait for Yahweh (Ps. 27.14).

44. McCarthy, 'An Installation Genre?', pp. 38-41.
45. McCarthy, 'An Installation Genre?', p. 40.
46. McCarthy, 'An Installation Genre?', p. 41.

> Love Yahweh, all his godly ones; Yahweh preserves the faithful, and fully recompences him who behaves proudly. Be strong and let your heart take courage (חזקו ויאמץ לבבם), all who hope in Yahweh (Ps. 31.24-25).

The idea of Yahweh's faithfulness in helping those who trust in him can be discerned in these Psalms (as McCarthy pointed out), but the surrounding terminology is completely different from the expression of the idea of Yahweh's presence and help in the third element of the schema, which is usually some form of עמך יהוה. Furthermore, the idea of Yahweh's assured help as a motive for encouragement is also central to the biblical ideology of warfare, particularly in the DH war oracles (Deut. 3.2, 22; 20.3-4; Josh. 8.1-2; 10.8; 11.6). The idea of Yahweh's faithfulness to those who trust in him is so general that it finds expression throughout the Bible in a wide variety of contexts, including covenantal theology (Deut. 7.9), Psalms (Pss. 4.4; 13.6; 128.4, etc.) and classical prophecy (Jer. 17.7-8). Apart from some similarity of terminology, the connection remains rather loose.

Nevertheless, McCarthy's point, that the presence in the Psalms of the phrase חזק ואמץ is noteworthy, should be taken seriously, even though the two words alone are not sufficient to link the origin of the entire genre to cult ritual. Probably the Psalmists were making use of an already-familiar stylized phrase, reinterpreting it for use in a cultic context, by deliberately bringing into play its military associations. Both Psalms 27 and 31 employ other military imagery. The first three verses of Psalm 27 may even be a loose play on the 'fear not' (אל תירא) military oracles:

> Yahweh is my light and my salvation (or 'victory וישעי).
> Whom shall I fear (אירא)?
> Yahweh is the stronghold of my life;
> Whom shall I dread (אפחד)?
> When evildoers came upon me to devour my flesh,
> My adversaries and my enemies, they stumbled and fell.
> Though an army (מחנה) encamp against me,
> My heart will not fear (לא־יירא לבי);
> Though war rise up against me (אם־תקום עלי מלחמה) in this I shall trust...

The repetition of the word ירא (the same root as in אל־תירא) in vv. 1ab and 3ab serves as a frame for 'when evildoers came upon me... my adversaries and my enemies they stumbled and fell', which is reminiscent of the idea that the enemy troops 'will not be able to stand before you' (Josh. 10.8 in an אל־תירא oracle) and that 'Yahweh will deliver them (the enemies) into your hand' (Deut. 3.2-4; Josh. 8.1,7; 10.8, 19 in אל־תירא oracles; Deut. 2.30-33; Josh. 10.30, 32; 11.8 in closely related war narratives). The concept of adversaries being 'unable to stand' before someone because of divine action (as distinguished from the concept of an ordinary military rout by human means) is drawn from the literary traditions of divine war (see previous chapter). The concept of being free from fear (ירא) because of the assurance that the deity will bring about victory in precisely this way is drawn primarily from the אל־תירא oracles.

The Psalmist is not talking about fear in a general sense in these verses (vv. 1-3); he specifically has in mind fear in the face of an opposing 'army encamped against' him and 'war' rising up against him. It is reasonable to suppose that the Psalmist was making conscious use of the literary conventions of war narratives. Psalm 27 seems to draw upon language and imagery from both the חזק ואמץ oracles and the (more numerous) אל־תירא oracles, as well as military terminology in general (תחנה מלחמה מחנה). Even the word ישע (v. 1), traditionally translated 'salvation', may be intended to have military connotations by calling to mind the other sense of the root ישע, 'victory' (cf. Pss. 33.16; 44.4; 98.1). The Psalmist may be playing on a double meaning.

B. *Amos*

One of the most interesting occurrences of חזק ואמץ (to which McCarthy also drew attention) is found in Amos 2:

> ...and his strength will not give force to the brave (וחזק לא יאמץ כחו, v. 14).
> Even the bravest among the warriors (ואמץ לבו בגבורים) will flee naked in that day, declares Yahweh (v. 16).

McCarthy (rightly) sees this passage as an example of Amos' favorite device of irony: 'Just as he turns the divine choice (3.2) and the day of Yahweh (5.18-20) against the faithless people, so here he mocks their confidence that Yahweh is at their side in battle. To be effective, such irony must play on a usage whose positive meaning is well known'.[47] To McCarthy's accurate analysis, I would add that Amos makes explicit reference to the conquest tradition just a few verses earlier: 'And it was I who brought you up from the land of Egypt...that you might take possession of the land of the Amorites' (v. 10). The prophet is turning the

---

47. McCarthy, 'An Installation Genre?', p. 38.

traditional holy war oracle on its head: instead of assured victory (as in the conquest stories), there will be assured defeat (vv. 14-16) because, instead of faithful obedience from the people, Yahweh has received the opposite, unfaithfulness (v. 12).

C. *1 Kings 2.1-9*

J.R. Porter has suggested that the חזק ואמץ passages in Deut. 31.5-8, 23, and Josh. 1.1-9 find their closest parallel in David's speech to Solomon in 1 Kgs 2.1-9.[48] While accepting the Installation Genre theory, Porter suggests that the succession of Joshua as presented in the DH has its roots in royal ideology. However, Porter outlines the central elements of the 1 Kings 2 passage rather differently from Lohfink's outline of the 'genre',[49] and his theory is particularly dependent upon the acceptance of the excursus on the law as an intrinsic part of the text:

a.   Solemn charge, v. 1: *piel* of צוה.
b.   Encouragement, v. 2: חזקת והיית לאיש.
c.   Exhortation to keep the law, v. 3.
d.   Assurance of divine help, v. 4.[50]

1 Kgs 2.1 contains terminology reminiscent of the war exhortations of the conquest narratives, but the language originally associated with battle against an external threat (Canaanites) is here applied to an internal threat, those who might be able to mount a successful coup d'état. The enemies in vv. 5-9 are the internal enemies of the dynasty whom Solomon needs to destroy in order to solidify his hold on the throne on behalf of the Davidic line. Joab in particular possessed the ruthlessness and military capability to challenge Solomon's hold on the throne should he try. The deaths of Abner and Amasa (v. 5) are given as justification for the action against Joab, but it is odd that David never felt the need to avenge their deaths during his own lifetime, if vengeance were his true motive. Considering his own twisted involvement with Joab's ruthlessness (2 Sam. 11.14-17), David knew the danger that Joab posed. The

48. J.R. Porter, 'The Succession of Joshua', in J.R. Porter and J.I. Durham (eds.), *Proclamation and Presence: Old Testament Essays in Honour of Gwynne Henton Davies* (London: SCM Press, 1970), pp. 102-34.

49. Although Porter quotes Lohfink's version of the elements of the 'genre' (pp. 104-105 of above-mentioned article), his discussion emphasizes features not mentioned by Lohfink, particularly the importance of צוה in the *piel*, which he says indicates a solemn charge to someone in, or entering, an official position.

50. Porter, 'The Succession of Joshua', p. 117.

stories about the deaths of Abner (2 Sam. 3.22-34) and Amasa (2 Sam. 20.4-13), alluded to in 1 Kgs 2.5, are specifically stories about Joab's ambition and jealousy for power. Solomon's hold on the throne could also be threatened by Shimei, who had shown himself to be disloyal to David in the rebellion of Absolom (2 Sam. 16.5-13), and had been allowed to live (2 Sam. 19.16-23). It is not unlikely that someone with a history of disloyalty to the throne might take advantage of the temporary instability caused by the succession. The theory that the basis for David's exhortation and advice to Solomon in 1 Kgs 2.1 (using the terminology of a battle exhortation) is that Shimei is perceived as a threat to the dynasty. This is born out in 1 Kgs 2.45. Just before Solomon put Shimei to death, he justified his action by saying that 'King Solomon shall be blessed and the throne of David shall be established before Yahweh forever'.

As in Josh. 1.1-9, the admonition to obey the law in 1 Kgs 2.1-9 interrupts the call to physical action introduced by חזק. Although it is possible that David's charge included more than one task, there is little likelihood that the call to action would originally have been interrupted and resumed without a smooth transition, particularly since the terminology of the exhortation in v. 2 is borrowed from military tradition and is more applicable to the context of armed struggle (vv. 5-9) than to legal matters (vv. 3-4).

Fishbane agrees that the subject matter of the passage is primarily military action against dynastic enemies.[51] The command to 'be strong' is articulated in military terms in vv. 1-2 and vv. 5-9, which Fishbane recognizes as 'a sequence unified by both subject matter and style', so that one is thoroughly struck by the intrusion of vv. 3-4, in which faithfulness to the Torah is the condition for success in this (military) venture (v. 3) and in the maintenance of the dynasty (v. 4). Fishbane points out that v. 4 is also a radical reinterpretation of the scripture it purports to cite, 2 Sam. 7.12-16, because in that passage, the dynastic promise is explicitly unconditional. Therefore, the redactor has transformed not only David's purely military advice to his son, but the unconditional promise of grace to the Davidic line as well.

That the expression 'take courage and be a man' in 1 Kgs 2.1 is a battle exhortation is demonstrated by its use in 1 Sam. 4.9: 'Take courage and be men, Oh Philistines...take courage and fight'. In the ensuing battle, the Philistines defeated the Hebrews and took the ark

51. Fishbane, *Biblical Interpretation*, p. 385.

captive (a dubious accomplishment, as it turned out, since Yahweh proved his divine powers by afflicting the Philistines with a painful malady as well as toppling their idol Dagon, 1 Sam. 4.10–6.21). There can be no doubt that the context of the exhortation in 1 Sam. 4.9 is a military situation with a religious dimension. The situation in 1 Kgs 2.1 is no less military although the enemies are internal.

D. *Postexilic Writings*

The phrase חזק ואמץ appears several times in postexilic writings, where its use is usually modelled on specific incidents in the DH. The phrase חזק ואמץ or something similar appears in the Chronicler's version of Solomon's accession to the throne (1 Chron. 22.13; 28.20, the latter in the variant form חזק ועשה), and in Ezra 10.4 (also in the variant form חזק ועשה), as well as in several battle exhortations and prophetic oracles related to warfare.

The phrase חזק ואמץ is fairly common in military situations in Chronicles. 2 Chron. 32.7 contains a complete version of the war oracle in its classic form, as Hezekiah urges his people not to fear the might of the Assyrian troops. Although some have argued that the instance in 2 Chron. 32.7 is an example of an installation genre (Lohfink, Porter), the situation is explicitly military. Hezekiah tells his assembled troops to be brave because the deity will help them and fight for them in the coming seige of Jerusalem. The language is clearly reminiscent of the war oracle in Joshua 1 which inaugurates the conquest of Canaan. The Chronicler is drawing a parallel between the two situations, implying that Yahweh would work through King Hezekiah just as he had worked through Joshua to make sure that the disputed territory (specifically the city of Jerusalem in the case of the Chronicler) is under Yahweh's dominion. Although the Chronicler is stretching the truth in ascribing to Hezekiah a victory, just as the Dtr stretched the truth about Joshua's 'conquest', the rhetoric is clearly military. However, the people of Jerusalem are not required to fight, because an angel of Yahweh does their fighting for them, as in the parallel passage 2 Kgs 19.35. (The phrase חזק ואמץ is absent from the Kings account of the event.)

Similarly, the exhortation to 'fear not' in 2 Chron. 20.15-17 is military in character. The people are ordered in a prophetic oracle to go out and face the enemy, but they are not required to fight the battle. Instead, Yahweh causes Judah's enemies to destroy each other (vv. 22-23).

In the battle between David's forces, led by Joab and the Arameans, (1 Chron. 19.12-13) the Chronicler at first downplays the actual fighting in favour of intimidation: Joab and his troops had only to approach the Arameans for battle, and they fled (v. 14). However, since the Chronicler is repeating the battle incident almost word for word from 2 Samuel 10, he does not shy away from reporting the carnage inflicted by David on Hadadezer's troops (vv. 17-19, cf. 2 Sam. 10.12-19). In any case, Joab is in a military situation as commander of David's troops when he gives the pre-battle exhortation (v. 13), just as he (Joab) is in the DH version of the event (2 Sam. 10.12).

2 Chronicles 14 and 15 also recount stories of battles in which human action is combined with divine help in military victory. Asa is exhorted by a prophet (2 Chron. 15.7), 'be strong and do not lose courage'. As in some of the passages inserted into the DH by the exilic editor, military victory is specifically linked to religious fidelity (for example, Josh. 1.7-8), but there is no parallel passage in the DH account of Asa's reign (1 Kgs 15.9-24). The DH account is entirely lacking the narrative of Asa's war with the Ethiopians, but in the Chronicler, the phrase (mentioned above) is sandwiched between the war with Ethiopia and the war with Baasha of Israel. Clearly the context is military.

The final occurrence of חזק in a battle situation (2 Chron. 25.8) contains a negative war oracle in which a prophet advises against entering a particular altercation. He tells the king that Yahweh will bring him down before the enemy, but says, 'If, however, you do go, be strong (חזק) for the battle', which provides further evidence that חזק may be part of a stylized battle exhortation rather than an installation ritual.

In conclusion, we find that most occurrences of חזק and related expressions in the Chronicles are found in military situations, with the exception of the succession of Solomon (1 Chron. 22.13; 28.20). Although the succession of Solomon is not presented by the Chronicler as a military situation, the Chronicler's version relies heavily on the DH account,[52] including the repetition of key words and phrases (חזק is one

52. H.G.M. Williamson, 'The Accession of Solomon in the Books of the Chronicles', *VT* 26 (1976), pp. 351-61. Williamson has argued convincingly that the language in 1 Chron. 28.20 alludes directly to the passage in Josh. 1.1-6, 9, and the parallel passages in Deuteronomy, in which Joshua succeeds Moses. Although Williamson gives more credence than I to the installation genre theory, his observation that the language in 1 Chron. 28.20 is apparently based on Joshua 1 actually strengthens my argument against the installation genre: since the wording serves to imply a similarity between Joshua's succession and Solomon's, then the important aspect of the wording is probably its allusive function (to Joshua 1), and not the fact that in this case a new role (king) is indeed involved. The possibility of an old

of them). The DH account of the succession of Solomon, as I have argued elsewhere, is a military context. The Chronicler's use of language in the succession account is derivative and tells us little about the original *Sitz* of the terminology.

The other postexilic occurrence of חזק which requires examination is in Ezra. Ezra 10.4 is neither a military situation nor is it an installation of a leader. Ezra is already established in his leadership role. Furthermore, he is told not that Yahweh will be with him, but that the people will be, which is clearly different from the battle exhortations in which divine presence in warfare is the major point. There still may be a literary allusion to the story of Joshua, however. Perhaps Ezra is being urged to 'be strong' (חזק) in driving out the Canaanites (and other foreigners) from their midst (by excluding them) just as Joshua was urged to 'be strong' in driving out the Canaanites in battle. Whether or not an allusion was intended may be a moot point since the passage in Ezra 10.4 is not a complete example of the installation genre schema as described by Lohfink or Porter in any case because the promise of divine presence and help is replaced by a promise of purely human community support.

Since Lohfink and Porter both relied heavily on examples from the postexilic writings to prove their case regarding the existence of an installation genre, it is significant that only one of the military incidents described above[53] also involves a person or persons being installed in a new position of leadership, 2 Chron. 32.7. Even though Hezekiah appoints new military officers in v. 6, the exhortation concerns having courage in the upcoming battle and is clearly directed at those facing an Assyrian siege of their city.

The existence of an installation ceremony underlying the exhortation to 'be strong and bold' is not supported by the evidence. The occurrences of the phrase and its variations in the DH are found in military situations, while those occurrences in the postexilic writings are either

installation ceremony underlying the words becomes increasingly remote when one considers that every postexilic occurrence of חזק is found to be either a military situation or an allusion to a military situation from the DH.

53. Again the succession of Solomon stands out as an exceptional case, because the Chronicler's version is emphatically not placed in a military context, although his version alludes to the language of DH narratives which are in military contexts. Perhaps the Chronicler was being careful to avoid placing Solomon in a military situation which would compromise his status as a man of peace, while still using military language to draw parallels to the succession stories of leaders in the DH.

allusions to particular DH passages, clearly martial in nature, or are themselves military situations.

V. *Other War Oracles in the DH*

War oracles in the DH consist of stock phrases, arranged in various combinations. The resulting form is fairly flexible because of the variety of possible combinations; although, the phrases which make up the oracle tend to be composed of a limited number of stylized terms. An examination of the language and form of war oracles reveals a large number of repetitive word pairs resembling the word pairs in the חזק ואמץ passages. Comparison shows that these חזק passages (Deut. 31.1-8, 23 and Josh. 1.1-6, 9) contain many stock war oracle phrases, and that the form of the חזק passages is well within the flexible boundaries of variation normal to the war oracles.

A. *Arise + Active Verb of Motion*
The command to 'arise' (קום), immediately followed by another imperative is common in war oracles. The second word in the pair is usually an active verb of motion, such as 'go up' (עלה), 'go down' (רד), 'cross over' (עבר), or simply 'go' (לך). קום ועבר (arise and cross over), the word pair in Josh. 1.2, is used not only in reference to crossing the Jordan in order to conquer the promised land, but appears in war oracles addressed to Moses as well:

Now arise (קמו), and cross over (ועברו) the brook Zered...(Deut. 2.13).

Arise! Set out and cross through (קומו סעו ועברו) the Valley of Arnon. Look, I have given Sihon the Amorite, King of Heshbon, and his land into your hand; begin to take possession (רש), and contend with him in battle (Deut. 2.24).

In the latter example, there is a string of imperatives, rather than the customary pair. The middle term סעו comes from the root נסע, meaning to set out, depart, or break camp. The *qal* is used repeatedly in Numbers 33 in reference to the journeying of the people each time they broke camp, as they marched 'by their armies under the leadership of Moses and Aaron' (Num. 33.1). In Josh. 10.31, עבר is used to describe Joshua's movement of the troops from one battle to the next:

Joshua and all Israel with him passed on (ויעבר) from Libnah to Lachish, and they camped by it and fought against it.

The same words are repeated in v. 34 as the troops move from Lachish to Eglon.

In the oracle of Deut. 10.11, Moses is ordered to 'arise' and proceed (לך) on the journey (מסע from the root נסע) ahead of the people (or army, עם), to go in (בוא) and take possession (ירש) of the land. In addition to the set of imperatives which introduces the oracle, קום with an active verb of motion (לך), this passage has the second set of verbs בוא and ירש. This pattern, a verb of motion + a 'take possession' verb, is discussed in a separate section below.

In the 'fear not' (אל־תירא) oracle of Josh. 8.1, Joshua and his army (עם המלחמה) are ordered to 'arise' (קום) and 'go up' (עלה) to Ai. Another passage which uses the word-pair קום עלה in an oracle is 2 Kgs 1.1-16. In his book on the 'fear not' oracles rooted in the conventional language of war, Edgar Conrad argues that Elijah is a war prophet who is addressed with language typically associated with the conduct of war:

> In 2 Kgs. 1.1-16 Elijah is ordered to be part of Yahweh's offense and to attack Ahaziah, the king, with words of judgment pronouncing the king's imminent death... The war connotations of this whole affair are strengthened by the response the king makes to the oracle. He repeatedly sends military troops... to seize Elijah (pp. 30-31).

Conrad's argument is further strenthened by the presence in the same passage of an אל תירא oracle (v. 15). In vv. 3-4, Elijah is commanded by Yahweh in an oracle to deliver the message:

> Arise, go up (קום עלה) to meet the messengers of the king of Samaria...

Later he is ordered to 'go down' (רד) and 'fear not' (v. 15). There is no repetition of 'arise' before this second imperative verb of motion (רד), but in the latter half of the same verse, we are told that Elijah 'arose and went down' (ויקם וירד).

Similarly, in the story of the oracle against Ahab and Jezebel (1 Kgs 21.14-29), Elijah is told to 'arise and go down to meet Ahab, king of Israel' in order to pronounce judgment against him (v. 18). In language which is a demonic parody[54] of a conquest oracle, Ahab is told by Jezebel to 'arise, take possession' (קום רש) of the vineyard of Naboth (v. 15). Jezebel is the instigator of Ahab's (evil) seizure of the land, using

---

54. 'Demonic parody' is a literary term used by N. Frye in *Anatomy of Criticism: Four Essays* (Princeton: Princeton University Press, 1957) to describe the mirroring device of good and bad versions of the same archetype or narrative pattern juxtaposed in the text.

conquest language which parodies the role of the deity in a true conquest oracle as the instigator of the actions of Moses, Joshua and other
leaders. Although not particularly concerned with war oracles, David
Jobling's literary analysis of the pattern of instigation to sin in the Elijah
stories is instructive: Jezebel instigates Ahab's sin, who leads the people
into sin (Jobling was discussing primarily chapters 16-18).[55] The pattern
Jezebel-Ahab-people is like a photographic negative of the positive pattern of obedience found in connection with the good leaders of the holy
war, Yahweh-leader-people, when Yahweh gives the directives for action
through oracles to the commander. An example of the positive version
of the pattern can be seen in Joshua 8:

> Now Yahweh said to Joshua, Do not fear or be dismayed. Take all the
> people of war with you and arise, go up to Ai. See, I have given into your
> hand the king of Ai, his people, his city, and his land (v. 1).

> ... So Joshua arose (וַיָּקָם) with all the people of war to go up (לַעֲלוֹת) to
> Ai... (v. 3)

Verse 8 reiterates the pattern of instigation, as Joshua says to the warriors, 'You shall do it according to the word of Yahweh. See, I have
commanded you'. Then the narrative goes on to tell the story of the
successful ambush, carried out according to Joshua's orders, which
Joshua in turn had received directly from Yahweh in the war oracle.

The phrase 'arise and go down' (קוּם רֵד) appears in an oracle in an
overtly military context, the oracle to David in 1 Sam. 23.4: 'Arise! Go
down to Keilah, for I will give the Philistines into your hand'. This
'arise'+ verb of motion oracle does not contain the words אַל תִּירָא, but
the stock holy war phrase 'I will give ___ into your hand' occurs frequently in 'fear not' oracles in conquest narratives (Deut. 3.2; Josh. 8.1-
2; 10.8). The phrase appears with 'arise' (קוּם) alone, not paired with a
verb of motion, and without 'fear not') in the war oracle of Judg. 4.14.
In Judg. 20.28, the phrase appears with a verb of motion alone, without
קוּם or 'fear not':

> And Yahweh said 'Go up, for tomorrow I will give them into your hand'
> (cf. Judg. 3.28).

55. D. Jobling, 'Ahab's Quest for Rain: Text and Context in 1 Kings 17–18',
The Sense of Biblical Narrative, I (JSOTSup, 7; Sheffield: Sheffield Academic
Press, 1978), pp. 85-86.

These examples demonstrate that although the vocabulary is stereo-typed, any number of different combinations is possible.

Deut. 1.42 is an inversion of a standard war oracle form, warning against military engagement in the absence of divine initiative. Using some of the typical divine war terminology, the oracle turns the double verbs into negatives: לא תעלו ולא תלחמו (do not go up and do not fight). The negative phrase 'for I am not among you' is reminiscent of its posi-tive counterpart, the assurance of divine presence. In the חזק ואמץ pas-sages (Deut. 31.7, 8, 23; Josh. 1.5, 9), the warrior is assured that no man will be able to stand before him (לפניך), which can be read as another variation of the standard promise of victory through divine assistance (Josh. 1.5). Josh. 10.8, which is not one of the חזק ואמץ passages, con-tains the same assurance in an אל תירא oracle. As Yahweh's presence brings victory, his absence is said to bring about defeat: אינני בקרבכם ולא תנגפו לפני איביכם.

B. *Active Verb of Motion + 'Take Possession'*
Some oracles have an active verb of motion (usually 'go in' בוא or 'go up' עלה) with 'take possession':

> See, I have placed the land before you; go in and take possession (באו ורשו) of the land... (Deut. 1.8).

> See, Yahweh your God has placed the land before you; go up, take pos-session (עלה רש), as Yahweh has spoken to you... (Deut. 1.21).

Moses' paraphrase of the war oracle of Kadesh Barnea in Deut. 9.23 repeats the same word pair, עלו ורשו. Joshua's words to his men at Ai are noteworthy, because the word 'arise' is used as a verb of motion with 'take possession':

> Arise from your ambush and take possession (והורשתם) of the city, for Yahweh your God will deliver it into your hand (Josh. 8.7).

'Arise' in this passage is meant literally, as a verb of motion, rather than merely as an introductory word to the oracle, although Josh. 8.1 also has the conventional pair, קום עלה. Another oracle mentioned in the previous section, Deut. 10.11, has both sets of word pairs together, 'arise' + a verb of motion (קום and לך), followed by a verb of motion + 'take pos-session' (בוא and רש). Jud. 18.9 has a similar combination, although slightly less regular in form, because it includes a string of infinitives, followed in v. 10 by 'God has given it into your hand'. Deut. 2.24 is also not quite regular: it opens with 'arise' and two verbs of motion

regular: it opens with 'arise' and two verbs of motion (סעו ועברו
קומו), then continues with 'begin to take possession'
(החל רש) and 'contend with him in battle' (והתגר בו מלחמה), after the
stock war oracle phrase 'I have given ___ into your hand'.

The use of the word pair בוא and נחל in the חזק passages (Deut. 31.7;
Josh. 1.6) does not differ substantially from the usage of the more
common verbs בוא and רש. נחל occurs in the *hiphil*, while ירש occurs
mostly in the *qal*, but והורשתם in Josh. 8.7 is *hiphil*, which shows that
some variation is allowable. In all of these war oracles, the verbs ירש and
נחל refer to seizing enemy territory in battle.

C. אל־תירא *and Synonyms*

The words אל־תירא (fear not) are extremely common in war oracles in
the DH.[56] Although 'fear not' often occurs alone in war oracles, it is
sometimes paired with a word which has the same or a similar meaning,
such as admonitions not be in dread, terror or dismay. אל־תירא is paired
with אל־תחת in Deut. 1.21, an oracle which also includes the pair 'go up'
and 'take possession' (רש) along with the stock war oracle phrase
'Yahweh your God has placed the land before you'. In v. 29, within the
same story, Moses reiterates the encouragement not to fear with the
words לא תערצון ולא תיראון, which resembles the pair in Deut. 31.6,
אל־תיראו ואל־תערצו. The חזק ואמץ oracle of Deut. 31.7-8 also has the
word pair תירא ולא תחת with a verb of motion and a 'take possession'
verb, similar to Deut. 1.21. Josh. 1.9 has the other two synonyms for 'fear
not' combined as a word pair אל־תערץ ואל־תחת, and the passage also
has the verb of motion + 'take possession' word pair, as well as חזק ואמץ.
The war oracle at Ai in Josh. 8.1 includes the pair אל־תירא ואל־תחת,
combined with the pair 'arise' + a verb of motion.

The ritualized expression of war oracle language in Deut. 20.3 has
four more or less synonymous (or very similar) 'fear' words strung
together: אל־ירך לבבכם אל־תיראו ואל־תחפזו ואל־תערצו, combined with
an assurance of divine presence. The two words תירא and תערץ are
not uncommon (as demonstrated above), but the other two phrases
אל־ירך לבבכם and אל־תחפזו are not found in any other war oracle. This
uniqueness raises the possibility that the passage may be an expanded
version of a familiar literary form.

In Deut. 11.25, the 'fear' and 'dread' words are used to describe the
opponents' state of mind. Yahweh is said to put the 'dread of you'
(פחדכם) and the 'fear of you' (מוראכם) on all the land (presumably on

56. Conrad, *Fear Not Warrior*, pp. 6-37.

the land's inhabitants). Verse 25 contains a promise of victory which resembles the language of Josh. 1.5: 'No man shall be able to stand before you'. In Deut. 2.24-25, the 'fear' and 'dread' word pair is used once again to describe the state of mind which Yahweh will bring about in the opponents: פחדך ויראתך. The oracle begins in v. 24 with 'arise' and two standard verbs of motion, followed by the assurance of victory, 'I have given ____ into your hand', and then a 'take possession' verb.

We can conclude that the elements in the oracles are combined in a variety of ways although the language tends to stay within a stock vocabulary. Any two of the three words תירא, תערץ and תחת may be paired together, using the negatives אל or לא. The resulting pair may occur with the other stock war oracle phrases, a verb of motion + a 'take possession' verb, 'arise' + a verb of motion, and/or an assurance of victory such as 'I have given ____ into your hand'. The assurance of divine support or victory may include other pairs of 'fear' words describing the opponents' state of mind (divinely induced).

The חזק ואמץ oracles fit easily within the general pattern. The examination of war oracle terminology demonstrates that the חזק ואמץ passages do not differ substantially from other war oracles, in either the vocabulary or the way in which the stock words and phrases are combined. In the light of my investigation of formulaic word pairs in the war oracles, the חזק ואמץ passages begin to look less like a separate genre and more like one of many variations in the pattern of war oracle language.

The structure of the חזק ואמץ passages is also less distinctive than the discussions of Lohfink, McCarthy and Porter have implied, in comparison with war oracles generally. The structure posited for the installation genre (1. Exhortation to bravery; 2. Statement of task; 3. Assurance of divine assistance) is no different from the typical war oracle structure, which also includes an encouragement, a statement of task and an assurance of divine assistance. In addition to 'Yahweh will be with you' as an assurance of divine assistance, the phrase 'I have given/will give ____ into your hand' (Deut. 2.24; 3.2; Josh. 6.2; 8.1, 7; 10.8, 19; Judg. 3.28; 4.14; 18.10; 20.28; 1 Sam. 23.4) also falls into this category, as do the phrases 'Yahweh your God is the one fighting for you' (Deut. 3.22; cf. Deut. 1.30; Josh. 10.14, 42) and 'I will deliver them slain' (Josh. 11.6).[57] Therefore, the best way to characterize the חזק ואמץ oracles is simply to

57. These phrases are discussed in more detail in my section on Assyrian influence.

call them war oracles which begin with an exhortation to bravery. The exhortation חזק, with or without אמץ, is not at all uncommon in military narratives, so its employment as an element in a war oracle is completely consistent with its meaning and usage elsewhere.

The concept of bravery, exemplified by the phrase חזק ואמץ, is not at all out of place in war oracles; on the contrary, war oracles are suffused with references to physical courage. In addition to the חזק exhortations, the phrase 'fear not', with or without another synonymous term, is common in war oracles, as we have seen. The state of fear which the deity will induce in the enemy warriors is another fairly common element (as discussed above). All of these encouragement formulae occur in various combinations with one another; none of them are necessarily mutually exclusive. Physical courage therefore emerges as one of the central concepts of the war oracle. Like other war oracle elements discussed in the present section, the encouragement formulae tend to consist of word pairs. The phrase חזק ואמץ therefore fits easily within the war oracle pattern.

VI. *Conclusion*

In this chapter, detailed attention has been focused on the passage which opens the conquest narratives in order to clarify the sort of language of which it consists. Now that the place of Josh. 1.1-6, 9 among the war oracles in the Hebrew Bible has been established, attention must be turned to the use of the war oracle phrase חזק ואמץ as part of a rhetoric of violence to establish boundaries of inclusion and exclusion in Josiah's kingdom.

Chapter 7

THE DISCURSIVE FUNCTION OF חזק ואמץ IN THE TEXT

I. *Introduction*

The focus of the previous chapter was the war oracle which opens the Book of Joshua. The purpose of the current chapter will be to discuss how the phrase חזק ואמץ functions elsewhere in the conquest narrative of Joshua 1–12. The phrase occurs twice (Josh. 1.18; 10.25), both times in a military context and both times in connection with an execution, actual (10.24-25) or threatened (1.16-18). Furthermore, both cases are concerned with Joshua's sovereignty and both are involved in the negotiation of boundaries of one kind or another. This chapter will be a New Historicist analysis of the part that the rhetoric of violence inherent in the phrase חזק ואמץ plays in the establishment and negotiation of the borders of inclusion and exclusion, with attention to the systems of power at work in the process.

Inherent in the question of inclusion and exclusion is the matter of identity. As New Historicist Steven Mullaney says, 'any culture defines itself in terms of its Others, whether imaginary or real'.[1] In the basic structure of the conquest narrative in Joshua, Israelites are insiders and Canaanites are outsiders (Others) to be utterly destroyed in battle; however, some of the Book of Joshua consists of a series of what Greenblatt terms 'negotiations and exchanges',[2] which determine who will be accepted and who will be categorized as the unacceptable Other.

In many of the incidents in the conquest narrative, the communal entity 'Israel' is presented as though it had clearly marked ethnic borders. Therefore, throughout the Book of Joshua there are a number of public assemblies or processions which include the entire nation, 'all

1.   S. Mullaney, *The Place of the Stage: License, Play, and Power in Renaissance England* (Chicago: University of Chicago Press, 1988), p. 92.
2.   Greenblatt, *Negotiations*, p.12.

Israel', or at least all of its male members. For example, the entity 'all Israel' crosses the Jordan as a unified group when it enters the land in a solemn procession, and then the crossing is given commemoration in a ceremony at which the entire group is said to be present.

The collective circumcision of the male population (5.1-12) functions as another ritual of communal identity. Whatever the practice may have meant in ancient times, the incident in the Book of Joshua is clearly a ceremony of inclusion and exclusion, sealing the borders of the community. All insiders are to be circumcised, outsiders are not. Circumcision confers a physical mark of insider status.

The ceremony at Ebal (8.30-35) also functions as a ritual of communal identity. While most scholars have sought evidence of an actual religious ceremony underlying the reading of the law mentioned in the text, an examination of the assembly's meaning in its literary context is a more fruitful approach. The point is not whether or not leaders in ancient Israel stood before the people and read from a Book of the Law; the more important point is that several different things are being linked together rhetorically. First, the gathering follows immediately after a victorious battle. As discussed below, battles function as rituals of inclusion and exclusion in a very basic way, drawing the boundaries of the community and its opponents. Second, since Yahweh is said to have given them their victory, the text reinforces the community's connection with Yahweh as a national deity. Third, the sovereignty of Yahweh is linked with the sovereignty-by-proxy of the national leaders in hierarchical order: Joshua, the elders, officers and judges (v. 33), and, most importantly, the legacy left behind by 'Moses the servant of Yahweh'. Therefore, obedience to the hierarchical chain of command is linked with faith in the deity and the heritage of the law, all of which converge in the person of King Josiah at the time of the composition of the DH.

Even the division of the land by lot to the tribes is presented as a cohesive public ceremony. Although the group was divided into separate tribes, the effect of making the division of the land into an assembly of the national entity as a whole places the emphasis on the communal nature of the act. The message is reinforced that tribal identity is to be regarded as a subcomponent of national identity.

In all the episodes mentioned above, the narrator informs us repeatedly that the events take place in an assembly of 'all Israel'. The emphasis on 'all Israel' indicates an attempt to assert that the existence of such a thing is unproblematic; that there is a national entity 'Israel' with clearly defined borders and an unequivocal identity. However, the heavy emphasis raises the question whether exactly the opposite may be the case. Otherwise, why would it require reinforcement with constant repetition? Further evidence that the borders are permeable is offered by the episodes, discussed below, in which inclusion is negotiated.

II. *Joshua 1.18 and the Boundaries of Community*

Joshua's first action, after receiving the war oracle ordering the conquest and urging him to be strong and bold with the phrase חזק ואמץ, is to pass through the military encampment, still on the far side of the Jordan River from the promised land, giving marching orders. The focus of the remainder of ch. 1, however, is on the transjordanian tribes, Reuben, Gad and the half-tribe of Manasseh, who have no personal stake in the territory to be conquered when the Jordan is crossed. They already posses their inheritance in the Transjordan. Their position is therefore liminal: they belong to the community designated 'all Israel', but they are to settle on the outside of the symbolic boundary which marks the territory targeted in the conquest narrative. Their speech to Joshua, in which they declare their fidelity to him and their solidarity to the cause of the conquest, is, therefore, crucial in determining their place in the communal identity. They affirm their position (as insiders) with military terminology: they agree to obey Joshua's commands and they promise to execute any among their number who refuse to co-operate in the conquest. Finally, their speech ends with the military exhortation חזק ואמץ which affirms their enthusiastic participation in the community's military enterprise.

A. *Military Language and its Part in Setting the Boundaries of Community*

A military narrative, almost by definition, requires two groups: a set of insiders, from whose point of view events are told, and a set of opponents, the Others. War is more than merely a background for working out how the community of insiders is constructed. In Josh. 1.16-18, a rhetoric of violence plays an important part in negotiating the social boundary.

A simple analogy from the anthropological literature illustrates how a rhetoric of violence may help to create and maintain communal identity. In his semiotic analysis of the relationship between literature and violence in north Arabia, anthropologist M.E. Meeker[3] discovered a revealing pattern in the oral literature of a tribe of camel-herding nomads, the Rwala, whose way of life involved them constantly in camel- and cattle-raiding expeditions and resultant tribal warfare. Meeker found that most Rwala literature was concerned with their life of raiding and warfare. It was this 'political adventurism', as Meeker termed it, which gave the Rwala their sense of identity as a tribal entity. Their recitation of formative events (raids and battles) in their history enabled them to make sense of their collective experiences, which forged them into a people with a shared past.

Although most of the Rwala literature concerns human warfare taking place in the earthly realm, Meeker found that they had a few myths about the life beyond. As in their poems and narratives of warfare, their paradise myths are also built around a structure of self (Rwala) and Other:

> Paradise and hell are not populated with those who have done right and wrong. They are seen in purely tribal terms. All the Rwala are in paradise. All their enemies are in hell... All the Rwala in paradise are free to raid their former, worldly enemies at will.[4]

At the same time, the Rwala valued above all the peaceful domesticity which they intended to enjoy in the afterlife:

> In paradise we find a fully formed and exuberant domesticity. There is an abundance of pasture. All the Rwala live together in harmony. Everyone is perpetually young. Everyone can marry. Everyone has many children... The herds are large. Each of these features suggests a high valuation of domestic life, and such a high valuation is the basis on which peace must be built among the camel-herding nomads.[5]

Similarly, one of the most striking aspects of the military narratives of the DH is the oddity of a society whose literature places a high value on peace and 'rest', while accepting, even glorifying, military violence and destruction on a grand scale. According to the Dtr, the point of the warfare which dominates the narrative is to reach the state of 'rest' from

3. M.E. Meeker, *Literature and Violence in North Arabia*. My discussion of Meeker's work in this section is not intended to be a thorough look at the anthropoligical literature on violence. Instead it is simply offered as a particularly appropriate example to illustrate certain points about the relationship between literature (written or oral) and violence.

4. Meeker, *Literature and Violence*, p. 105.

5. Meeker, *Literature and Violence*, p. 105.

enemies whom they will defeat with Yahweh's help (Deut. 12.10; 25.19; Josh. 21.44; 2 Sam. 7.1). Rwala literature also put the quest for an outcome of peace in terms of insiders and outsiders (Others), and like the Dtr, the Rwala perceived a divine order to the arrangement of inclusion and exclusion.

In another Rwala myth of a paradise located beyond the horizon, Meeker again found a vision of a peaceful domestic structure, which was associated explicitly with Allah. Regarding this structure, Meeker concluded that:

> Among the Bedouins, the hope for the existence of a moral authority, which would protect and support human life, is linked with the possibility of perceiving an order in the world... which favors a domestic way of life.[6]

At the same time, the Rwala also believed in divine intervention in warfare. Although they and their opponents were all of the same religion (Muslim), the Rwala viewed Allah as a transcendent actor in their disputes. In some of the war narratives Meeker examined, battle was inaugurated with an invocation of the deity:

> Let Allah decide between us and him... Oh ye Arabs, shoe your horses and get your supplies ready, for tomorrow we shall go on a raid as ordered by our highest commander.

> Let Allah judge between them and us! Up and at the Beni Sakhr![7]

The 'highest commander' is the deity, who sends the Rwala into battle. Meeker points out that the literal meaning of the Arabic root translated as 'decide' or 'judge' is 'to see', and this emphasis on visual perception is an indication that the Rwala perceive the manifestation of the deity's authority as a divine act of 'looking' from one man or tribe to the next in order to judge in connection with political struggles. In some cases, warfare is seen as a response to provocation, which causes an ethical element to be introduced. For example, Meeker cites a narrative in which a wise and judicious tribal chief who desires peace has no alternative but to go into battle against an aggressive adventurer whose provocations cannot be ignored. However, Meeker's main point is that most of the Rwala literature contains not even a pretense of a coherent philosophy of ethics governing the insider/outsider distinction. The

6. Meeker, *Literature and Violence*, p. 107.
7. Meeker, *Literature and Violence*, pp. 101-102.

Rwala perceived Allah's authority, according to Meeker, in terms of a strategic response to political circumstances, rather than in the form of a systematic political or ethical theory.[8] In the examples above, as in other Rwala war narratives, 'human passions are the real and concrete roots of these dreadful events',[9] and the 'passions' of which Meeker speaks are centered around feelings of group identity, self and Other.

Like the war narratives in the Bible, the Rwala literature reveals an attempt to make sense of human experience, to discern some divine design in human affairs, including the violent side of human life. By using literature, the Rwala bards gave shape to their community's experience of warfare, which was one of the constitutive experiences in the formation of its identity. Although peace is presented as ideal, the literature of warfare gives form and meaning to the struggle to attain the ideal and, in doing so, creates the boundaries of affinity and estrangement which mark where the community begins and ends.

One of the functions of war literature, both ancient and modern, is the shaping of national (or group) identity, according to Catherine Savage Brosman.[10] She correctly points out that while the literature of war is voluminous, the secondary scholarly treatments of the subject deal mostly with the history of the theme and its mode of expression, rather than with the functions that war literature serves. Although the focus of her article is the modern period, some of her observations apply universally.

War literature may be used to inspire a warlike spirit in the population. It may also serve the collective purpose of memorializing great military deeds as part of the history of a people, forming a sense of identity in solidarity. Conversely, especially in the modern period, war literature may function as a way of discrediting the idea that war is glorious. She cites as an example the post-Vietnam films in America, but one could multiply examples from other cultures, such as the rise of a certain branch of German Expressionism after World War I, including the paintings of Max Beckman and the plays of Hans Borchert. Some of the Hebrew prophets, Amos for example (mentioned in a previous chapter), used military rhetoric in a similarly ironic way, to undermine the standard ideologies of war prevalent in the dominant culture.

8. Meeker, *Literature and Violence*, p. 102.
9. Meeker, *Literature and Violence*, p. 104.
10. C.S. Brosman, 'The Functions of War Literature', *South Central Review* 9.1 (1992), pp. 85-98.

Nevertheless, says Brosman, even the artistic critiques of war are evidence of its centrality to the human experience, demonstrating war's ability to 'appeal to what is deepest in human beings', both individually and communally. In the modern period, war literature may inspire not just a sense of national purpose, but of personal challenge. Because of the Romantic and post-Romantic priveleging of the self, modern war literature may foreground the personal encounter with fear and the question of conduct under fire. However, she notes, even the expression of individual valour is collective; valour is defined by, exercised on behalf of, and ratified by the community.[11]

The function of war literature, ancient as well as modern, also includes another communal dimension: the working out of the question of identity within the national context. Brosman mentions the plethora of films and novels featuring the Jewish soldier or the Hispanic soldier in modern America.[12] The issue of forging diverse subgroups into a national entity is equally central to the Book of Joshua.

Shakespeare's *Henry V* provides another good analogy. By yoking together diverse peoples, the Welshman, Irishman, and Scot who fight at Agincourt alongside the Englishmen, King Hal symbolically tames the last wild areas in the British Isles, areas that in the sixteenth century represented the last vestiges of a vanishing tribalism. The three characters are each made to speak in stereotypical accents, representing not what is truly alien but what is predictable and automatic. According to Greenblatt:

> ...they give pleasure because they persuade an audience of its own mobility and complexity; even a spectator gaping passively at the play's sights and manipulated by its rhetoric is freer than these puppets jerked on the strings of their own absurd accents.[13]

---

11. Brosman, 'Functions', p. 86.

12. She mentions specifically Norman Mailer's *The Naked and the Dead*, but ethnic and regional diversity is almost a cliché in American war films. The World War II "bomber crew" always seems to include a mixture of Northern and Southern, rural and urban, and an eclectic ethnic mix. Even modern films which attempt to discredit the enterprise of war often use the same formula. For example, the anti-war film *Apocalypse Now* had a boat crew consisting of an urban African American from the Northeast, a blond surfer from California, and a chef from New Orleans. The issue of subgroup and national identity may be worked out whether the war itself is presented as worthwhile or as senseless.

13. Greenblatt, *Negotiations*, pp. 56-57.

Through language, Shakespeare managed (at least within the play) to civilize symbolically the untamable Celtic tribes, something which was impossible for Queen Elizabeth to accomplish (nor has it been accomplished since) in the historical context which gave birth to the 'history plays'.

A similar use of history to address the issues of a different sociological context is seen in the Book of Joshua. Like Shakespeare, the Dtr was concerned with forging 'the martial national state', as Greenblatt said of *Henry V*,[14] out of a diverse population. Like Shakespeare, the Dtr also was concerned with the monarchy's role in the formation and maintenance of national identity. In Joshua, the tribal leaders are given a particular place in the hierarchy of dominance: under the central authority of Joshua and Yahweh. Tribal identity, therefore, is cemented firmly into place as secondary, under the umbrella of 'all Israel'. Tribal and regional concerns are to be subordinated to national ones in the 'martial state' being forged by Josiah, just as tribal identity and authority were subordinated under Joshua in the (alleged) original formation of early Israel as a nation, in the Dtr's telling of the narrative.

The relationship between force and discourse is also explored by Bruce Lincoln in his book on discourse and the construction of societal boundaries.[15] Lincoln defines force as the exercise or threat of physical violence. It is regularly employed by those in power to compel obedience and suppress deviance. That way, the elite group in power is not only able to preserve social stability but is also able to preserve a specific configuration in which they and certain others occupy positions of privilege. Further, says Lincoln, the elites may use force to effect social change. For example, in the case of imperial expansion, they direct the force at their disposal outside their own borders in campaigns of conquest through which ever-larger social aggregates with more complex patterns of organization can be constructed.

However, although new territories may be taken by conquest, successful control of the population within those territories depends upon the transformation of the peoples' consciousness so that they come to consider themselves members of the larger imperial society rather than vanquished subjects of a foreign power. Such a radical recasting of collective identity, which amounts to the dismantling of a previously

14. Greenblatt, *Negotiations*, p. 56.
15. B. Lincoln, *Discourse and the Construction of Society: Comparative Studies of Myth, Ritual and Classification* (Oxford: Oxford University Press, 1989).

significant sociopolitical border and the corollary construction of a new, encompassing sociopolitical aggregate, can hardly be accomplished through force alone. Physical force is also not an adequate long-term response to the episodes of revolt and rebellion that occur in empires within which conquered peoples remain imperfectly integrated and retain their pre-conquest loyalties. Force can quell these outbreaks only at the cost of further alienating subject populations. Ultimately, Lincoln goes on to say, that which either holds a society together or takes it apart is sentiment, and the chief instrument with which such sentiment may be aroused and manipulated is discourse.

Discourse supplements force in several important ways. Lincoln reminds us that a society is basically a grouping of people who feel bound together as a collectivity and who feel themselves separate from others who fall outside their group. Various factors help to mark and enforce such social boundaries, such as language, topography, diet, patterns of economic exchange, customs, moral values, aesthetic taste, and so forth. When groups and individuals note similarities and dissimilarities of whatever sort between themselves and others, they can employ these as instruments to evoke specific sentiments out of which social borders are constructed. Lincoln refers to these as affinity and estrangement, feelings of likeness and mutual attachment, or feelings of alienation and otherness. In order to be successful, a discourse must be able to command a following by eliciting those sentiments out of which new social formations can be constructed.

Discourse may be verbal, such as political speeches, or a written text such as the DH, but discourse may also take other forms, such as the symbolic discourses of spectacle, gesture, costume, edifice, icon, musical performance, and any number of rituals. Those in power may employ discourse to mystify the inequalities of the social order and win the consent of those over whom power is exercised, thereby obviating the need for the direct use of force. Yet discourse can also serve members of subordinate classes in their attempts to demystify, delegitimate, and dismantle the established norms and institutions that play a role in constructing their subordination. Because there are virtually infinite grounds on which individual and group similarity and dissimilarity may be perceived and corresponding sentiments of affinity and estrangement may be evoked, the borders of society are never a simple matter. In reality, there are always potential bases for dissociating oneself and one's group from others, and the majority of social sentiments are ambivalent mixes in which potential sources of affinity are overlooked or suppressed in the interests of establishing a clear social border.

Although Lincoln's analysis sheds some light on the issue of boundaries and power, a fundamental problem emerges when he uses the term 'elite', because it implies a static relationship of dominance and submission. According to Foucault, power relations are not simply a matter of dominance and submission, but rather, are a:

> ...power exercised rather than possessed; it is not the 'privilege', acquired or preserved, of the dominant class, but the overall effect of its strategic positions—an effect that is manifested and sometimes extended by the position of those who are dominated...[16]

Foucault goes on to say that this power is not simply forced upon those who do not 'have it' by those who do, but rather is transmitted by them and through them, so that these relations go down into the depths of society, constituting society's very structure.

The structure of boundaries and hierarchy in the Book of Joshua pivots around the concept of voluntary submission to authority. Those who submit voluntarily to the authority of Joshua (and by analogy King Josiah) are afforded insider status; they are allowed to live within the borders, ethnic and geographic, of the community. Those who resist or dissent are stigmatized as Other, and the punishment for Otherness is death. Therefore, the mechanism of voluntary submission to authority in the Joshua text is one of the primary ways that the power relations being asserted are transmitted by and through those who are dominated.

Greenblatt's example of the Celtic tribes, mentioned above, is relevant once again. Although they represent the 'foreign', their presence at Agincourt represents the taming of foreignness and demonstrates how sovereignty is transmitted through the voluntary actions and words of the dominated. As another critic of Shakespeare's history plays observed, 'The right people of the play merge into a larger order; the wrong people resist or misuse that larger order'.[17]

Although the rituals of inclusion and the rhetoric of violence against Others give an impression of clear social borders, the distinction between Israel and the Others based on ethnic, cultural and religious differences begins to break down immediately in the Book of Joshua, as noted

---

16. M. Foucault, *Surveiller et punir*, p. 30 (pp. 26-27 in the Eng.).

17. Norman N. Holland, *2 Henry IV* (New York: New American Library, 1965), p. xxxvi; cf. Greenblatt, *Negotiations*, p.52.

above. The ostensible ideology, in which the cohesive group 'all Israel' is to take control of the promised land inside the boundary[18] and institute pure Yahweh worship there, is already undermined in the first chapter by the presence of the Transjordanians on the margins of the community, but they merge into the larger order by taking part in the military violence associated with the conquest of a territory which is not for their own occupation. Their participation has a symbolic significance beyond what their numbers could be expected to contribute to the success of the conquest. By their co-operation and obedience, they negotiate their position from marginality to inclusion.

B. *Negotiating the Margins: the Transjordanians Compared with the Gibeonites*

The Transjordanians are addressed by Joshua in a public assembly. In negotiating their place in the larger order, they answer him with an oath of loyalty (Josh. 1.18), using the war oracle language that opens the Book of Joshua: חזק ואמץ.

The book of Joshua begins with a clear delineation of the lines of authority: Yahweh, as the national deity, is to be supreme commander of military affairs. Since Moses, the servant of Yahweh is dead, Joshua the servant of Moses is elevated to second in command, representing Yahweh on earth. The people are represented as a cohesive entity under the central authority of Joshua. Although they are arranged hierarchically under tribal authority, the text continually reinforces the idea that the people are to find their primary identity as parts of the unified whole, 'all Israel'; tribal identity is to be secondary.

The military hierarchy continues to receive emphasis after Yahweh puts Joshua in charge. The first thing Joshua does when the deity has finished giving him his orders to cross the Jordan and conquer the territory, is command the officers of the people, telling them to pass through the camp, commanding (in turn) the people, with exactly the same orders.

> Pass through the midst of the camp and command the people, saying, 'Prepare provisions for yourselves. Within three days you are to cross this Jordan to go in and take possession of this land, which Yahweh your god is giving you to possess' (Josh. 1.11).

18. D. Jobling, 'The Jordan a Boundary: Transjordan in Israel's Ideological Geography', *The Sense of Biblical Narrative*, II (JSOTSup, 39; Sheffield: Sheffield Academic Press, 1986), pp. 88-134.

The repetitiousness underscores the hierarchical military values of the text.

Once the lines of authority have been established and commands given, Joshua turns to the Transjordanians, his first marginal case. His words include them as part of the whole. He tells them to cross over with the rest and help them to take possession; afterwards, they may return to their own possessions on the other side of the Jordan. They willingly place themselves under Joshua's authority: '...all that you have commanded us we will do, and wherever you send us we will go' (Josh. 1.16). The lines of military hierarchy are once again reinforced when they promise to obey Joshua, just as they obeyed Moses 'in all things' (v. 17). The most telling part of their submission to authority, however, is their elaboration on their willingness to obey and to enforce obedience in their own internal ranks, in v. 18: 'Anyone who rebels against your command and does not obey your words in everything which you command us, he shall be put to death'. Anyone who steps outside the lines of authority incurs the same fate as the Others, the enemy troops: death.

Further light may be shed on the Transjordanians by comparing their situation to that of another group at the margins of the community, the Gibeonites. The Transjordanians have the right ethnicity, the right patriarchal lineage, but they receive their inheritance outside the symbolic boundary, the Jordan: right ethnicity (qualified for insider status), wrong geographical location (outside). On the other hand, the Gibeonites are a group of people in exactly the obverse situation: wrong ethnicity, but inside the boundary of the 'pure' geographical location. A look at this pair of marginal cases demonstrates that the price of inclusion is voluntary submission to the authority structure represented by Joshua and his military men, and the alternative is the standard punishment for otherness: death.

The Gibeonites in ch. 9 also voluntarily submit to Joshua's central authority and take a place in the hierarchy. 'We are your servants', they announce to Joshua in v. 8. With elaborate trickery, they get Israel to make a covenant by presenting themselves as inhabitants of a land faraway when they are actually ethnic outsiders living in the promised land. So their problem is the obverse of the Transjordanians: the Transjordanians were the right people on the wrong land, while the Gibeonites were the wrong people on the right land. Their motive for submitting to Joshua is their fear of his, and Yahweh's, military prowess.

They had heard of what Yahweh and Joshua had done to destroy other opponents. Joshua made a covenant with them, backed up by an oath sworn by the leaders of the congregation: 'Joshua made peace with them and made a covenant with them, to let them live...' (v. 15). Then when their trickery was discovered, the congregation became annoyed because of the deception, but the leaders said:

> We have sworn by Yahweh, god of Israel, so we cannot touch them. This will we do for them: let them live, lest wrath be upon us for the oath which we swore to them. The leaders said, 'Let them live' (vv. 19-21).

In return for their deception, the Gibeonites were made into permanent slaves, to hew wood and draw water for Israel, which does not seem like a very appealing covenant from the Gibeonite point of view. The Gibeonites, however, seemed to accept their lowly status with gratitude for their lives.

> we greatly feared for our lives because of you, and we have done this thing (meaning the deception). Now, behold, we are in your hand. As it seems good and right in your eyes to do unto us, do it. So he did unto them. He delivered them out of the hand of the sons of Israel, so that they did not slay them (vv. 24-26).

Thus they were spared the usual punishment for Otherness, which was death, because of their voluntary submission to Joshua's and Yahweh's authority. They were allowed to live and even to stay within the geographical boundaries of the promised land, but they had to take a lowly place in the hierarchy and remain in it forever.

Like the many examples above of incidents staged as public assemblies, the negotiations with both the Transjordanians (1.10-18) and the Gibeonites (9.19) took place in public situations. The Transjordanians in particular were addressed by Joshua in a public ceremony of national identity, unity and cohesion, using the rhetoric of violence which had just been introduced in the war oracle that opens the Book of Joshua: חזק ואמץ. The Transjordanians (1.16-18) are presented as a unit, speaking the words with one voice.

Jobling pointed out the importance of the Jordan River as a boundary in Israel's ideological geography in his structural analysis of the Transjordanians' situation. He observed that the idea of Israelites living east of the Jordan symbolically broke the integrity of Israel: 'One people about to enter one land becomes two groups with different territorial intentions'.[19] Although the Transjordanians are living outside the boundary of the promised land, says Jobling, their problematic situation may be neutralized by crossing the Jordan for the service of Yahweh.[20] The point is worth making that the 'service' required of them is specifically military service. Even though Jobling's essay moves in a different direction, the concept of military action playing a role in the creation of boundaries by inspiring a sense of communal identity once again arises as a primary theme in the Dtr's tale.

In the resolution of the Transjordanian problem in Joshua 22, the envoy of chieftains sent to deal with the Transjordanians (after they have built an altar) is said to speak collectively for 'the whole congregation of Yahweh' (v.16). When the altar-building on the far side of the symbolic boundary, the Jordan, raises the possibility that the Transjordanians might establish an independent cult community,[21] the word used to describe their iniquity, מעל (22.16), is the same as that used for Achan's action (Josh. 7.1; 22.20). The fact that the name of Achan is raised in the speech to the Transjordanians in 22.20 indicates an analogy in their situations, the commitment of an 'iniquity' which breaks the symbolic unity of 'all Israel' under its national deity. The Transjordanians are pointedly reminded that Achan died alone in his iniquity (v. 20). The situation is negotiated to a peaceful conclusion only when the Transjordanians emphasize that Yahweh is indeed the deity to whom they are pledged (v. 22) and that they have no intention of setting themselves up as a rival cult performing sacrificial offerings (vv. 26-28). If a peaceful solution had not been reached, the result for the transjordanians would have been the usual punishment for Otherness: destruction (v. 33).

III. *Joshua 10.24-26 and Public Execution*

While the Transjordanian situation is successfully resolved in the text, the Gibeonites remain marginal. Their presence poses a crucial problem: by their trickery, they had created an opening at the ethnic boundaries of the community. As Mullaney points out, 'any structure of ideas, values, or beliefs, whether it takes the shape of a political philosophy, a religion, or a ceremonial city, is vulnerable at its margins'.[22] The same applies to

---

19. Jobling, *Sense of Biblical Narrative*, II, p. 103.
20. Jobling, *Sense of Biblical Narrative*, II, p. 106.
21. Mayes, *The Story of Israel*, p. 41.
22. Mullaney, *The Place of the Stage*, pp. 37-38.

an ethnic community. The execution of the enemy kings in 10.25 serves
to reaffirm the margins of insider/outsider status with a display of power.

A. *Otherness and Obedience*

The incident is staged as a public ceremony of national identity, unity
and cohesion against outside enemies. Like the Achan incident
(discussed below), Josh. 10.24-26 is a ritual of execution, but, in this
case, the ritual involves the execution of enemy kings who clearly fall
into the category of Others as the enemies of Israel. How they come to
be described as Israel's enemies, however, is noteworthy: they become
Israel's foes because of the Gibeonites (Josh. 10.1-7). The Gibeonites are
placed on the same side (as Israel) of the boundary of identity and
Otherness when the enemies of Gibeon become the enemies of Israel.

At the same time that the rhetoric of violence functions in precisely
orchestrated ways to make examples of the Others, it simultaneously
serves to control the lines of authority within the community. Like the
other rituals of inclusion and exclusion discussed above, the incident in
Josh. 10.24-26 takes place before all Israel, or at least its male members:
'Joshua summoned all the men of Israel' (v. 24). The hierarchical system
is reinforced once again by having the military chiefs take part physically
in the ritual by placing their feet on the necks of the defeated rulers. The
enemy kings embodied their peoples' national identities just as Joshua
served as the embodiment of the nation Israel. By having the chiefs take
part in the ritual in such a graphic manner, Joshua was, in one gesture,
sharing his power with those just under him in the hierarchy as an integral part of the national entity and, at the same time, containing that
power under his central authority, making it clearly subordinate to him.

Furthermore, Yahweh's place at the top of the hierarchy is reinforced
by the assurance of future military victories in Yahweh's name: 'Thus
will Yahweh do to all your enemies...' (v. 25). The message is clear that
the people are to find their military success through their identification
with their national deity. National spirit, religious sentiment and authority
structure are all to be one unified whole which makes them who they
are as a people.

The assurance of further victories follows immediately after Joshua's
words echoing the war oracle language that Yahweh had used speaking
to him in the original oracle of Joshua 1 that inaugurated the conquest
narrative and established Joshua's place in the hierarchy. The same
rhetoric of violence that had been used to express the national purpose

in Josh. 1.1-9, אל־תיראו ואל־תחתו חזקו ואמצו, is being reiterated in Josh. 10.25 to retrace the boundaries of Otherness which had already been established by the battle stories preceding it. Both scenes take place in the same military setting: the camp of the army.

The scene in Josh. 10.24-26 is far grislier, however. The dead enemy kings, the exemplary Others, are hung on trees in public view after Joshua 'smote them' (v. 26). As Boling makes clear, the intent is again a discursive one: 'This is not death by hanging nor crucifixion, but the public exposure of the corpses after execution so as to inspire fear',[23] a typical Assyrian tactic in psychological warfare. A number of Assyrian palace reliefs show scenes in which corpses or parts of corpses of defeated enemies are graphically displayed hanging from trees or poles.

The parallel with an Assyrian rhetoric of violence goes even further. In the Annals of Tukulti-Ninurta I, the Assyrian king humiliates the captured Babylonian king in the same way that Joshua and his men humiliate their captives: 'His royal neck I trod with my foot, like a footstool'. Clearly the blatant allusion to Assyrian tactics on the part of the Dtr was intended to inspire fear and obedience in his readership, the subjects of King Josiah.

Anthropologist David Riches says that violent acts constitute a performance,[24] and that violence itself has a symbolic as well as an instrumental function.

> violent acts fulfill both instrumental and expressive functions... a particular act of violence will, at the same time, transform the social environment in a practical sense and strikingly dramatize important social ideas.[25]

Furthermore, Riches goes on to say, the same act or image of violence will achieve more than one expressive purpose: the act or image offers to the perpetrator's own group a statement about his 'worth as a political associate', and to the rival group, a statement about his own group's political and social capabilities.[26]

Riches' observations refer to acts of violence in general, but his principles take on a distinctive cast when applied to a sacred text in which the violence is attributed to a deity. The text of Joshua indicates that the

23. Boling, *Joshua*, p. 286.
24. D. Riches, *The Anthropology of Violence* (Oxford: Oxford University Press, 1986). Riches uses the word 'performance' in a way which is similar to Foucault's use of the word 'ritual' below.
25. Riches, *The Anthropology of Violence*, p. 11.
26. Riches, *The Anthropology of Violence*, p. 14.

deity's purpose in perpetrating violence is to advertise his worth as a political associate:

> Yahweh gave them rest on every side according to all that he had sworn to their fathers, and not one of all their enemies stood before them. Yahweh gave all their enemies into their hand (Josh. 21.44).

Evidently, to the Dtr, the reward for adhering to this particular god is victorious occupation of the disputed territory and subjugation of enemies. The point is made even more explicitly in Joshua 2 when the deity's mighty military deeds are given as the reason that Rahab chooses to pledge her fidelity to Yahweh. The deity's worth as a political associate extends also to his human representatives. Rahab seeks the protection of Joshua's men when she says to the spies:

> I know that Yahweh has given you the land, and the terror of you has fallen on us... (Josh.2.9)... For we have heard how Yahweh dried up the water of the Red Sea before you... and what you did to the two kings of the Amorites who were beyond the Jordan, Sihon and Og, whom you utterly destroyed (Josh. 2.10).

Several expressive purposes are thus accomplished at once. The deity receives the credit/blame, enabling the people to distance themselves from responsibility for the perpetration of violence. Secondly, the hierarchical authority structure represented by the deity Yahweh and his human delegates is rhetorically reinforced: the men under Yahweh's military command receive homage from Rahab precisely because of their ability utterly to destroy opponents (Sihon and Og) in battle. Likewise in the battle reports of Joshua 10 and 11, the emphasis is on total destruction of the enemy.

> Joshua captured Makkedah... he utterly destroyed it and every person in it. He left no survivor (Josh.10.28).

> And Yahweh gave it (Libnah) with its king into the hands of Israel, and he struck it and every person who was in it with the edge of the sword. He left no survivor (Josh.10.30).

> And Joshua and all Israel with him passed on from Lachish to Eglon, and they camped by it and fought against it. And on that day they captured it and struck it with the edge of the sword, and utterly destroyed every person who was in it... (Josh.10.34-35).

The pattern continues through ch. 11. Time after time the same words are repeated: 'he utterly destroyed every person who was in it; he left no survivor'. The text makes its point absolutely clear: the punishment for Otherness is death.

Therefore, one ideological purpose of the conquest narrative is to send a message to Josiah's potential enemies. The text is more concerned with demonstrating to the populace the extent of the governing authorities' strength, and therefore their worth as political associates, than with sending to external rival groups a statement about their capabilities. For the in-group, in the case of the conquest narrative, there is the need to constitute themselves as a power structure in the wake of imperial domination.

Yahweh's advertisement of himself and his representatives as worthwhile political associates carries within it an implicit warning: a worthwhile ally is, by definition, a dangerous foe to those who refuse to align themselves with the right side by voluntary submission to its authority structures.

However, Foucault would point out that power relations are not univocal:

> they define innumerable points of confrontation, focuses of instability, each of which has its own risks of conflict, of struggles...[27]

In other words, rather than two solid blocks on either side of a boundary, the entire field of relations is a complex series of social interactions. Inclusion and exclusion are therefore not simple matters. By finding or constructing an Other, the boundaries are made to appear, at least to a limited extent, reconstituted. After the rupture caused by the admission of the Gibeonites, the public execution in Josh. 10.25 recreated the illusion of a seamless boundary.

B. *Another Public Execution: the Achan Incident*

The Achan incident in Joshua 7 is the only other example in the Book of Joshua of a public execution. Therefore, it requires attention as a point of comparison and also for the context it supplies for the execution in Joshua 10.

The execution of Achan can be described as discourse (in Lincoln's sense of the term, above) on two interrelated levels. Historical writing is one type of discourse because telling the story of a particular group is intended to evoke feelings of affinity within the group and to construct boundaries of identity, as in the example of the Rwala (above). The Dtr is using discourse at that level to evoke feelings and to draw boundaries which define the community of Josiah's constituents.

27. Foucault, *Surveiller*, p. 31 (ET p. 27).

Within the text, the leader Joshua is also using another type of discourse, particularly certain rituals that establish boundaries of insider/outsider status. The public execution of Achan is one such ritual. The public execution, says Foucault, has a 'juridico-political function. It is a ceremonial by which a momentarily injured sovereignty is reconstituted'. According to Foucault, the public execution belongs to a whole series of great rituals in which power is eclipsed and restored, such as coronation, entry of the king into a conquered city, and the submission of rebellious subjects. The criminal represents an element of disorder. His execution in public is not intended merely to re-establish justice. It is, instead, a reactivation of power.

Foucault calls public execution one of the 'ceremonies by which power is manifested'. He further explains that execution is a political ritual in which the right to punish becomes 'an aspect of the sovereign's right to make war on his enemies'. Because the law represents the will of the sovereign, a breach of the law is also an attack on him and all that he stands for, the monarch and the monarchy as an institution, as well as the realm over which he reigns. Therefore, committing a crime places the sovereign in contempt, deploying before all eyes, as Foucault says, a force which must be countered.

The force employed against the criminal must, therefore, be out of proportion to the actual crime, in order to display the strength of the all-powerful sovereign, to make everyone aware of the unrestrained presence of the sovereign. The word sovereign has a more complicated meaning in the DH than it does in Foucault's examples from French history because, in the text of Joshua, the sovereign is really Yahweh. Therefore, Joshua, King Josiah's stand-in, can appear to be motivated only by loyalty and obedience to the deity, rather than by an attempt to assert his own power. This is one of the rhetorical devices employed to mystify the inequities of the social order and to advance the power of the monarchy. The rhetoric depends upon the evocation of sentiment by employing a kind of false modesty: Yahweh is really in charge. Joshua (and by extension Josiah) poses merely as Yahweh's humble servant, acting as his proxy. However, since Joshua is functioning as the deity's proxy, Joshua happens to be the most powerful of all human beings since he and only he has been chosen by Yahweh (according to the internal logic of the text) as an instrument of the deity's sovereignty. Furthermore, since Joshua is standing in as the embodiment of national identity for King Josiah, the discourse of and within the text is more politically self-serving and not quite as selflessly pious as it appears on the surface. The things that Joshua and King Josiah do in apparently humble servitude for Yahweh, the sovereign, happen to enhance their own power and sovereignty immeasurably. One of the uses of the Joshua story for King Josiah is a solidification of the monarchy's role.

The rhetoric of the centralization of power is already encoded in the text of Joshua, particularly in Joshua's words to Achan. The hierarchy under Yahweh is further delineated by the repetition of Joshua's name in both the posing of the question and Achan's answer:

> Then Joshua said to Achan, 'My son, I implore you, give glory to Yahweh, the god of Israel, and give praise to him; and tell me now what you have done. Do not hide it from me'. So Achan answered Joshua and said, 'Truly I have sinned against Yahweh, the god of Israel, and this is what I did...' (Josh. 7.19-20).

The Dtr equates confession to Joshua, the human leader, with giving glory and praise to Yahweh. Then the words of Achan himself reconfirm the equation by confessing that his disobedience to Joshua was primarily a transgression against Yahweh. In his confession to Joshua, Achan acknowledges the deity Yahweh as the one against whom he has ultimately committed his act of insubordination (Josh. 7.20).

In the space of just a few lines, the text has told us not once, but twice, that Yahweh is the 'god of Israel' and that Joshua is his human representative to whom Achan is answerable. Central to Michel Foucault's analysis of power-relations is the issue of who has the right (power) to pose questions and who is obligated to answer them. The text is highlighting Joshua's authority, second only to Yahweh's in the hierarchy.

On a deeper level, the text also presents the transgression of the individual Achan as an affront to the entire community since Yahweh, as their national god, represents the people, and since their leader (Joshua, or Josiah) functions as the embodiment of national identity. The Achan incident, therefore, serves as an assertion of power through discourse in two ways: it places the national leader in an important position as the deity's proxy, solidifying the position of the monarch Josiah, and it also plays a role in the creation of social boundaries. The people 'all Israel' are much more than observers in the execution of Achan. They are themselves the executioners. They all join together as a group to stone Achan. By making the people the executioners, the people are presented as having a personal stake in ousting the disorder which has come within their boundaries. The purpose is to make the members of the community, individually and collectively, appear to feel wronged by Achan's action and to feel a part of the collective entity that is joining together to punish him. In doing so, they are drawing a border around themselves with Achan on the outside. The Dtr is using discourse to evoke the sentiments of the people reading or hearing the story in the 7th century BCE: not only are they not to identify with the disobedient Achan, or potential dissenters of any kind in their own society, but they might even actively feel motivated to exclude or punish the Achans among them. They are encouraged to feel themselves a part of the national enterprise by falling into line under King Josiah's sovereignty. Therefore, in the Achan incident, sovereignty is reconstituted by the ritual of public execution and by making the community the executioner. Sovereign power is reinforced by the construction of social boundaries which enhance the position of the central government headed by the monarch.

Achan's significance can be further explored by looking at the events which immediately precede his execution. The Achan incident occurs after (and, in a sense, as a result of) the Battle of Jericho, from which the prostitute Rahab was saved (Josh. 6.22-25). Therefore, the implications of the two episodes may be explored in conjunction with each other since the Rahab and Achan stories serve as an obverse pair in the negotiations which are involved in creating the boundaries of the community.

In several important respects, Achan (Joshua 7) is the obverse of Rahab (Joshua 2 and 6). If Rahab, a woman and a prostitute as well as a Canaanite, was the ultimate 'Other' who became an insider by voluntarily submitting and pledging her allegiance to Yahweh's hierarchy, represented by Joshua's military machine, then Achan was the exemplary insider (with the right lineage) who made himself 'Other' by his lack of submission to the hierarchical authority headed by Yahweh.

Achan's initial insider status is emphasized in the text by the double citation of his parentage and affiliation in precise, patrilineal terms. The hierarchical order is given twice (forward and backward) within the space of a few lines:

> Joshua arose early in the morning and brought Israel near by tribes, and the tribe of Judah was taken. And he brought the families of Judah near and the family of the Zerahites was taken; and he brought the family of the Zerahites near, man by man, and Zabdi was taken. And he brought his household near, man by man, and Achan, son of Carmi, son of Zabdi, son of Zerah, from the tribe of Judah, was taken (Josh. 7.16-18).

The strong overcoding of the lines of authority in the text makes the power assertion inherent within it perfectly clear: individuals belong to households, which belong to families; the families are subordinate to the patriarchal heads of the tribes, who, in turn, are to find their identity primarily as components of the entity 'Israel', whose god is Yahweh. The deity's chosen representative on earth, to whom Yahweh gives commands and to whom the people are answerable, is Joshua. Everyone has a particular place in the centralized system, and everyone ('all Israel') belongs firmly under Joshua's control. Achan, the individual who has tried to step out from under the lines of authority, is therefore subject to punishment not only by Joshua but by 'all Israel', the cohesive yet stratified entity:

> Joshua and all Israel with him took Achan the son of Zerah, the silver, the mantle, the bar of gold, his sons, his daughters, his oxen, his donkeys, his sheep, his tent and all that belonged to him; and they brought them up to the Valley of Achor. And Joshua said, 'Why have you troubled us? Yahweh will trouble you this day'. And all Israel stoned them with stones, and they burned them with fire after they had stoned them with stones (Josh. 7.24-25).

Everything which falls underneath Achan's control in the patriarchal system, namely his offspring and possessions, is destroyed along with him, which serves to emphasize further the hierarchical aspect of the political arrangement. The total destruction of Achan and everything under him is also reminiscent of the ban, which Achan had violated in his insubordination. By hoarding the booty from Jericho, he had infected the entire community with its presence among them. In order to restore purity, the source of the pollution—Achan himself, possessor of the banned items—and everyone in close proximity to him had to be removed from the community. (The purity/impurity aspect of the ban is emphasized also in Deut. 7.22-26 and 13.13-17.) Impurity is often projected on to the opponents in literature of violence in an attempt to justify the action taken against them.[28]

Rahab's function as an obverse image of Achan is reinforced by her reappearance in the text (Josh. 6.22-25) immediately before the Achan incident of Joshua 7. Although Rahab is a woman, she is described as a head of household in patriarchal language, almost as though she were a man:

28. N. Carroll, *The Philosophy of Horror* (New York: Routledge, 1990) pp. 28-35.

> So the young men who were spies went in and brought out Rahab and her
> father and her mother and her brothers and all she had; they also brought
> out all her relatives and placed them outside the camp of Israel (Josh.
> 6.23).

While she remains in a transitional situation 'outside the camp of Israel',
her femaleness is temporarily ignored in the text, and so is her low status
as a prostitute; for once she is simply 'Rahab' rather than 'Rahab the
harlot', her usual appellation. Then in v. 25, she is put into her hierarchical 'place' (in accordance with the patriarchal values of the text), with
her father designated as head of the household, as she and her relatives
settle permanently in the midst of Israel:

> However, Rahab the harlot, and her father's household and all that she
> had, Joshua spared; and she has lived in the midst of Israel to this day...
> (Josh.6.25).

Thus Rahab and her family were 'spared' the usual punishment for
Otherness (death). The contrasting fate of the rest of the inhabitants of
Jericho is graphically spelled out:

> And they (Joshua's men) utterly destroyed all in the city, both man and
> woman, young and old, and ox and sheep and donkey, with the edge of
> the sword (Josh. 6.21).

As in the battle reports of chs. 10 and 11 (cited earlier), the emphasis is
on total destruction. By her voluntary submission to Joshua's authority
and her acknowledgement of Yahweh (Josh. 2.11), Rahab was
transformed from the quintessential Other into an insider deemed
worthy of protection (and life). She accepted the structures of control
and was allowed a place within the hierarchy of insiders. Achan, on the
other hand, forfeited his place within the hierarchical system, although
he was a born insider, by his attempt to circumvent the structures of
control. His lack of submission to the lines of authority placed him
(along with his offspring, because of the patriarchal nature of the system)
outside the boundaries of control, thereby earning him (and them) the
standard punishment for Otherness: a violent death.

The pairing of the Rahab and Achan episodes back-to-back in chs. 6
and 7 undermines the initial impression, given by the battle narratives in
the text, that ethnicity is paramount. The two stories illustrate the process of negotiations and exchanges by which insiders may become outsiders and outsiders may become insiders. Comparison of Rahab's
behaviour and fate (chs. 2 and 6) with Achan's (ch. 7) reveals that the

true organizing principle of the narrative is not primarily ethnic identity but voluntary submission to authority structures, including the patriarchal political arrangement as well as the central ruling establishment represented by Joshua. The usual punishment for Otherness is death, as demonstrated by the many incidents in which all the Canaanites of a city or territory were 'slain with a great slaughter' or 'struck with the edge of the sword', leaving 'no survivor'. Yet the Canaanite Rahab is spared, along with everyone and everything under her (possessions and relatives), while Achan, along with his possessions and relatives, is violently destroyed.

Although Rahab is included by her voluntary submission to authority, the enemy kings in Josh. 10.24-26 stand for absolute externality. Ceremonies of power at the margins of community, such as public executions, amount to 'ritual demarcations of the limits of social and political authority', according to Mullaney.[29] Achan, the former insider who makes himself an outlaw, is a liminal figure, whose presence shows the social location of the threshold of the community. It is a threshold through which he exits when his disobedience places him outside the law. In his discussion of execution in the English Renaissance, Mullaney prefers the word 'outlaw' over Foucault's term 'criminal'. Mullaney points out that when an individual is conveyed to his execution, his place is that of 'an outlaw rather than a criminal' because the latter is a modern concept, while the former is a fitting description of the place the condemned occupies in the cultural landscape, having removed himself from the human community by his actions. 'Whether alive or in the throes of a protracted death', Mullaney says, the person being executed serves at once as 'a sign of power and authority in its fullest manifestation, and as a marker of authority's limit, of the place where law, authority and community gave way to something else, something Other'.[30] The kings executed in Josh. 10.24-26 are the exemplary Others, the kind of Others whom Achan joins in death by placing himself on the outside of the boundaries of the community.

The incident in Josh. 10.24-26 is an example of a rhetoric of violence used in several ways at once: to build community by inspiring a feeling of belonging, to create a bond of loyalty to that community and its hierarchy of authority through a bellicose spirit of nationalism, and to intimidate potential enemies within and without, but especially within the

29. Mullaney, *The Place of the Stage*, p. 40.
30. Mullaney, *The Place of the Stage*, p. 40.

boundaries of the community. The potential enemies could be individual opportunists like Achan (Joshua 7), or they could be politically motivated rebels with rival claims to the loyalty of the people. In either case, the incident serves as a deterrent to disobedience through its threat of death to those guilty of Otherness, combined with the rallying of community spirit among the insiders.

IV. *Conclusion*

The incidents in Josh. 1.16-18 and Josh. 10.24-26 serve as what Foucault calls spectacular displays of power. By the term 'spectacular', he means that the event is presented as a public spectacle with significance for the entire community, which acts as a participant, not merely passive audience. The executions and threatened executions in Joshua, therefore, are more than spectacle; the community becomes the executioner. When the Transjordanians use the military phrase חזק ואמץ in their speech to Joshua to affirm their solidarity against the Others (the Canaanites), and when in the same speech, they affirm their willingness to execute any among their ranks who break that solidarity, they are transmitting the community's values and simultaneously taking their own place in the hierarchy. Likewise, when the officers place their feet on the necks of the enemy kings executed in 10.25 as Joshua speaks, using the phrase חזק ואמץ, before the community, the officers become active participants in destroying the Others, but they also are reaffirming their own place in the hierarchy under Joshua. The phrase חזק ואמץ, therefore, is part of a rhetoric of violence in the text which functions simultaneously in the negotiation of boundaries and as an instrument of power within the hierarchical structure of the community.

Chapter 8

CONCLUSION

In this book I have sought to analyze the use of the phrase ואמץ חזק in the conquest narrative of the Book of Joshua. In order to do so, I have adapted a methodology called the 'New Historicism' from Renaissance literature studies and combined it with more traditional approaches from the field of biblical studies in order to shed new light on the rhetoric of violence in the conquest narrative. Unlike most New Historicists, I was working with an unknown historical context. As part of my discussion, therefore, I briefly sketched the most important of the arguments concerning the historical context in which the Book of Joshua was likely to have been composed. In agreement with R.D. Nelson, I concluded that it is probably a document of Josiah's reform, and that the conquest narrative, along with the rest of the DH, plays a part in King Josiah's centralization of power. Like Nelson, I think that Joshua is a thinly disguised Josiah.

My primary interest, however, has not been merely in contributing to the debate about the dating of the DH. My goal has been to analyze how the rhetoric of violence expressed in the military language of Joshua functions as an assertion of power in the construction of community, both in negotiating its boundaries and in solidifying its internal hierarchy. As a step towards this goal, I attempted to establish the place of the phrase ואמץ חזק among the military terminology of the DH and the rest of the Bible. I also have attempted to demonstrate the similarity between the rhetoric of violence in the DH and that of the neo-Assyrians, in order to set up my discussion of the Dtr's use of Assyrian modes of discourse to accomplish his ideological purposes.

In the wake of colonial oppression, a community may attempt to find its (previously submerged) identity by seeking to differentiate itself from the culture of the oppressor in two complementary ways, one of which involves looking inward at itself, and one of which involves looking outward. On the one hand, a community's attempts at self-definition may involve looking inward by doing such things as restoring a heritage, resurrecting past folk heroes or reconstructing narratives about themselves.[1] In other words, a community may turn to history in order to construct an identity for its own context out of the past, as the Dtr did in his telling of the conquest narrative.

As Lloyd Kramer has pointed out, structures of thought and symbolic meaning are an integral part of everything we know as history.[2] He explains that the imaginative aspect in all accounts of events does not necessarily mean that the events did not happen. It means that any attempt to describe events, even as they are occurring, must rely on 'various forms of imagination'. Every attempt to describe events necessarily relies on narratives that display the coherence, integrity, fulness and closure of an image of life that is and can only be imaginary.[3] The conquest narrative in the Book of Joshua is such an 'imaginary' use of the past.

On the other hand, a community's attempts at self-definition may involve looking outward in order to differentiate itself from the oppressor. When a community does so, however, it participates in the dominant culture's structure of meaning. In the attempt to construct a sense of identity and purpose, observes John Tagg, nationalist discourses run the risk of 'their own essentialising of a dominant frame of differentiation' by 'remaining prisoner to the very terms and structures they seek to reverse, mirroring their fixities and exclusions'. Furthermore, he goes on to say, there is a deeper contradiction at the core of such discourses:

> ... the attachment is also deeper and its effects more pervasive and unconscious, as nationalisms are fractured by the drive of a desire for the very Other they constitute, denigrate and expel, yet to which they continue to attribute enormous powers.[4]

1. J. Tagg, *Grounds of Dispute: Art History, Cultural Politics and the Discursive Field* (Minneapolis: University of Minnesota Press, 1992), p. 193.
2. L.S. Kramer, 'Literature, Criticism, and Historical Imagination', in L. Hunt (ed.), *The New Cultural History* (Berkeley: University of California Press, 1989), pp. 97-128. The present Chapter is not intended to be a discussion of the secondary literature on historiography or nationalism, but includes a few observations from scholars in historical and cultural studies merely to aid in articulating a few concluding remarks consistent with a New Historicist point of view.
3. Kramer, 'Imagination', pp. 98-101.
4. Tagg, *Grounds*, p. 193.

Josiah's monarchy was based on the concept of a cohesive identity under a highly centralized government. The authorities asserting their power through the religious, political, military and cultural control mechanisms were using the text to establish boundaries of acceptability in the society they were creating. In the wake of Assyrian collapse, the previously existing power structures and military values remained. Removal of the Assyrian Empire did not remove the mechanisms of power assertion. As part of their imperial strategy, the Assyrians had undermined the sense of identity of the nations they conquered. Identity was being reasserted in the Joshua story, but it was done by adopting the violent ideology of the oppressors. The same ideology that had undermined their identity was now being used to exert their identity.

The rhetoric of violence appropriated from the oppressor is turned by the oppressed into a vehicle of self-reconstitution. Although the Canaanites are the ostensible victims in Joshua, the goal is not to incite literal violence against a particular ethnic group. The text of Joshua is concerned with voluntary submission to a set of rules and norms; it is directed primarily at Josiah's own subjects, not at real (ethnic) outsiders, but at insiders who pose a threat to the hierarchy being asserted. The message is that the punishment of Otherness is death, and that insiders can easily become outsiders (Others) by failure to submit. The purpose of the rhetoric of violence in the conquest narrative is to serve as a warning to the people of Josiah's kingdom that the post-imperial power of the central government could and would be unleashed upon any who resisted its assertion of control.

Although I have attempted to shed new light on the usage of a particular phrase, חזק ואמץ, in the conquest narrative, I have said little about the remainder of the Book of Joshua and even less about the other parts of the DH. Many other narratives in the DH are fertile ground for New Historicist analysis, but unfortunately are beyond the scope of the present study, and will have to wait until sometime in the future.

BIBLIOGRAPHY

Albrektson, B., *History and the Gods: An Essay on the Idea of Historical Events as Divine Manifestations in the Ancient Near East and in Israel* (Lund: C.W.K. Gleerup, 1967).

Albright, W.F., 'The Israelite Conquest of Canaan in the Light of Archaeology', *BASOR* 74 (1939), pp. 11-23.

—'Some Remarks on the Song of Moses in Deuteronomy XXXII', *VT* 9 (1959), pp. 339-46.

—*Yahweh and the Gods of Canaan* (Garden City: Doubleday, 1968).

Alter, R., *The Art of Biblical Narrative* (New York: Basic Books, 1991).

—*The Pleasures of Reading in an Age of Ideology* (Berkeley: University of California Press, 1990).

Bach, R., *Die Aufforderungen zur Flucht und zum Kampf im Alttestamentlichen Prophetenspruch* (WMANT, 9; Neukirchen: Neukirchener Verlag, 1962).

Barker, M., *The Older Testament: The Survival of Themes from the Ancient Royal Cult in Sectarian Judaism and Early Christianity* (London: SPCK, 1987).

Baumann, E., 'Das Lied Moses (Dtn. 32, 1-43)', *VT* 6 (1956), pp. 414-24.

Becking, B., *The Fall of Samaria: An Historical and Archaeological Study* (Leiden: Brill, 1992).

Bersani, L., and U. Dutoit, *The Forms of Violence: Narrative in Assyrian Art and Modern Culture* (New York: Schocken Books, 1985).

Breasted, J.H., *Ancient Records of Egypt* (Chicago: University of Chicago Press, 1906).

Brosman, C.S., 'The Functions of War Literature', *South Central Review* 9.1 (1992), pp. 85-98.

Butler, T.C., *Joshua* (WBC; Waco: Word Books, 1983).

Carpenter, J.E., and G. Harford-Battersby, *The Hexateuch* (2 vols.; London: Longmans, Green, 1900).

Carroll, N., *The Philosophy of Horror* (New York: Routledge, 1990).

Ceram, C.W., *The Secret of the Hittites* (trans. R. and C. Winston; New York: Dorset Press, 1955).

Christensen, D.L., *Transformations of the War Oracle in Old Testament Prophecy* (Harvard Dissertations in Religion, 3; Missoula, MT: Scholars Press, 1975).

Clements, R.E., 'The Isaiah Narrative of II Kings 20:12-19 and the Date of the Deuteronomistic History', in A. Rofé and Y. Zakovitch (eds.), *Isaac Leo Seeligmann Volume: Essays on the Bible and the Ancient World* (3 vols.; Jerusalem: Magnes Press, 1983).

Clifford, R.J., 'Cosmogonies in the Ugaritic Texts and in the Bible', *Or* 53 (1984), pp. 183-201.

Coats, G.W., 'An Exposition for the Conquest Theme', *CBQ* 47 (1985), pp. 47-54.

—'Legendary Motifs in the Moses Death Reports', *CBQ* 39 (1977), pp. 34-44.

Cogan, M., 'The Chronicler's Use of Chronology as Illuminated by Neo-Assyrian Royal Inscriptions', in J.H. Tigay (ed.), *Empirical Models for Biblical Criticism* (Philadelphia: University of Pennsylvania Press, 1985), pp. 197-209.

Cohn, R.L., 'Convention and Creativity in the Book of Kings: The Case of the Dying Monarch', *CBQ* 47 (1985), pp. 603-16.

Conrad, E.W., *Fear Not Warrior: A Study of 'al tira' Pericopes in the Hebrew Scriptures* (Chico, CA: Scolars Press, 1985).

Coote, R.B., and M.P. Coote, *Power, Politics and the Making of the Bible: An Introduction* (Minneapolis: Fortress Press, 1990).

Craigie, P., *The Problem of War in the Old Testament* (Grand Rapids: W.B. Eerdmans Publishing, 1978).

Cross, F.M., *Canaanite Myth and Hebrew Epic* (Cambridge, MA: Harvard University Press, 1973).

—'The Divine Warrior in Israel's Early Cult', in A. Altmann (ed.), *Biblical Motifs* (Cambridge, MA: Harvard Universty Press, 1966).

Dearman, J.A., 'Historical Reconstruction and the Mesha Inscription' in *idem* (ed.), *Studies in the Mesha Inscription and Moab* (Atlanta: Scholars Press, 1989), pp. 155-210.

—*Religion and Culture in Ancient Israel* (Peabody: Hendrickson Publishers, 1992).

De Vries, S.J., 'Temporal Terms as Structural Elements in the Holy-War Tradition', *VT* 25 (1975), pp. 80-105.

Dietrich, W., *Prophetie und Geschichte* (FRLANT; Göttingen: Vandenhoeck & Ruprecht, 1972).

Dillmann, A., *Numeri, Deuteronomium und Josua* (KEH; Leipzig, 1886).

Dion, H.M., 'The "Fear Not" Formula and Holy War', *CBQ* 32 (1970), pp. 565-70.

—'The Patriarchal Traditions and the Literary Form of the "Oracle of Salvation"', *CBQ* 29 (1967), pp. 198-206.

Drinkard, J., 'The Literary Genre of the Mesha Inscription', in J.A. Dearman (ed.), *Studies in the Mesha Inscription and Moab* (Atlanta, GA: Scholars Press, 1989), pp. 131-54.

Driver, G.R., 'Three Notes', *VT* 2 (1952), pp. 356-57.

Driver, S.R., *A Critical and Exegetical Commentary on Deuteronomy* (ICC; Edinburgh: T. & T. Clark, 1895).

—*An Introduction to the Literature of the Old Testament* (ITL; Edinburgh: T. & T. Clark, 9th edn, 1909).

Eagleton, T., *Criticism and Ideology* (London: New Left Books, 1976).

Eissfeldt, O., 'El and Yahweh', *JSS* 1 (1956), pp. 25-37.

Fishbane, M., *Biblical Interpretation in Ancient Israel* (Oxford; Clarendon Press, 1985).

Finkelstein, J.J., 'The So-called "Old Babylonian Kutha Legend"', *JCS* 11 (1957), pp. 83-88.

Flanagan, J.W., 'Court History or Succession Document? A Study of 2 Samuel 9–20 and I Kings 1–2', *JBL* 91 (1972), pp. 172-81.

Forshey, H.O., 'The Construct Chain nᵃḥalat YHWH/ᵖᵉlōhîm', *BASOR* 220 (1975), pp. 51-53.

Foucault, M., *Power/Knowledge: Selected Interviews and Other Writings, 1972–1977* (ed. C. Gordon; New York: Pantheon, 1980).

—*Surveiller et Punir* (Paris: éditions Gallimard, 1975); available in English (trans. A. Sheridan) as *Discipline and Punish: The Birth of the Prison* (New York: Vintage Books, 1979).

Frankfort, H., *Kingship and the Gods: A Study of Ancient Near Eastern Religion as the Integration of Society and Nature* (Chicago: University of Chicago Press, 1948).

Fraser, J., *Violence in the Arts* (Cambridge: Cambridge University Press, 1974).

Fredriksson, H., *Jahwe als Krieger* (Lund: C.W.K. Gleerup, 1945).

Friedman, R.E., *The Exile and Biblical Narrative: The Formation of the Deuteronomistic and Priestly Works* (Chico, CA: Scholars Press, 1981).

Frye, N., *Anatomy of Criticism: Four Essays* (Princeton: Princeton University Press, 1957).

Geertz, C., 'Ideology as a Cultural System', in *The Interpretation of Cultures* (New York: Basic Books, 1973), pp. 193-233..

Gerbrandt, G.E., *Kingship According to the Deuteronomistic History* (Atlanta: Scholars Press, 1986).

Gerleman, G., 'Nutzrecht und Wohnrecht: Zur Bedeutung von אחזה und נחלה', *ZAW* 89 (1977), pp. 313-25.

Gesenius, W., *Hebrew and Chaldee Lexicon to the Old Testament Scriptures* (trans. S.P. Tregelles; Grand Rapids: Eerdmans Publishing, 1949).

Goetze, A., *Die Annalen des Muršilis* (6 vols.; MVAG, 38; Leipzig: Hinrichs, 1933).

Good, R.M., 'The Just War in Ancient Israel', *JBL* 104.3 (1985), pp. 385-400.

—*The Sheep of His Pasture: A Study of the Hebrew Noun 'Am(m) and Its Semitic Cognates* (Chico, CA: Scholars Press, 1983).

Gordon, C.H., *Ugaritic Literature: A Comprehensive Translation of the Poetic and Prose Texts* (Rome: Pontifical Biblical Institute, 1949).

Gottwald, N.K., *The Hebrew Bible: A Socio-Literary Introduction* (Philadelphia: Fortress Press, 1985).

—*Tribes of Yahweh* (Maryknoll: Orbis, 1975).

Graff, G., 'The Nonpolitics of PC', *Tikkun* 6.4 (1991), pp. 50-52.

Gray, J., *Joshua, Judges, Ruth* (NBC; Grand Rapids: Eerdmans Publishing, 1986).

—*I & II Kings: A Commentary* (Philadelphia: Westminster Press, 1962).

Gray, R., *Writing the South* (Cambridge: Cambridge University Press, 1986).

Greenblatt, S., *The Power of Forms in the English Renaissance* (Norman: University of Oklahoma Press, 1982).

—*Shakespearean Negotiations: The Circulation of Social Energy in Renaissance England* (Berkeley, CA: University of California Press, 1988).

Grossfeld, B., 'Targum Neofiti 1 to Deut. 31.7', *JBL* 91 (1972), pp. 533-34.

Gunn, D.M., 'The "Battle Report": Oral or Scribal Convention', *JBL* 93 (1974), pp. 513-18.

—*The Story of King David: Genre and Interpretation* (Sheffield: Sheffield Academic Press, 1978).

Gurney, O.R., 'The Sultantepe Tablets: The Cuthean Legend of Naram-sin', *AS* 5 (1955). pp. 93-113.

Güterbock, H.G., 'The Deeds of Suppiluliuma as Told by His Son, Muršili II', *JCS* 10 (1956), pp. 41-130.

—'Die historische Tradition und ihre literarische Gestaltung bei Babyloniern und Hethitern bis 1200', *ZA* 44 (1938), pp. 49-61.

Halpern, B., *The First Historians: The Hebrew Bible and History* (San Francisco: Harper & Row, 1988).

—*The Constitution of the Monarchy in Israel* (Chico, CA: Scholars Press, 1981).

—*The Emergence of Israel in Canaan* (Chico, CA: Scholars Press, 1983).

—'Gibeon: Israelite Diplomacy in the Conquest Era', *CBQ* 37 (1975), pp. 303-16.

Hawk, C.D., *Every Promise Fulfilled: Contending Plots in Joshua* (Louisville: Westminster Press, 1991).

Heidel, A., *The Gilgamesh Epic* (Chicago: University of Chicago Press, 1949).

Heinz, J.G., 'Oracles prophétiques et "geurre sainte" selon les archives royales de Mari et l'Ancien Testament', *VT* 17 (1969), pp. 112-38.

Helck, W., *Urkunden der 18. Dynastie* (Berlin: Akademie Verlag, 1955).

Hermann, J.P., *Allegories of War: Language and Violence in Old English Poetry* (Ann Arbor: University of Michigan Press, 1989).

Hobbs, T.R., *A Time for War: A Study of Warfare in the Old Testament* (Wilmington: Michael Glazier, 1989).

—'2 Kings 1 and 2: Their Unity and Purpose', *SR* 13 (1984), pp. 327-34.

Holland, N.N., *2 Henry IV* (New York: New American Library, 1965), p. xxxvi.

Holzinger, H., *Das Buch Josua* (KHC; Tübingen: J.C.B. Mohr, 1901).

Horst, F., 'Zwei Begriffe für Eigentum (Besitz): נחלה und אחזה', in A. Kuschke (ed.), *Verbannung und Heimkehr* (Tübingen: J.C.B. Mohr, 1961), pp. 135-56.

Ishida, T., *The Royal Dynasties in Ancient Israel: A Study on the Formation and Development of Royal-Dynastic Ideology* (Berlin: de Gruyter, 1977).

Jameson, F., *The Political Unconscious* (London: Methuen, 1981).

Jenni, E., *Das hebräische Piel* (Zürich: EVZ-verlag, 1968), p. 213.

Jobling, D., 'Ahab's Quest for Rain: Text and Context in I Kings 17-18', *The Sense of Biblical Narrative*, I (JSOTSup, 9; Sheffield: Sheffield Academic Press, 1983), pp. 66-88.

—'The Jordan a Boundary: Transjordan in Israel's Ideological Geography', *The Sense of Biblical Narrative*, II (JSOTSup, 39; Sheffield: Sheffield Academic Press, 1986), pp. 88-134.

Jones, G.H., 'Holy War or YHWH War?' *VT* 25 (1975), pp. 642-58.

Kang, S.-M., *Divine War in the Old Testament and in the Ancient Near East* (Berlin: de Gruyter, 1989).

Kaufmann, Y., *The Biblical Account of the Conquest of Palestine* (Jerusalem: Magnes Press, 1953).

Kearney, P.J., 'The Role of the Gibeonites in the Deuteronomic History', *CBQ* 35 (1973), pp. 1-19.

Kramer, L.S., 'Literature, Criticism, and Historical Imagination', in L. Hunt (ed.), *The New Cultural History* (Berkeley, CA: University of California Press, 1989).

Kristeva, J., *La Révolution de la langue poétique* (Paris: Seuil, 1974).

—*Séméiotiké: Recherches pour une Sémanalyse* (Paris: Seuil, 1969).

Kuenen, A., *The Hexateuch* (Leiden: Brill, 1885).

Kümmel, H., 'Hethitische Texte', in M. Dietrich, H.M. Kümmel, O. Loretz, and H. Otten (eds.), *Rechts- und Wirtschaftsurkunden* (Gütersloh: Gütersloher Verlagshaus, 1985), pp. 452-80.

Lambert, W.G., 'Destiny and Divine Intervention in Babylon and Israel', *OTS* 17 (1972), pp. 65-72.

Lemaire, A., 'Vers L'histoire de la Rédaction des livres de Rois', *ZAW* 98 (1986), pp. 221-36.

Lichtheim, M., *Ancient Egyptian Literature: A Book of Readings* (Berkeley: University of California Press, 1973–1980).

Lincoln, B., *Discourse and the Construction of Society: Comparative Studies in Myth, Ritual and Classification* (Oxford: Oxford University Press, 1989).

Lind, M.C., *Yahweh is a Warrior: The Theology of Warfare in Ancient Israel* (Scottsdale, Herald Press, 1980).

Liver, J., 'The Literary History of Joshua IX', *JSS* (1963), pp. 227-43.

Liver, J. (ed.), *The Military History of the Land of Israel in Biblical Times* (Jerusalem: Magnes Press, 1964).

Lohfink, N., 'Die deuteronomistische Darstellung des Übergangs der Féhrung Israels von Moses auf Josue: Ein Beitrag zur alttestamentliche Theologie des Amtes', *Scholastik* 37 (1962), pp. 32-44.

Long, B.O., '2 Kings III and Genres of Prophetic Narrative', *VT* 23 (1973), pp. 337-48.

Longman, T., III, *Fictional Akkadian Autobiography: A Generic and Comparative Study* (Winona Lake: Eisenbrauns, 1991).

Malamat, A., 'The Ban in Mari and the Bible', in *idem*, *Biblical Essays 1966* (Pretoria: Stellenbosch, 1967), pp. 40-49.

Mann, T.W., *Divine Presence and Guidance in Israelite Traditions* (Baltimore: The Johns Hopkins University Press, 1977).

Mayes, A.D.H., *Deuteronomy* (NCBC; Grand Rapids: W.B. Eerdmans Publishing, 1979).

—*The Story of Israel between Settlement and Exile: A Redactional Study of the Deuteronomistic History* (London: SCM Press, 1983).

McCarter, P.K., Jr, *I Samuel* (AB; Garden City: Doubleday, 1980).

McCarthy, D.J., 'An Installation Genre?' *JBL* 90 (1971), pp. 31-41.

—*Old Testament Covenant: A Survey of Current Opinions* (Oxford: Oxford University Press, 1972).

—'Some Holy War Vocabulary in Joshua 2', *CBQ* 33 (1971), pp. 227-28.

—'The Theology of Leadership in Joshua 1-9', *Bib* 52 (1971), pp. 165-75.

—*Treaty and Covenant* (Rome: Pontifical Biblical Institute, 1963).

McKenzie, S., *The Trouble with Kings* (VTSup, 42; Leiden: Brill, 1992).

Meeker, M.E., *Literature and Violence in North Arabia* (Cambridge: Cambridge University Press, 1979).

Meyer, R. 'Die Bedeutung von Deuteronomium 32, 8f.43 (4Q) für die Auslegung des Moseliedes', in A. Kuschke (ed.), *Verbannung und Heimkehr* (Tübingen: J.C.B. Mohr, 1961), pp. 197-210.

Miller, J.M., 'The Mesha Stela as a Memorial Inscription', *PEQ* 106 (1974), pp. 9-18.

Miller, P.D., 'The Divine Council and the Prophetic Call to War', *VT* 18 (1968), pp. 100-107.

—*The Divine Warrior in Early Israel* (Cambridge, MA: Harvard University Press, 1973).

—'God the Warrior', *Int* 19 (1965), pp. 39-46.

Moran, W.L., 'New Evidence from Mari on the History of Prophecy', *Bib* 50 (1969), pp. 15-56.

Muilenburg, J., 'A Study in Hebrew Rhetoric: Repetition and Style' in *Congress Volume Copenhagen 1953* (SVT; Leiden: Brill, 1953), pp. 97-111.

—'Form Criticism and Beyond', *JBL* 88 (1969), pp. 1-18.

Mullaney, S., The Place of the Stage: License, Play, and Power in Renaissance England (Chicago: University of Chicago Press, 1988).

Mullen, E.T., *The Divine Council in Canaanite and Early Hebrew Literature* (Chico, CA: Scholars Press, 1980).

Na'aman, N., 'The Kingdom of Judah Under Josiah', *Tel Aviv* (1991), pp. 3-71.

Nelson, R.D., *The Double Redaction of the Deuteronomistic History* (JSOTSup, 18; Sheffield: Sheffield Academic Press, 1981).

—'Josiah in the Book of Joshua', *JBL* 100.4 (1981), pp. 531-40.

Norris, C. *The Contest of Faculties* (London: Methuen Press, 1985).

Noth, M., *Das Buch Josua* (HAT; Tübingen: J.C.B. Mohr, 1953).

—*Gesammelte Studien zum Alten Testament* (München: Kaiser, 1957).

—*Überlieferungsgeschichtliche Studien* (Halle: Scriften der Konigsberger Gelehrten Gesellschaft, 1943).

O'Brien, M.A., *The Deuteronomistic History Hypothesis: A Reassessment* (Göttingen: Vandenhoeck & Ruprecht, 1989).

Oettli, S., *Das Deuteronimum und die Bücher Josua und Richter* (München, 1893).

Oppenheim, A.L., *Ancient Mesopotamia: Portrait of a Dead Civilization* (Chicago: University of Chicago Press, 1977 [1964]).

Otten, H., 'Neue Fragmente zu den Annalen des Murüili', *MIO* 3 (1955), pp. 153-79.

Polzin, R., *Moses and the Deuteronomist: A Literary Study of the Deuteronomic History* (New York: Seabury Press, 1980).

Porter, J.R., 'The Succession of Joshua', in J.I. Durham and J.R. Porter (eds.), *Proclamation and Presence: Old Testament Essays in Honour of Gwynne Henton Davies* (London: SCM Press, 1970), pp. 102-32.

Provan, I.W., Hezekiah and the Books of Kings: A Contribution to the Debate about the Composition of the Deuteronomistic History (BZAW; Berlin: de Gruyter, 1988).

Rad, G. von, *Der heilige Krieg im alten Israel* (Göttingen: Vandenhoeck & Ruprecht, 1962).

—*Deuteronomy* (London: SCM Press, 1966).

Ransom, J.C., 'Art and the Human Economy', *Kenyon Review* (1945), pp. 683-38.

—'Reconstructed but Unregenerate' in *I'll Take My Stand* (ed; 'Twelve Southerners'; New York: Harper & Brothers, 1930), pp. 1-27.

Riches, D., *The Anthropology of Violence* (Oxford: Oxford University Press, 1986).

Ryrie, C., *The Ryrie Study Bible* (Chicago: Moody Press, 1978).

Saggs, H.W.F., 'Assyrian Warfare in the Sargonid Period', *Iraq* 25 (1963), pp. 145-60.

—*The Encounter with the Divine in Mesopotamia and Israel* (London: Athlone Press, 1978).

—*The Might That Was Assyria* (London: Sidgwick & Jackson, 1984).

Schultz, W., 'Stilkritische Untersuchungen zur Deuteronomistischen Literatur', *TLZ* 102 (1977), pp. 853-55.

Schwally, F., *Semitische Kriegsaltertumer I: Der heilige Krieg im alten Israel* (Leipzig: Dieterich, 1901).

Scruton, R., *The Aesthetic Understanding: Essays in the Philosophy of Art and Culture* (London, Methuen, 1983).

Skehan, P.W., 'The Structure of the Song of Moses in Deuteronomy', *CBQ* 13 (1951), pp. 153-63.

—'A Fragment of the "Song of Moses" (Deut. 32) from Qumran', *BASOR* 136 (1954), pp. 12-15.

Smend, R., 'Das Gesetz und die Völker: Ein Beitrag zur deuteronomistischen Redaktionsgeschichte', in H.W. Wolff (ed.), *Probleme biblischer Theologie: Gerhard von Rad zum 70. Geburtstag* (München: Kaiser, 1971), pp. 494-509.

—*Die Bundesformel* (Zürich: Theologischer Verlag, 1963).

—*Jahwekrieg und Stämmebund* (Göttingen: Vandenhoeck & Ruprecht, 1963).

Smith, M.S., *The Early History of God: Yahweh and the Other Dieties in Ancient Israel* (San Francisco: Harper & Row, 1990).

Soggin, J.A., *Das Königtum in Israel* (Berlin: de Gruyter, 1967).

—*Joshua* (trans. R.A. Wilson; OTL; Philadelphia: Westminster Press, 1972).

Stern, P.D., *The Biblical Herem: A Window on Israel's Religious Experience* (Atlanta: Scholars Press, 1991).

Sternberg, M., *The Poetics of Biblical Narrative: Ideological Literature and the Drama of Reading* (Bloomington: Indiana University Press, 1985).

Steuernagel, C., *Übersetzung und Erklärung der Bücher Deuteronomium, Josua, und Allgemeine Einleitung in den Hexateuch* (Göttingen: Vandenhoeck & Ruprecht, 1900).

Stolz, F., *Jahwes und Israels Kriege: Kriegstheorien und Kriegserfahrungen im Glauben des alten Israel* (Zürich: Zwingli Verlag, 1972).

Tagg, J., *Grounds of Dispute: Art History, Cultural Politics and the Discursive Field* (Minneapolis: University of Minnesota Press, 1992).

Tigay, J.H., *The Evolution of the Gilgamesh Epic* (Philadelphia: University of Pennsylvania Press, 1982).

Van der Lingen, A., Les Guerres de Yahvé: L'implication de YHWH dans les guerres d'Isräel selon les livres historiques de l'Ancien Testament (LD, 139; Paris: Cerf, 1990).

Van Seters, J., 'The Conquest of Sihon's Kingdom: A Literary Examination' *JBL* 91 (1972), pp. 182-97.

—*In Search of History: Historiography in the Ancient World and the Origins of Biblical History* (New Haven: Yale University Press, 1983).

Vater, A.M., 'Story Patterns for a Sitz: A Form- or Literary-Critical Concern?', *JSOT* 11 (1979), pp. 47-56.

Veijola, T., Das Königtum in der Beurteilung der Deuteronomistischen Historiographie: Eine redaktionsgeschichtliche Untersuchung (AASF/B, 198; Helsinki: Suomalainen Tiedeakatemia, 1977).

—Die ewige Dynastie: David und die Entstehung seiner Dynastie nach der deuteronomistischen Darstellung (AASF/B, 193; Helsinki: Suomalainen Tiedeakatemia, 1975).

Vriezen, T.C., *An Outline of Old Testament Theology* (Oxford: Oxford University Pres, 1958).

Walker, C.B.F., 'The Second Tablet of ṭupšenna pitema: An Old Babylonian Naram Sin Legend?', *JCS* 33 (1981), pp. 191-95.

Weimar, P., 'Die Jahwekriegserzählungen in Exodus 14, Josua 10, Richter 4 und 1 Samuel 7', *Bib* 57 (1976), pp. 38-73.

Weinfeld, M., *Deuteronomy and the Deuteronomic School* (Oxford: Clarendon Press, 1972).

—'Divine Intervention in War in Ancient Israel and in the Ancient Near East', in M. Weinfeld and H. Tadmor, *History, Historiography and Interpretation: Studies in Biblical and Cuneiform Literatures* (Jerusalem: Magnes Press, 1983), pp. 121-47.

Weippert, H., 'Das deuteronomistische Geschichtswerk: Sein Ziel und Ende in der neueren Forschung', *TRu* NS 50 (1985), pp. 213-49.

—'Die "deuteronomistischen" Beurteilungen der Könige von Israel und Juda und das Problem der Redaktion der Königsbucher', *Bib* 53 (1972), pp. 301-39.

Weippert, M., ' "Heiliger Krieg" in Israel und Assyrien: Kritische Anmerkungen zu Gerhard von Rads Konzept des "Heiligen Krieges im alten Israel" ', *ZAW* 84 (1972), pp. 460-93.

—*The Settlement of the Israelite Tribes in Palestine* (London: SCM Press, 1971).

Wellhausen, J., *Die Composition des Hexateuchs und der historischen Bücher des Alten Testaments* (Berlin: de Gruyter, 1876–77).

Wenham, G., 'The Deuteronomic Theology of the Book of Joshua', *JBL* 90 (1971) pp. 141-42.

Widengren, G., 'King and Covenant', *JSS* 2 (1957), pp. 1-32.

Williamson, H.G.M., 'The Accession of Solomon in the Books of the Chronicles', *VT* 26 (1976), pp. 351-61.

—'The Death of Josiah and the Continuing Development of the Deuteronomistic History', *VT* 32 (1982), pp. 242-47.

—*1 and 2 Chronicles* (NCB; Grand Rapids: Eerdmans Publishing, 1982).

Willis, J.T. 'The Song of Hannah and Psalm 113', *CBQ* 35 (1973), pp. 139-54.

Winter, P., 'Der Begriff "Söhne Gottes" im Moselied Dtn 32 1-43', *ZAW* 67 (1955), pp. 40-48.

Wright, G.E., and R.G. Boling, *Joshua* (AB; Garden City: Doubleday, 1982).

Wuellner, W., 'Where Is Rhetorical Criticism Taking Us?', *CBQ* 40.3 (1987), pp. 448-63.

Würthwein, E., *The Text of the Old Testament: An Introduction to the Biblia Hebraica* (Grand Rapids: Eerdmans Publishing, 1979).

Yadin, Y., *The Art of Warfare in Biblical Lands* (New York: McGraw–Hill, 1962).

Younger, K.L., *Ancient Conquest Accounts: A Study in Ancient Near Eastern and Biblical History Writing* (JSOTSup, 98; Sheffield: Sheffield Academic Press, 1990).

INDEXES

INDEX OF REFERENCES

OLD TESTAMENT

INDEX OF AUTHORS

JOURNAL FOR THE STUDY OF THE OLD TESTAMENT
SUPPLEMENT SERIES